EVIL AND
THE EVIDENCE
FOR GOD

EVIL AND THE EVIDENCE FOR GOD

The Challenge of John Hick's Theodicy

R. DOUGLAS GEIVETT

Afterword by John Hick

Temple University Press
Philadelphia

Temple University Press, Philadelphia 19122
Copyright © 1993 by Temple University. All rights reserved
Published 1993
Printed in the United States of America

Library of Congress Cataloging-in-Publication Data
Geivett, R. Douglas.
    Evil and the evidence for God : the challenge of John Hick's
theodicy / R. Douglas Geivett ; afterword by John Hick.
        p.   cm.
    Includes bibliographical references and index.
    ISBN 1-56639-094-X (alk. paper)
    1. Hick, John—Contributions in theodicy.   2. Theodicy—
History of doctrines—20th century.   I. Title.
BT160.G358   1993
214'.092—dc20   93-205

To
Dianne,
Kaitlyn,
and
Erin

CONTENTS

PREFACE

As an eminent philosopher of religion, John Hick has met with both praise and criticism. His work ranges over all of the territory normally associated with the philosophy of religion. He has produced influential books and articles on religious epistemology, the arguments for the existence of God, the problem of evil, religious language, religious experience, and the relationships among diverse religious perspectives. Much of his work ventures into the border region of philosophical theology. His book *Philosophy of Religion,* published in several editions, surveys the whole field of philosophy of religion. *An Interpretation of Religion: Human Responses to the Transcendent* (1989), Hick's crowning achievement, has been highly celebrated and widely discussed.

Numerous essays and books critically analyze various aspects of Hick's work in these areas. The vast literature that his writings have inspired is impressive and continues to grow. This book is an appraisal of his work on the specific topic of theodicy—his effort to cope philosophically with the problem of evil from within the Judeo–Christian tradition.

My interest in writing this book grew out of the convergence of several observations. First, no challenge to the system of Christian truth claims has been more enduring than the problem of evil. The long history of this objection to Christian theism testifies to its tenacity in comparison with virtually all other criticisms of the tradition.

Second, owing to his own recognition of this state of affairs, Hick has attempted to redress this difficulty in modern terms, inviting the close attention of both religious believers and nonbelievers. Perhaps no book on Christian theodicy is better known today than is his *Evil and the God of Love.*

Third, Hick's work on God and evil is, in at least one important respect, revolutionary. For he intends his theodicy hypothesis to supplant the venerable Augustinian tradition of theodicy, which he thinks is inadequate for the needs and demands of contemporary human society.

Finally, Hick's theodicy may now be studied in the context of his work on all the other major topics in the philosophy of religion. While he continues to contribute actively to the range of topics included in the philosophy of religion, his work is now complete in the sense that it addresses all major issues that concern philosophers of religion, and it does so with a remarkable degree of consistency and uniformity.

Because I share Hick's interest in responding to the chief philosophical challenges brought against the Christian tradition, and since evil continues to provide the detractors of Christianity with the greatest skeptical fodder, but also because I take exception to his belief that the Augustinian tradition is in sufficient disrepair to warrant the construction of a new "theodicy for today," I have undertaken to analyze Hick's theodicy from within the free-will tradition of Augustine and to recommend this classical tradition anew.

In the process of writing this book I have come to believe that a fresh appraisal of Hick's theodicy hypothesis may serve to restore the respectability of the tradition he criticizes. This book enters a plea to give the Augustinian tradition of theodicy another sympathetic look and to see whether it can meet the challenge of John Hick's theodicy.

PLAN OF THE BOOK

This book is in three parts. Part I supplies the background needed for a proper appreciation of the critical points advanced in subsequent chapters. Here two competing traditions in Christian theodicy are given exposition. Chapter 1 describes the problem of evil, a problem that uniquely confronts the Christian theist. Chapter 2 surveys the classical Augustinian response to this perennial difficulty. This is carried out through a comparison of three influential exponents of the tradition, St. Augustine, St. Thomas Aquinas, and Gottfried Leibniz. Special stress is laid upon the important role played by natural theology within this tradition.

Chapter 3 presents an exposition of the main points of Hick's "soul-making" theodicy, which is then contrasted with the Augustinian tradition. This overview of Hick's theodicy will enable those unfamiliar with Hick's proposal to follow the argument throughout this book.

Part II deals with two alternative approaches to religious epistemology, or inquiry into the justification of belief in God. This is very much the heart of the book, for it deals with general epistemological issues that operate in the background for many who write on the problem of evil. The idea in this section is to clarify the role that positive support for belief in God might play in formulating a theodicy. Chapter 4 begins this task by noting the crucial significance of Hick's religious epistemology for his own system of theodicy and stresses the value of natural theology as a prolegomenon for theodicy proper. Chapter 5 spells out the consequences of his negative judgment regarding the possibility of natural theology to justify belief in God.

A major thesis of this book is that an adequate response to the problem of evil depends upon the possibility of natural theology, or of providing good evidence for the existence of God. Chapters 6 and 7 represent my attempt to sketch the outline of a natural theology that will serve as a fitting prolegomenon to framing a viable theodicy. In Chapter 8 I respond to two types of criticism that Hick would be likely to make against my position.

Part III focuses on theodicy proper, with a close examination of the main points of Hick's specific theodicy proposal. Chapters 9 through 12 offer an appraisal of the teleological, anthropological, and eschatological dimensions of his theodicy, in that order. These chapters follow the organization of the material in Chapter 3. Two of these chapters (9 and 10) are devoted to the central problem of relating the reality of evil to the divine will for humanity. Throughout this section the Augustinian theodicy is presented as a desirable alternative to Hick's approach.

Often during my preparation of this volume I have had the opportunity to talk with Professor Hick about various points. I gratefully acknowledge his contribution to this volume and his interest in the project of comparing the relative merits of two systems of theodicy. He joins the discussion in a very welcome Afterword.

ACKNOWLEDGMENTS

I wish to express special thanks to Frank and Dixie Smith for their many hours of help in typing and processing an early version of the manuscript. Others have read all or parts of this book, making helpful suggestions to me along the way. I thank my good friends Paul House, Greg Jesson, J. P. Moreland, and Brendan Sweetman for the many hours of stimulating and fruitful conversation we have had on this and other topics of great human significance; my teachers Norman Geisler, Wayne Pomerleau, and Dallas Willard for their contribution to my philosophical development; Janet Levin, Donald Miller, Ronald Nash, Richard Purtill, William Rowe, Merold Westphal, and Keith Yandell for their thoughtful comments and suggestions regarding various parts of the book; and Barry Freedman, who offered me very helpful stylistic advice. It has been a delight for me to get to know and to work with my editor, Jane Cullen, and the others at Temple University Press. My colleagues at Taylor University, where I worked on the final phase of this project, also supported me through many kindnesses.

I especially acknowledge the unfailing encouragement of my wife, Dianne, and the inspiring joy of my daughters, Kaitlyn and Erin. At great personal sacrifice, Dianne and Kaitlyn helped see this project through to completion. Erin joined our family during the final editing. I gratefully dedicate this book to the three of them. They are the most concrete and enduring signs of divine goodness in my life.

PART I
TWO TRADITIONS

1
The Problem of Evil

In his expansive autobiography, the great twentieth-century British philosopher Bertrand Russell wrote:

> Three passions, simple but overwhelmingly strong, have governed my life: the longing for love, the search for knowledge, and unbearable pity for the suffering of mankind. These passions, like great winds, have blown me hither and thither, in a wayward course, over a deep ocean of anguish, reaching to the very verge of despair. . . .
>
> Love and knowledge, so far as they were possible, led upward toward the heavens. But always pity brought me back to earth. Echoes of cries of pain reverberate in my heart. Children in famine, victims tortured by oppressors, helpless old people a hated burden to their sons, and the whole world of loneliness, poverty, and pain make a mockery of what human life should be. I long to alleviate the evil, but I cannot, and I too suffer.[1]

While the problem of evil has exercised the minds of philosophers for centuries, it is no mere philosopher's conundrum. It does not take an encounter with the peculiar logical difficulties regarding evil to realize that there is a problem of evil. In philosophical environs the question of evil assumes a sequestered significance. But Everyman is just as aware of the problem as any philosopher is. Distinguishing between the existential problem of evil picked out by ordinary human experience and the more academic logical problem that concerns most philosophers as philosophers is now commonplace. The former is the problem of evil encountered in the "real" world of blood, sweat, and tears; the latter the problem considered from the relatively more comfortable perspective of the ivory tower. Of course, the logical problem of evil and the existential problem of evil are not unrelated in their purview. Rather, they represent different perspectives from which to regard what is fundamentally the same issue. The problem of evil must be felt before it can be pondered. Nevertheless, it is the same fact of evil that gives rise to the concern, whether that concern is essentially practical or distinctively theoretical. The practical and the theoretical represent merely different points on a single continuum of concern with our experience of evil.

Some philosophers have been rather adroit in their expression of this theme. For Gabriel Marcel, the only problem of evil is what is sometimes called the "existential" mode of the problem. If Marcel is correct, this language intrudes a pseudodistinction and the so-called logical problem of evil becomes a pseudoproblem, or a mystery degraded to the level of a problem. To seek "the causes or the secret aims" of experienced evil, the professed goal of any theodicy, is to view evil "from outside," where evil no longer "*touches* me" and is therefore "no longer evil which is suffered." And evil that ceases to be suffered "ceases to be evil." So the only evil that exists is the evil that we encounter in our prereflective lived experience. Our ivory tower incursions into logical territory miss the heart of the matter.[2]

Even if we accept Marcel's corrective, and it is salutary that we learn to appreciate the priority that is to be reserved for evil as experienced, his insight does not entail that philosophical puzzles in this connection are simply about nothing. Furthermore, in the controversy about evil, the lofty realm of philosophical speculation and the mundane arena of hard personal experience are not mutually exclusive. Their respective concerns do not ride along parallel tracks, never to converge. The logical puzzles that preoccupy philosophers are generated by certain undesirable features of our experience (that is, particular evils) together with certain beliefs that we, or at least some people, hold about the divine nature. In fact, our very recognition of evil within experience involves the application of appropriate concepts and an appeal to distinctions we are given to making between what is good and what is evil. Langdon Gilkey observes:

> Persons are thinking and reflective as well as merely existing beings. They have unanswered puzzles in their minds as well as unrelieved estrangement in their souls. They have skeptical doubts about the truth they possess as well as despair about the meaning of the life that is theirs. They are curious about intellectual answers as well as hungry for a new mode of being or existing. And clearly these two levels, the existential and the intellectual–reflective, are interacting and interrelated all the time.[3]

What Gilkey says here seems to be especially well illustrated in connection with the problem of evil.

All intelligent persons, and not philosophers only, are constrained to seek an explanation for our experience of pain and suffering. This observation finds subtle confirmation in the best of fictional literature. The literary imagination exploits an abundance of archetypes in its ruminations about this ubiquitous ingredient of human experience.

Who can read Albert Camus, or Fyodor Dostoyevsky, or Thomas Hardy without noticing the role evil plays in the lives of their characters and their interest in coming to terms with evil in their experience? The experienced reality of evil, as a central feature of the "human condition," begs the attention of all who are sensitive to the permutations of human existence.[4]

That serious discussion of the problem of evil is not the exclusive domain of professional philosophers is further evidenced by the numerous popular nonfictional treatments of the problem. It is interesting to note that even these display a marked regard for the logical and philosophical difficulties attending the question of evil, despite disclaimers to the contrary. Consider two examples. Rabbi Harold Kushner warns at the very outset of his national bestseller *When Bad Things Happen to Good People* that "this is not an abstract book about God and theology.... This is a very personal book."[5] Kushner intends for his book to fill a rift in the landscape of theodicy, for he says regarding the other books he turned to in the face of personal tragedy that they "were more concerned with defending God's honor, with logical proof that bad is really good and that evil is necessary to make this a good world.... I hope that this book is not like those. I did not set out to write a book that would explain or defend God."[6] Nevertheless, in reaching for an answer to his fundamental question of why "bad things" happen to "good people," Kushner not only betrays familiarity with the ordinary logical issues inherent in the problem of evil but even rejects traditional arguments purporting to solve the problem, and this precisely because of their inadequacy on logical grounds. His effort to formulate objections on this score is nothing if not a distinctly philosophical enterprise, however informally conducted.

In the inspirational book *Where Is God When It Hurts?* Christian author Philip Yancey asserts, "I will not attempt to address philosophers with this book. . . . Most of our problems with pain are not mental gymnastics." Yet he says, apparently with a sense of inevitability, that "some large philosophical questions I will leave *almost* untouched."[7] Yancey's footnotes reveal a mixture of references both to popular writings and to semiphilosophical works. Both Kushner and Yancey exhibit a concern to redress the especially human side of theodicy. Yet they seem to recognize that, given this emphasis, their reflections and conclusions must remain sensitive to the principles of philosophy. A concern with the philosophical dimensions of the problem of evil appears unavoidable.

It seems that the popularity of the highly publicized problem of evil, even in airy philosophical circles, is due largely to the existential forcibleness of evil in routine human experience. It is the felt reality of evil that impels even the philosopher; doubtless, no philosopher ever sought to address the matter who did not first sense that "all climates are not equally genial, that perpetual spring does not reign throughout the year, that all God's creatures do not possess the same advantages, that clouds and tempests sometimes darken the natural world and vice and misery the moral world, and that all the works of the creation are not formed with equal perfection."[8]

The most casual encounter with the philosophical literature on the subject of evil yields the impression that diverse formulations of the problem come down to essentially the same thing. In the final analysis, the greatest difference between diverse expressions of the problem of evil is their comparative degree of sophistication. The relative ease of posing the problem of evil philosophically is illustrated by two famous examples. The aristocratic Roman philosopher Boethius (c. A.D. 480–524) articulated the problem of evil with utmost economy of language: "If there be a God, from whence proceed so many evils?"[9] Who cannot identify with this imposing question? The classic expression of the problem comes from David Hume's *Dialogues Concerning Natural Religion.* Here Philo says to Demea, "Epicurus's old questions are yet unanswered. Is he [the Deity] willing to prevent evil, but not able? then is he impotent. Is he able, but not willing? then is he malevolent. Is he both able and willing? whence then is evil?"[10] Martin Gardner notes that "this argument, deadly and incisive, has been repeated endlessly by philosophers of all persuasions. I suspect that in every age and place, if you asked an ordinary atheist why he or she did not believe in God you would get some version of Epicurus's argument."[11]

Skeptics are by no means the only ones who have formulated the problem of evil with such keen logical forcefulness and daring simplicity. The next chapter describes the manner in which the Christian thinkers St. Augustine, St. Thomas Aquinas, and Gottfried Leibniz have defined and addressed the problem of evil. But first, it is useful to delineate the distinctiveness of the problem of evil for theistic belief.

In its logical form the problem of evil is typically sketched against the backdrop of belief in a God having certain specific attributes. This is the God of classical theism, whose problematic attributes include omniscience, omnipotence, and omnibenevolence. Hume's formulation of the problem of evil is clearly directed against this Judeo–Christian conception of God.

Of course, it is true that monotheistic faith is not the only religious orientation that has had to face the problem of evil generally. "All religions take account of this; some, indeed, make it the basis of all they have to say."[12] The history of religions attests that evil is everyone's problem. Even the sophisticated atheist is not exempt, for in a very important sense the problem of evil is not overcome by denying the existence of God. Though the experience of evil does not present the same theoretical problem for atheists that it does for religious believers of various kinds, the conceptual difficulty of accounting for the reality of evil and the practical challenge of coping with the experience of evil remain.[13]

Some theists have argued that, apart from some ultimate objective basis for assigning moral distinctions, there is the problem of adequately defining evil from an atheistic point of view. Nicolas Berdyaev, for example, appeals to this difficulty in explicit connection with the philosophical problem of evil: "The ethical problem presupposes a theodicy, without which there can be no ethics. If there is a distinction between good and evil, and if evil exists, God must be justified, since the justification of God is the solution of the problem of evil. If there were no evil and no distinction between good and evil, there could be no ethics and no theodicy."[14] In response to this sort of claim, Kai Nielsen, for example, has objected to the accusation that there can be no basis for affirming the meaningfulness of human existence and of ethical norms without reference to religious values of some kind.[15]

This debate reflects an area of concern for atheists when confronted with the reality of evil that faces any person, believer or nonbeliever. The atheist certainly does not accept the thesis that the nature of evil cannot even be properly conceived without reference to some moral ultimate that inheres in a personal Being. And yet it would seem unsatisfactory for the atheist to deny the reality of evil for the sake of disbelief in God. There are two reasons for this. The experience of evil seems too immediate to warrant such a denial, and atheists have tended to rely on the reality of evil in framing their most compelling objections to the claim that God exists. Even objections that consist primarily in decrying confusion about impossible conceptions of God often refer, en passant, to the reality of evil.

Despite this universal concern with the problem of evil, when speaking of "the problem of evil" in this book I have in mind the particular difficulty (or cluster of difficulties) arising when Christian theistic faith encounters the reality of evil in the world and in human experience. This restriction of discussion to Christian theistic belief is due in part to the realization that the encounter between Christian faith and the experience of evil is internal to that faith itself. The redemptive aspects of Christian theology are central to the Christian tradition. In their redemptive nature these components are responses to the presence of evil.

Furthermore, the problem of evil has traditionally been associated with the truth claims of the Christian religion. Historically, "the problem of evil" is the official label for a difficulty uniquely attending Christian theism, with its affirmation of divine omnipotence and omnibenevolence. While theoretical problems regarding evil may be posed for other religious traditions, the prima facie conceptual difficulties for these alternative religious perspectives can often be assuaged in ways not open to the Christian theist. This latter point calls for some independent explanation.

In almost every other religious orientation the specific logical difficulties attending evil vary according to their respective orientation's conceptions of God and evil, and prima facie solutions at their disposal are discoverable along one of two general avenues. Either the nature of evil itself is defined in a way that does not seem to risk contradiction with belief in the existence of God, or else the nature and character of God is conceived in such a way as to mitigate the difficulty that the reality of evil would otherwise pose. Often an alteration in the conception both of the divine nature and of the essence of evil go hand in hand. Either strategy has the effect of dissolving the theoretical–philosophical problem of evil by conceiving either of evil or of God's nature (or both) in such a way as to eliminate the appearance that these realities are ultimately irreconcilable. (A further strategy that is sometimes suggested involves some fine-tuning of the conception of human freedom.)

In the first strategy, that of redefining evil, two alternatives immediately present themselves. These are the antithetical positions of either concluding that evil is an unreality (as we find in the Christian Science of Mary Baker Eddy, Theosophy, Buddhism, and some forms of Hinduism) or regarding evil as a real metaphysical principle that coexists with the principle of good (as taught in Zoroastrianism). If either of these options is adopted, the *logical* problem of evil recedes into the background, more or less regardless of one's conception of the divine nature. It does so, however, at a price that the traditional Christian theist is unwilling to pay. The Christian believer must not deny the reality of evil, for then the redemptive aspect of Christian faith would be entirely superfluous.

The philosophical options concerning the nature of God are more numerous. They are, in fact, representative of a rather wide range of metaphysical viewpoints. At least three alternative conceptions of God each allow for the simultaneous existence of both God and evil by altering the concept of God in some way. This result is obtained when it is denied either that God is capable of destroying evil, that God is willing to destroy evil, or that God is capable of foreseeing evil. The most common of these three strategies is the first, which allows for a limitation on divine power to prevent or overcome evil. John Stuart Mill and William James adopted this strategy, and so have the process theists Alfred North Whitehead, Charles Hartshorne, and John Cobb. A fourth option concerning God is atheism, which denies God's existence altogether. This too has been a popular approach among twentieth-century thinkers.

The whole point of this taxonomy of alternative positions is that no one of these philosophical options, either concerning evil or concerning God, is open to the orthodox Christian theistic believer. Not only, therefore, do "the terms of the problem of evil vary with the character of the religious beliefs which give rise to it,"[16] but there is a distinctive problem of evil for the tradition under consideration in this book.

Henceforth, the problem of evil treated here is the problem of reconciling a minimum of three propositions that have traditionally been taken as essential to Christian theism. These are (1) that God is all-powerful, (2) that God is completely good, and (3) that evil really exists. The resulting "trilemma" arises in that, as J. L. Mackie suggests, "there seems to be some contradiction between these three propositions, so that if any two of them were true the third would be false."[17] Or, as Antony Flew writes, "The issue is whether to assert at the same time first that there is an infinitely good God, second that he is an all-powerful Creator, and third that there are evils in his universe, is to contradict yourself."[18] Indeed, the problem of evil refers to what "many people regard as the clearest indication that there could not be a God."[19]

The effort to reconcile three propositions apparently germane to a particular theological system demands a clarification of the meaning of the term "reconcile." Apart from a well-defined context, this term is admittedly ambiguous.[20] In the context of our discussion, "reconcile" refers to the attempt to demonstrate that the three minimal propositions cited above are not logically incompatible. The term is appropriate for designating the task confronting the theodicist who wishes to respond to deductive or a priori formulations of the problem of evil, formulations that purport to show that Christian theism entails belief in logically contradictory notions. The so-called inductive or a posteriori problem of evil is another matter. Here the theodicist must defend the *plausibility* of theistic belief in the face of evil.

The problem of evil, then, has been subjected to centuries-long discussion. The next chapter is devoted to surveying the main features of a tradition that has developed in response to the problem of evil. The purpose is to show that there is historical precedent for my central claim: that the significance of the problem of evil and the possibility of constructing an adequate theodicy both depend upon the fortunes of natural theology.

2
The Augustinian Tradition

This chapter focuses on three key theodicists who have endeavored to reconcile the existence of evil with the traditional Christian conception of God and who subscribe to the same general strategy in their formulation of a theodicy. While St. Augustine, St. Thomas Aquinas, and Gottfried Leibniz made distinctive contributions to the project of theodicy, each of their proposals for dealing with the problem of evil stresses the role of natural theology (the attempt to demonstrate the rationality of belief in God by appealing to evidence from the natural world).

In general, their position is that the development of natural theology is a noneliminable first step toward formulating an adequate theodicy. I emphasize the importance that each of these thinkers has placed upon the possibility of demonstrating the existence of God. For these figures the problem of evil is the problem of explaining the existence of evil, given that the existence of God has already been rendered rationally credible by one or more arguments. In other words, it is the problem of understanding the reasons (or possible reasons) God has for permitting evil.

Others, who also identify with the Christian tradition, have not approached theodicy in this way. For John Hick, for example, the problem is whether one may hold that God exists, given that evil exists, without losing all rational credibility. His conception of the problem, and of the proper way to address it, is in part a consequence of his judgment that natural theology cannot succeed.

ST. AUGUSTINE

The uncontested precursor of the theodicy tradition espoused in this book is St. Augustine of Hippo (A.D. 354–430). Hick has called Augustine "the greatest theodicist of all,"[1] an appellation well deserved in light of his originality and subsequent influence on both medieval and Reformation religious thought.

The problem of evil was a lifelong preoccupation for Augustine. In its practical aspect it was for him a stumbling block of immense proportions, effectively postponing his conversion to Christianity for some time. It is well known that he initially aligned himself with Manichaeism for its "admirably plausible solution to a difficulty which appeared to [him] insoluble on the premises of orthodox Christianity: the problem of evil."[2]

As an adherent of Manichaeism for nine years, Augustine envisioned a resolution of the problem of evil by means of a metaphysical dualism. He affirmed the coexistence of two primal principles or substances, namely, the divine principle of the good or light and the conflicting principle of evil or darkness. He believed these opposing principles to have roughly the same ontological status. The important point is that he regarded evil as a real independent substance. In the Manichaean theory, the world of the here and now was represented as "the locus of dramatic conflict between the two primal principles. . . . Man himself is ambivalent, embodying the conflict of the two principles."[3] Seeking refuge from this bondage, the Manichaean anticipated unification with the good principle through a gnosis, or true knowledge, of the human condition. Augustine eventually became disenchanted with this approach, for it proved ineffectual in his own experience with moral turpitude.

Augustine's bout with Manichaeism was one factor that led ultimately to his conversion to Christianity and to his subsequent formulation of an alternative theodicy that begins with an altogether different conception of the nature of evil. His treatise *De libero arbitrio voluntatis (On Free Choice of the Will)* in effect charts his pilgrimage from Manichaeism to the Christian faith. As it happens, the problem of evil is the central issue addressed in this significant writing. It is interesting to note that Augustine began his treatise only two years after his conversion to Christianity, though it was not completed until seven or eight years later. By this time he had become an ordained priest of the Church at Hippo Regius. This remarkably rapid ascent to such a position of authority was vouchsafed by his obvious critical acumen as a Christian scholar as well as his commitment to Christian piety. One can safely surmise that the treatise on free will represented Augustine's mature analysis and earned for him the reputation that he enjoyed within the church.

Augustine composed his treatise in the form of a dialogue between himself and a friend named Evodius. The dialogue begins very appropriately with a request from Evodius: "Tell me, please, whether God is not the cause of evil." Augustine replies: "But if you know or believe that God is good (and it is not right to believe otherwise), God does not do evil."[4] What follows in the rest of the discourse is Augustine's attempt to justify this initial reply by means of rational argumentation. The resulting theodicy is now regarded within the Christian tradition as the classic reply to the problem of evil. It is even possible to speak, as Hick often does, of an "Augustinian tradition" in theodicy, a tradition that has influenced Christian theodicists for centuries.

Augustine's initial response to the problem of evil is ingeniously proleptic of his overall strategy for framing a theodicy. When he answers Evodius, it is evident that for Augustine a prior commitment to the goodness of God precludes the very possibility of assigning God as the cause of evil. He insists, rather, that if God is good in any meaningful sense then the search for the cause of evil must lead elsewhere. Everything that God creates is necessarily good. This follows if God himself, the Creator, is good. This reply has the form of a conditional proposition: *if* you know or believe that God is good, then God is not the cause of evil.

Not surprisingly, therefore, Augustine's procedure for constructing an adequate account of the origin of evil begins with his argument for the existence of God as the omnibenevolent Creator. His proof for God's existence plays a crucial role in his treatise *On Free Choice of the Will.* This fact cannot be overemphasized. Much of book 2, the central portion of the treatise, is devoted to this philosophical argument for the existence of God. Augustine's theodicy can be understood only to the extent that one fully appreciates the importance he places on the possibility of demonstrating that a good God exists. This has not always been recognized by his readers.[5]

The starting point in Augustine's proof for God's existence is the self-consciousness of the questioning individual. The individual's own real personal existence is undeniable, for the possibility of being deceived about one's existence presupposes that one exists. That is, doubt is itself intractable evidence that the one who doubts actually exists. (It is said that when asked by an anxious skeptic, "Augustine, do I exist?" the saint answered with rhetorical flare, "Who wants to know?") Whereas one's mind itself is neither immutable nor timeless but a contingent fact, the undeniability of one's existence is a timeless and immutable truth. While our minds may change or pass away, the judgment that we have minds, that we exist as conscious entities, is unchangeable. The intentional act of the mind grasps an unchangeable reality, even though the object the mind intends is contingent. If it is true that I exist at time t_1, that truth will remain long after I cease to exist. If the proposition "I exist at t_1" is ever true, then it must be true for all time. It does not matter whether truth's object is a contingent reality or a necessary reality, the truth itself is immutable. The mind often apprehends truths that are immutable and timeless but happen not to be about contingent entities—that seven plus three is ten, for instance. But it is not a necessary condition for the immutability of any truth that it have as its object a noncontingent reality. Etienne Gilson remarks that, according to Augustine, "even in the simplest judgment, provided only it be a true one, there is a sufficient foundation for a proof of the existence of God."[6]

The initial step in Augustine's argument for the existence of God is to establish that there are eternal truths "more excellent" than our minds that entertain them. In the sequel, God is posited as the necessary ground of these eternal truths. Inasmuch as all eternal truths prove, in principle, to be superior to finite human minds, their source must be an immutable Mind. Augustine's argument takes the following form:

1. If there is something immutable and superior to reason, then God exists.
2. Truth is immutable and superior to reason.
3. Therefore, God exists.

Augustine proposes that by this "sure though somewhat tenuous form of reasoning" one cannot deny that God exists; it is, he says, an "indubitable fact."[7] However opaque the terms of the second premise may seem, one is impressed with the strong language he uses to characterize what he takes to be the force of his argument. He is not entirely self-assured about the *persuasive* capacity of his argument, for he acknowledges its tenuousness. Nevertheless, he believes that the argument is logically secure; that is, it provides support for the conclusion that God exists, whether or not any nonbeliever is ever actually convinced by the argument.

Having argued in this way for the existence of God, Augustine does not leave his reader to conjecture about the divine nature. He proceeds to offer a demonstration that God is "Creator of all good things which He Himself transcends in excellence."[8] Hence, there exists an important distinction between the goodness of God and the derivative goodness of the created order. God is a necessary good, whereas all created things are contingent goods.

Here Augustine's Platonistic propensity is most evident, for he identifies God, as the ground of eternal truth, with eternal Form, through which "every temporal thing can receive its form,"[9] explaining that "nothing can give itself form, since nothing can give to itself what it does not have."[10] All contingent forms depend for their existence upon the eternal Form. "Existing things cease to exist when form is completely taken away."[11] This argument that eternal Form is the provenance of all existing things leads Augustine to conclude that "all good things, whether great or small, can come only from God."[12] This means, conversely, both that the form of a thing is a good and that only goods proceed from God. As a consequence, things "tend toward nonexistence" when they suffer a deficiency in their form. "No matter how much creatures may lack, and however much they tend toward nonexistence by virtue of their deficiency, nevertheless some form remains in them, so that they somehow exist. Moreover, whatever form remains in a deficient object comes from that Form which knows no lack."[13] This belief in the existence and omnibenevolence of God as Creator is *the cornerstone of Augustine's theodicy*. With these truths firmly in place, both piety and reason require the believer to dissociate God from the cause of evil.

It may be tempting to object straight off to Augustine's apparent assumption that to cause evil is always to do evil. The temptation is reinforced by the fact that Augustine's immediate reply to the question Does God cause evil? is that God does not do evil, leaving the impression that causing is to be identified with doing. But this is not an assumption that Augustine makes, for there is a sense in which God does cause evil even though he does not do evil.

Augustine's insistence that God does not do evil is bound up with a distinction he makes between evil that is done and evil that is suffered. Divine punishment of an evildoer, though experienced as evil by the one punished, is not a case of God doing evil. Nevertheless, since it is experienced as evil by the one God punishes, it can be said somewhat loosely that God causes this evil, for God exacts the punishment. This is what his justice requires, and, since it is a function of his justice, the performance of the punishment cannot be evil. Indeed, it is good that God should punish a wicked person, even though the person loses certain desired goods (such as freedom of concourse in society) as a consequence. Here the loss of some good is a condition for the realization of another good. The presumption is that the latter good is of a higher order since it is the one promoted by God, who cannot do evil.[14]

Having excluded the possibility that God is the cause of evil, Augustine locates the source of evil elsewhere, namely, in the free will of human persons: "Either the will is the first cause of sin, or else there is no first cause."[15] He means that by the exercise of human free will comes all distortion to created goods, that is, evil.

Here one must note how Augustine defines evil. Evil is the corruption of a good. Such a corruption is never total lest that in which the evil inheres ceases to exist altogether. Every being is good insofar as it has being. Evil is a parasite on being; it is not a substance as such. Rather, it is a privation in a substance. A thing is evil to the extent that it lacks some particular good that is appropriate to it. The human will itself is created by God and is, therefore, a created good. Nevertheless, it can be abused, as it is when it is directed away from the good. Since the will is free, such abuse is possible. But free will itself is a good because, says Augustine, "no righteous act could be performed except by free choice of the will, and . . . God gave it for this reason."[16] Augustine's account depends upon a subtle distinction between the *having* of human free will and the *exercise* of human free will. The former obtains through divine agency, the latter through human agency.

Augustine's apology for the goodness of human free will begins with the deductive argument that free will must be a good since it is given by God, but his apology does not end there. He further asseverates that there are good inductive grounds for judging that free choice is a good. He argues that "even men who lead the most evil lives agree that they cannot live rightly" apart from having free will.[17] It would appear that freedom is a necessary condition for all moral behavior. By "living rightly" he means leading a righteous life. Such a life is one that is morally praiseworthy or commendable. It is a life for the direction of which the individual is personally and directly responsible.

In this free-will account of the origin of evil, evil consists in the movement of the will from immutable to transient goods.[18] When the search for happiness, proper in and of itself, is directed at temporal things rather than eternal things, the unhappy misdirectedness of this search is symptomatic of an abuse of free will, and the result is the production of evil.[19] This movement of the will is voluntary rather than compulsory since the will is free; therefore, the *exercise* of free will is not from God. Augustine denies that the movement of the will to lesser goods is natural to it, for this would imply necessity in the performance of evil, which in turn would obviate personal moral accountability. "We conclude, therefore, that the movement which, for the sake of pleasure, turns the will from the Creator to the creature belongs to the will itself."[20] Free persons are under no necessity to act immorally.

At this point Augustine anticipates a common objection to the possibility of human freedom within a theistic universe, namely, that God's foreknowledge makes real freedom impossible since all that God foreknows must come to pass, unless there is some deficiency in God's foreknowledge. If these two propositions, "that [1] God has foreknowledge of all future events, and that [2] we do not sin by necessity but by free will," are ultimately inconsistent, then it seems that one must choose between "the blasphemous denial of God's foreknowledge or . . . the admission that we sin by necessity, not by will."[21]

Augustine seems to think that the appearance of inconsistency between divine foreknowledge and human freedom is due to a shift in meaning of the term "necessary." If God foreknows all future states of affairs, then it is right to maintain that those states of affairs must occur. This must be so because God can never be wrong about what he knows. But if the objects of God's knowledge include free acts, then by definition these acts cannot be necessary. Indeed, as free acts they are not necessary in the same sense that they are necessary as objects of God's knowledge. If the alleged inconsistency arises only by committing the fallacy of equivocation, then no genuine contradiction between divine foreknowledge and human freedom has been demonstrated.

But Augustine does not leave the matter here. He goes on to offer a reductio ad absurdum response to this objection to free will when he asks: "How could it be that nothing happens otherwise than as God foreknew, if He foreknows that something is going to be willed when nothing is going to be willed?"[22] He argues that God's foreknowledge, far from removing freedom, guarantees that humans will have the power to exercise freedom in the future.

> For when [God] has foreknowledge of our will, it is going to be the will that He has foreknown. Therefore, the will is going to be a will because God has foreknowledge of it. Nor can it be a will if it is not in our power. Therefore, God also has knowledge of our power over it. So the power is not taken from me by His foreknowledge; but because of His foreknowledge, the power to will will more certainly be present in me, since God, whose foreknowledge does not err, has foreknown that I shall have the power.[23]

This particular claim may not seem very convincing.[24] It does, however, illustrate how confident Augustine was that divine foreknowledge and human free will are compatible. And just as God's foreknowledge does not attenuate real human freedom, so it does not mitigate human responsibility when such freedom is exercised.[25] Human creatures are therefore obliged to worship the Creator for the manifest order and goodness of his creation, which includes free moral persons who are able to do evil.[26]

The position here adumbrated by Augustine has come to be called the free-will defense. This title aptly identifies the manner in which Augustine attempts to account for the origin of evil. Human free will is the first cause of evil. For Augustine, the task of theodicy consists in properly accounting for the reality of evil in the world in light of the indubitable existence of God, who is the omnibenevolent Creator and who has bestowed the good of freedom upon human persons. On strictly independent grounds, Augustine argues positively for the existence of God. This is a non-negotiable first step in his theodicy. Because God is good, he cannot be the cause of evil.

Yet evil is real; there must, therefore, be *some* cause. Here Augustine's controversial metaphysical doctrine of privation comes into play. Evil, no less real for being a privation, is a deficiency in some created good. Human free will, itself a created good, is susceptible of just such a deficiency because, being free, it can be directed away from the good. In other words, the will is corruptible. However, the possibility that freedom would be abused, and the fact that it has been abused, in no way diminishes the omniscience of God, which includes foreknowledge. Indeed, even the abuse of freedom is subject to the sovereign wisdom of God, who gave humans free will in the first place. Hence, it is to be expected that God, the omnibenevolent Creator and wise Bestower of human free will, both can and will bring ultimate good out of all evil. With admirable terseness, Norman Geisler and Winfried Corduan summarize all of these essential elements in the theodicy formulated by Augustine: "An absolutely good God created a finitely good universe containing good creatures who freely chose the lesser good of themselves to the higher good of God, thus corrupting creation. God nevertheless is able to use the evil of the parts for the greater good of the whole according to His own good purposes."[27]

ST. THOMAS AQUINAS

St. Thomas Aquinas (c. 1225–1274) self-consciously constructed his own theodicy upon the foundation prepared by his predecessor, Augustine. Whereas Augustine clearly addressed the problem of evil as a matter of deep personal concern, Aquinas wrote more "in an abstract and detached manner."[28] In contradistinction to Augustine, it is possible to say with Thomas Gilby that "few voluminous writers have been less autobiographical than St. Thomas."[29] Nevertheless, although Augustine may have given this issue relatively more attention in his writings, particularly in terms of addressing the existential side of the problem, Aquinas was far from diffident in his approach to the problem of evil. He understood well that evil had been proposed as a serious objection to the existence of God, for in the *Summa theolo-*

giae the problem of evil first appears under the heading "Whether God Exists?": "It seems that God does not exist; because if one of two contraries be infinite, the other would be altogether destroyed. But the name *God* means that He is infinite goodness. If, therefore, God existed, there would be no evil discoverable; but there is evil in the world. Therefore God does not exist."[30] Aquinas subsequently acknowledged a less forcible objection regarding God's existence, one that is not presumed to demonstrate that God does not exist. This second objection is intended, rather, to show that "there is no need to suppose God's existence," and this on the supposition that nature can itself account for "everything we see in the world."[31]

Evidently, Aquinas believed that the presence of evil in the world is the basis for the most threatening argument against the existence of God. He apparently also thought that the best defense against this kind of objection is a good offense, for he did not initially reply by framing a theodicy per se. Instead, his initial response was to marshal five positive arguments for the existence of God. It is instructive to note that Aquinas's famous *quinque viae* ("five ways") are introduced in this context. He firmly maintained that "the existence of God, in so far as it is not self-evident to us, can be demonstrated from those of His effects which are known to us,"[32] the presence of evil in the world notwithstanding.

The effects that Aquinas considered to be demonstrative of the existence of God include motion, efficient causality, possibility and necessity (his argument from contingency), gradation in things, and the governance of the world.[33] He was unequivocal about what he regarded as the essential first step in answering any objections to God's existence on the basis of evil in the world. The crucial step consists in the formulation of a cosmological a posteriori argument for the existence of God. His explicit reply to the problem of evil is postponed and only briefly foreshadowed in a quote from Augustine: "As Augustine says: *Since God is the highest good, He would not allow any evil to exist in His works, unless His omnipotence and goodness were such as to bring good even out of evil.* This is part of the infinite goodness of God, that He should allow evil to exist, and out of it produce good."[34]

From this succinct statement the essence of Aquinas's theodicy can be expressed by a single proposition: God, being good, must have a morally sufficient reason for permitting the existence of evil in this world. What must be shown, then, is that God is indeed good and that evil can be reconciled with this truth. The Angelic Doctor moves from his fivefold demonstration of God's existence to a consideration of the *manner* of God's existence.

This paves the way for any proper understanding of God's essence, that is, of the particular attributes properly ascribed to God. Aquinas has this procedural point in mind when he writes, "When the existence of a thing has been ascertained, there remains the further question of the manner of its existence, in order that we may know its essence."[35] Following his efforts to demonstrate the existence of God, Aquinas proceeds with his attempt to show how "all perfections found in anything at all must originally and superabundantly be present in God."[36] This follows in that "the name for a perfection should be applied more forcibly to the cause than to the effect."[37] Or, in the words of the *Summa theologiae*, "everything brought to perfection pre-exists in the producing cause in a more excellent mode."[38] God "contains within himself the whole perfection of existence: all perfections are embraced in the perfection of existence, and therefore no single perfection is lacking in God."[39]

From the divine perfection it is but a short step to the goodness of God, for "each thing is good from the fact that it is perfect."[40] Aquinas even says in book 1 of the *Summa contra gentiles*, "From the divine perfection, which we have shown, we can conclude to the goodness of God."[41] Furthermore, one of the five ways of demonstrating God's existence ostensibly establishes that

> there is a certain first unmoved mover, namely, God. This mover moves as a completely unmoved mover, which is as something desired. Therefore, since God is the first unmoved mover, He is the first desired. But something is desired in two ways, namely, either because it is good or because it appears to be good. The first desired is what is good, since the apparent good does not move through itself but according as it has a certain appearance of the good, whereas the good moves through itself. The first desired, therefore, God, is truly good.[42]

From the demonstration that God, as the first unmoved mover, is good, two things follow: first, that "God is goodness itself"[43] and second, that "there cannot be evil in God."[44]

Having thus prepared the way by demonstrating both the existence and the essential goodness of God on independent grounds, Aquinas has merely to show that the existence of evil is compatible with this conclusion. It is at this point that he finally addresses the problem of evil directly. With the really difficult work behind him, his efforts here look rather like a mopping-up exercise. Again, his approach is recognizably Augustinian.

As for the nature of evil, Aquinas considers it a privation of good: "Evil indicates the absence of good. But not every absence of good is evil. For absence of good can be taken in a privative and in a negative sense. Absence of good, taken negatively, is not evil. . . . But the absence of good, taken in a privative sense, is an evil."[45] Furthermore, "evil cannot wholly consume good."[46] By calling evil a privation Aquinas is not denying the reality of evil. Evil is a real privation inherent in a good.

Frederick Copleston is sensitive to the spirit of Aquinas's analysis when he explains the relevance of this conception of the nature of evil: "If God created all things, and if evil is a thing, we should have to say that God created evil directly. . . . But if evil is a privation, it is not necessary to speak of it as having been created by God on the ground that God created all things."[47] If evil were a substantial entity, God would necessarily be its cause. Because it is not, however, God is not directly responsible for its existence.

Does this analysis of evil as a privation absolve Aquinas from seeking a cause for evil? No indeed, for he says, "It must be said that every evil in some way has a cause. For evil is the absence of the good which is natural and due to a thing. But that anything fall short of its natural and due disposition can come only from some cause drawing it out of its proper disposition."[48] So for Aquinas, even privation in being requires a cause, and it is precisely in terms of the peculiar nature of a privation that he seeks to ascertain the cause of evil: "But evil has no formal cause, but is rather a privation of form. So, too, neither has it a final cause, but is rather a privation of order to the proper end; since it is not only the end which has the nature of good, but also the useful, which is ordered to the end."[49] In other words, a privation as such is susceptible to neither a formal cause nor a final cause. Hence, the proper way to speak of the cause of evil, if evil is a privation, is "by way of an agent, not directly, but accidentally."[50]

According to Aquinas, *all* evil is caused accidentally. It is imperative to understand the subtlety of the terminology employed here. By "accidental cause" he means that evil arises as the byproduct of some good desired. Evil is produced as an incidental effect of some good that is sought. On this analysis, it is admissible to conceive of God as the *accidental* cause of some physical evils without assigning moral culpability to God for the existence of evil. In *Summa theologiae* 1a.49.2 Aquinas attempts to show how God can be regarded as the accidental cause of natural or physical evils. In his *Tour of the Summa* Paul Glenn paraphrases this passage as follows: "Thus God wills physical evils *per accidens* inasmuch as these are incidental to the working of good. But God wills no evil *per se*."[51]

God permits certain physical evils since they are necessary con-comitants to a world with the kinds of goods God wills. Yet not all physical evils fit into this analysis. Some are byproducts of moral activity, and though these too are brought about accidentally, the agent here is the human person. Human beings are the *per accidens* cause of all physical evils that are not willed *per accidens* by God. This is because such physical evils are themselves byproducts of moral evils, all of which are caused *per accidens* by finite human individuals in the exercise of free will. One acts immorally when "he causes evil *per accidens* in his quest for good."[52] So the efficient cause, indirect always, of all moral evils and, consequently, of many physical evils, is the human person. Therefore, finite human individuals are responsi-ble for the existence of all such evils.

This outline of a theodicy from Thomas Aquinas has salient affini-ties with Augustine's analysis. If it appears that the "solution" prof-fered by Aquinas raises further questions about why God, while perhaps not the cause of any evil per se and only the cause of certain physical evils *per accidens,* would permit any evil that he certainly could have foreseen and forestalled, then the crucial matter is to recall that Aquinas was "convinced that the metaphysician can prove the existence of God independently of the problem of evil, and that we therefore know that there is a solution to the problem even though we cannot provide it."[53]

Aquinas's theodicy cannot be fully appreciated, or even properly understood, apart from grasping his conviction that one could first positively establish that God exists. The question of evil arises natu-rally enough for him, but only as a residual problem once the existence of God has already been demonstrated. In other words, evil does not undermine the force of the proofs for God's existence. Rather, the truth that God exists delimits the range of possibilities for properly apprehending the reality of evil. This prior commitment to God's existence and absolute goodness is programmatic for Aquinas's theod-icy. For him, the problem of evil consists in reconciling the reality of evil with the previously established truth of God's omnibenevolent existence. If one fails in the attempt to reconcile these two existential realities, this failure has no bearing on the final certainty either of God's existence or of his goodness. Naturally, the believer should seek to understand this relationship as fully as possible, for "though evil is neither good nor of God, nevertheless to understand it is both good and from God."[54] The subtlety of this strategy for constructing a theodicy vindicates Ninian Smart's judgment that "the proofs are central to Aquinas' whole exposition of natural theology."[55]

GOTTFRIED WILHELM VON LEIBNIZ

It is commonplace to credit the great German thinker Gottfried Wilhelm von Leibniz (1646–1716) with coining the term "theodicy" in his treatise *Theodicee* (1710). By the time this monograph had been written and published in Amsterdam, Leibniz had already composed his *Discourse on Metaphysics* (1686), which reflects his mature thoughts on a complete metaphysical system. He evidently entertained a lifelong interest in the problem of evil. Some, however, criticize him for not being concerned enough. This is Hick's assessment when he says of Leibniz's *Theodicee* that "the problem of evil was for its author an intellectual puzzle rather than a terrifying threat to all the meaning that he had found in life."[56] Historically, Leibniz's philosophical treatment of the problem of evil was occasioned by the peculiar circumstances in which he found himself.

In 1676 Leibniz became tutor and librarian to the ducal court of Brunswick–Luneburg at Hanover, where he taught, among others, the Queen of Prussia, a very capable student. While at Hanover, one of his contemporaries, Pierre Bayle (1647–1706) emerged as a figure noted for stressing the problem of evil in his writings. So disturbing and influential was Bayle's religious skepticism that Leibniz was induced at the solicitation of the queen to formulate a refutation. The result was his *Essais de Theodicee sur la bonte de Dieu, la liberte de l'homme, et l'origine du mal (Theodicy; Essays on the Goodness of God, the Freedom of Man, and the Origin of Evil)*. One of the few philosophical works he published during his lifetime, Leibniz's *Theodicee* was written in response to an article in Bayle's *Dictionnaire historique et critique (Historical and Critical Dictionary)* (1696). Here is how Leibniz himself, in correspondence with Thomas Burnet, described the circumstances that led to his writing on the problem of evil:

> The greater part of the work was composed piece by piece, at a time when the late Queen of Prussia and I were having discussions of these matters in connection with Bayle's Dictionary and other writings, which were being widely read. In our conversations I generally answered the objections raised by Bayle and contrived to show that they are not so powerful as certain people who are not well disposed to religion would have us believe. Her Majesty frequently commanded me to set down my answers in writing, so that one could think them through more carefully. After the death of this great princess I gathered the pieces together, at the instigation of friends who had heard about them, and, with some additions, produced the book in question. It is a book of considerable size. As I have reflected upon this topic since my youth, I dare say that I have treated it thoroughly.[57]

Bayle, who has been described as "the most important and most influential skeptic of the late seventeenth century,"[58] challenged rationalist philosophers to demonstrate how the divine character could be reconciled with the reality of evil. It was his opinion that God's goodness and power were an impenetrable mystery in view of evil. The alleged purpose behind Bayle's incisive skepticism "was not . . . to foster atheism. His negative aim was to undermine any philosophical and theological defense of religious faith."[59] The *Dictionnaire historique et critique,* his chief work, "is a compendium of sceptical arguments against theological and philosophical theories, drawing the conclusion that rational endeavour is useless and man must turn to faith to justify his belief that things exist and that God is not a deceiver."[60]

Bayle believed that one could (and, sometimes at least, should) "accept as true that which a geometrical demonstration shows is completely false." He observed that "there is no contradiction between these two things: (1) The light of reason teaches that this is false; (2) I believe it nonetheless because I am convinced that this light is not infallible and because I prefer to submit to the proofs of feeling and to the impressions of conscience, in short, to the Word of God, than to a metaphysical demonstration." Not only is it psychologically possible for one to entertain such a combination of views; it is positively commendable when the light of reason is in conflict with the light of revelation.[61] On the relation between faith and reason, then, Bayle adopted the fideistic stance.

> One must necessarily choose between philosophy and the Gospel. If you do not want to believe anything but what is evident and in conformity with the common notions, choose philosophy and leave Christianity. If you are willing to believe the incomprehensible mysteries of religion, choose Christianity and leave philosophy. . . . A choice must necessarily be made. . . . Once again, a true Christian, well versed in the characteristics of supernatural truths and firm on the principles that are peculiar to the Gospel, will only laugh at the subtleties of the philosophers, and especially those of the Pyrrhonists. Faith will place him above the regions where the tempests of disputation reign. . . . Every Christian who allows himself to be disconcerted by the objections of the unbelievers, and to be scandalized by them, has one foot in the same grave as they do.[62]

In antithesis to Bayle's fideistic outlook, Leibniz felt that "philosophy has an ultimately religious and moral orientation in that it directs the mind to contemplation and love of God."[63] Leibniz pressed for certainty in metaphysics through rational demonstration. His fundamental outlook was clearly at cross-purposes with Bayle's "underlying conviction that reason should always remain skeptical toward religious affirmations and that the man of faith should forswear all concords and remain content with naturally inevident and unintelligible mysteries."[64]

These basic epistemological differences between Bayle and Leibniz are further exemplified in their respective attitudes toward the problem of evil. It is worth noting, however, that Bayle not only questioned the possibility of constructing a viable theodicy, but he also expended considerable effort to show that the truth of God's existence could not be demonstrated. It is advisable that students of the Leibnizian theodicy be fully appraised of the degree of Bayle's "historical Pyrrhonism" so that the relevance that this historical context has for Leibniz's response to the problem of evil can be fully appreciated.

As a rationalist, Leibniz was quite convinced that God's existence was capable of rational demonstration. He sought to deduce the existence of God by means of a sophisticated version of the ontological argument in which he sought to prove that God (or the necessary Being) is possible. The possibility of the existence of a necessary Being, in turn, would require that such a Being does actually exist.[65] Furthermore, Leibniz appealed to the "principle of sufficient reason" in his formulation of a cosmological argument, suggesting that "the ultimate [or sufficient] reason of all things must subsist in a necessary substance, in which all particular changes may exist only virtually as in its source: this substance is what we call *God.*"[66] This was his answer to the question, Why is there something rather than nothing?

Turning now to review Leibniz's theodicy proper, an insightful comment by H. J. McCloskey seems especially apposite: "Leibniz simply sought to bring out what is implied by the thesis that God exists."[67] M. B. Ahern is in basic agreement when he limns Leibniz's position as follows: "Leibniz believed that the existence of God can be established independently of evil. Consequently, problems about God and evil are in no way problems of how to account for evil since an omnipotent and wholly good God exists."[68] Given the existence of God, "the concept of the will of God has an important part to play in the philosophy of Leibniz" in that "it serves as an instrument of a priori construction."[69] If God exists, then certain truths follow out of hypothetical necessity. "Being all-perfect, he must create the best possible world, for there would be an imperfection in God if he chose to create a less good world when a better world is possible."[70]

John S. Feinberg has stated the matter plainly: "In a Leibnizian universe God exists by logical necessity, for He is the being whose nature is such that it is impossible for Him not to exist. The primary activity of God is to pick the best world out of an infinity of possible contingent worlds."[71] In Leibniz's metaphysical system God is the infinitely perfect Being. This is the conclusion of his theistic proofs. This infinitely perfect Being, when he acts, can do no less than his best when faced with a variety of possibilities or choices. He always does that which is the best he can do, and since God has "complete concepts" of all individual substances, he is able to select the best. It follows, therefore, that if there are a number of possible worlds, including no world at all, God must create the best one. Hence, Leibniz deduces that the actual world is—because it must be—the best of all possible worlds, any empirical evidence to the contrary notwithstanding.

Feinberg's use of "infinity" here may seem ill advised, for, as McCloskey understands Leibniz, "there must be a best possible world, for otherwise it would always be possible for God to have created a better world, *ad infinitum,* in which case he would not have created any world at all."[72] Indeed, it does not seem coherent to speak of God choosing the "best" among an infinity of contingent possibilities. This incoherence, however, may be latent in Leibniz's own thought, in which case Feinberg has stated the matter with accuracy. The point is an interesting one, but it does not affect my purpose in citing Feinberg's comment. I merely want to stress something important about Leibniz's view of the relationship between the judgment that God's existence is logically necessary and the judgment that the present world arrangment is optimal.

Now Leibniz does not mean to suggest that our experience of evil is merely a kind of "optical illusion" extrapolated to the level of all five senses. He writes, "It must be confessed that there is evil in this world which God has created, and that it was possible to make a world without any evil or even not to create a world at all, for its creation depended upon the free will of God."[73] Since he seriously admits the reality of evil, it is incumbent upon him to clarify what he means by calling this the "best possible world."

Leibniz begins the summary section of his *Theodicee* by anticipating the following objection:

> Whoever does not choose the best is lacking either in power or in knowledge or in goodness.
> God did not choose the best in creating this world.
> Therefore God was lacking either in power or in knowledge or in goodness.[74]

As one might expect, Leibniz takes issue with the second premise of this syllogism. He confidently accepts the first premise, and he would have to acquiesce in the conclusion if he could not show how this world, the world that God did create, is the best choice. He seeks to justify his rejection of the second premise "by showing that the best course is not always that which seeks to avoid evil, since it is possible that the evil is accompanied by a greater good."[75] He maintains that the objection will be sufficiently refuted if he can show "that a world which contains evil may be better than one without evil."[76] Since God could conceivably rectify the matter by some ultimate future perfection of the world, this possibility is established easily enough. In this Leibniz self-consciously aligns himself with the views of Augustine and Aquinas. He expostulates, however, that in the main part of the *Theodicee* he succeeds in doing more than demonstrating the mere possibility that evil is accompanied by a greater good. He boasts of proving the more ambitious proposition that "this world must in reality be better than any other possible world."[77]

Leibniz analyzes the notion of best possible world in terms of maximal good. The best world is one that exemplifies the greatest balance of complex intricacy on the one hand and order on the other. It must be a world in which both of these factors are simultaneously present to the greatest degree possible. In other words, in such a world no more complexity would be possible without a consequent sacrifice of order. Or conversely, more order would not be possible without a proportionate sacrifice in the level of complexity. This quintessential cosmic balance is obtained at the price of allowing a certain measure of evil into the system: "The permission of some evils and the exclusion of some goods, as is demanded by the best possible plan of the universe."[78] Leibniz further argues that this balance is in fact preserved in the world God has created as long as the amount of good in the overall system continues to outweigh that of evil.[79] It would not be too much to say of this proposal that evil is something of a hypothetical necessity, or "happy necessity," entailed by God's logically necessary choice of the best possible world.

Is God therefore responsible for "creating" evil? Leibniz's reply is grounded in his conception of the nature of evil. Although he readily acknowledges the reality of evil, he insists upon a distinction regarding the term "real" and, in doing so, proposes a way to understand evil that is once again reminiscent of that of Augustine and Aquinas. " 'Real' refers either to that which is positive only or it includes also privative beings."[80] Evil, in Leibniz's view, is a privative reality. It is an imperfection that comes from limitation. But since the infinitely perfect Being, God, cannot cause imperfection but only perfect positive realities, the imperfection of the privative reality denoted by the term "evil" must have some other cause. Here Leibniz identifies the human creature as the "deficient cause" of evil in the world. He even suggests that "privation is effective in an accidental way," perhaps alluding to the notion of *per accidens* causation in Aquinas.[81] In the tradition of Augustine and Aquinas, he affirms that human free will is the agency responsible for the occurrence of evil, or, in the case of some physical evils, it is the condition that prescribes the structure of the physical world wherein evil is a perfectly natural concomitant.

Before closing this discussion of Leibniz it is fitting to recall Voltaire's well-known satirical reaction to the Leibnizian theodicy in his droll tale *Candide*. *Candide, ou L'Optimisme* (1759) was written to mock the strange optimism that Voltaire believed to be inherent in Leibniz's theodicy. For Voltaire, this represented an irrational optimism. But Martin Gardner thinks that Voltaire's criticism "does not even touch [Leibniz's] argument."[82] This interesting consideration is included here because it throws a relatively unimposing aspect of Leibniz's theodicy into sharper relief: "The main point of *Candide* is that at this stage of history we live in what is not the best possible world, a point so obvious that Leibniz took it for granted. . . . Leibniz's world is the best possible only in its incomprehensible totality, and in the long run, which of course includes an afterlife."[83]

If this assessment is correct, and it does seem that Leibniz can be interpreted in this way, then here again Leibniz stands firmly within the tradition of Augustine and Aquinas by incorporating this eschatological assumption into his solution to the problem of evil. It may well be that Leibniz intended his best-world hypothesis to include the entire space–time universe, past, present, and future, including an eternity following this life where rewards and punishments will be meted out to morally deserving individuals with free wills. As the German theologian Wolfhart Pannenberg has observed, the Christian tradition affirms "an imminent end of this world that in some way invades the present even now."[84] Perhaps Leibniz envisioned something like this in his conception of the best possible world.

This brief excursion into the theodicy proposed by Gottfried Leibniz illustrates his solidarity with the tradition established by his precursors Augustine and Aquinas. Nevertheless, it is evident that he further developed the broad themes characteristic of Christian theodicy and even introduced certain peculiar notions not explicitly shared by otherwise like-minded theodicists. Leibniz's theodicy can be conveniently summarized in his own words:

> In this I have followed the view of St. Augustine, who said a hundred times that God has allowed evil in order to bring about good, i.e. a greater good, and that of Thomas Aquinas (in *libr.* II, *sent.*, *dist.* 32,

qu. I, *art.* i), that the permitting of evil tends to the good of the universe. . . . And for the clearer understanding of the matter I added, following many good authors, that it was in accord with order and the general good that God should allow certain creatures the opportunity for exercising their freedom, even when He foresaw that they would opt for evils: for God could so easily rectify the matter. For it was not proper that in order to counteract sin God should always act in an extraordinary manner.[85]

There can be no doubt that Leibniz deliberately placed himself within the tradition of his forebears Augustine and Aquinas. And it is noteworthy that in framing a satisfactory theodicy he shared their conviction about the important role of traditional arguments for the existence of God.

3
John Hick's Theodicy

The relevance of the problem of evil for the philosophy of religion has already been noted. The brief historical survey conducted in the previous chapter illustrates the urgency with which the problem has been addressed by theodicists for centuries. The first two chapters were general and preparatory for a more extensive treatment of a single important contemporary protagonist in the perennial debate, namely, John Hick.

The selection of Hick is easy to justify in view of his reputation as perhaps "the most influential thinker in the field of religious philosophy in the English speaking world."[1] As Jerry Gill remarks, the position Hick occupies "makes his thought 'fair game' for detailed attention and critical analysis."[2] With respect to the problem of evil in particular, Hick represents what some now view as the dominant trend in theodicy among modern Protestant thinkers.[3] William Rowe calls Hick the "foremost theodicist of our time."[4] Hick's efforts reflect a recent attempt to treat the problem of evil in light of modern scientific exigencies and to frame a theodicy that stands up under contemporary philosophical constraints. Further justification for devoting an entire monograph to the critical examination of Hick's theodicy can be found in a remark by the Catholic philosopher Illtyd Trethowan: "Dr. Hick has done so much excellent work in the philosophy of religion that anyone who ventures to disagree with him must give his reasons for doing so at some length."[5]

Since Hick's theodicy is intended as an alternative to the centuries-old Augustinian theodicy, his position is interesting for its ostensible promise to yield a better defense of Christian theism vis-à-vis evil in the world. This also makes his viewpoint susceptible to analysis through critical comparison with the tradition developed by Augustine, Aquinas, and Leibniz. It is the purpose of this book to provide a critical evaluation of Hick's theodicy and a defense of the Augustinian tradition by means of comparative analysis on several key points. To the extent that I find myself in agreement with Hick, my perspective will remain critical in the neutral sense of careful analysis and judgment. That is to say, not everything contained here will be censorious, for there is much in Hick's position that is instructive, whether one accepts it wholesale or not.

The procedure followed here in dealing with Hick's theodicy is first to provide a summary exposition of the main elements of his position in a way that adequately reflects their logical relationships and then to begin a reflective analysis and evaluation of certain of the most distinctive aspects of his system. The former is the lesser task and is executed in the remainder of this chapter. Subsequent chapters will take up the more engaging project of closer inspection. A defense of the Augustinian tradition is attempted along the way as the strengths and weaknesses of Hick's theodicy hypothesis come under critical scrutiny.

THE MAIN FEATURES OF HICK'S THEODICY

A number of philosophers have attempted to summarize the distinctive aspects of his theodicy before proceeding with an evaluation of some part or parts of his system. So, for instance, David Ray Griffin enumerates eight points central to Hick's position in preparation for his evaluation of the doctrine of omnipotence inherent in it.[6] Since Griffin's purpose in his book is to improve upon the concept of omnipotence utilized by various proponents of Christian theodicy, his summary of Hick naturally reflects an emphasis upon those matters that pertain to the concept of divine power. Others have fastened on different aspects of this theodicy in their evaluations, reflecting in their respective outlines of Hick's position the particular purposes they have set for themselves.[7]

In addition to these critical essays useful for determining the shape of his theodicy, there are several instances of exposition by Hick himself, varying in length and detail according to the context and purpose of his writing. His book *Evil and the God of Love* contains his most thorough treatment of the problem of evil and has become a well-known text on the subject of theodicy.[8] One must observe, however, that Hick's 389-page book (in its revised edition) is not confined to the development of his own theodicy. It also includes an extensive historical survey of the debate about God and evil. It is arguable that much of the popularity of the book derives from its usefulness as a historical text.

Still, Hick's own account of evil is original and provocative. The book as a whole may best be described as an attempt to formulate a theodicy that is relevant to the modern situation in contrast to that brand of Christian theodicy that has constituted the "majority report" since Augustine. Hick suggests the following as a full descriptive title for his book: "A critical study of the two responses to the problem of evil that have been developed within Christian thought, and an attempt to formulate a theodicy for today."[9] In an essay where he responds to one of his critics, he candidly acknowledges that "the Augustinian–Thomist approach to the problem of evil is the main target of the critical part of the book."[10] In other words, he develops his theodicy within a specific historical–philosophical context that must be understood before his own position can be fully appreciated. For him, the Augustinian tradition provides an apposite foil for advancing a new and improved theodicy.

At any rate, the space Hick's theodicy proper occupies in his book is comparatively small; historical concerns receive considerably more attention. Chapter 2 of this book is an attempt to fill in much of the background needed to interact meaningfully with Hick's alternative outlook. In keeping with the purposes of this book, my analysis here bypasses most of the historical matter in Hick's book and is confined to those details that are more directly pertinent to the construction of his own particular theodicy. Although *Evil and the God of Love* is the chief source for Hick's approach to the problem of evil, this exposition and evaluation of his theodicy includes a consideration of as much of the relevant literature, such as various shorter essays by Hick, as possible.

In the following exposition of the main features of Hick's theodicy, it should be kept in mind that he advances his system in deliberate opposition to the Augustinian tradition. Particular points of agreement and disagreement enunciated by Hick himself are explicated at the end of the chapter. In the following exposition, his theodicy is analyzed under four general headings: epistemology, teleology, anthropology, and eschatology. It is in terms of these categories that we can best understand the distinguishing features of his theodicy.

Epistemology

Paul Edwards has suggested that "Hick is a fideist, and before presenting some of the highlights of his theodicy, something should be said about the nature of his fideism."[11] Since I am concerned here with more than a few select highlights of Hick's theodicy, it seems all the more appropriate to begin at the epistemological level and look closely at what Edwards refers to as Hick's fideism. There is ample justification for beginning with his epistemology. In an autobiographical note entitled "A Spiritual Journey," Hick traces the development of his own philosophical theology, according to which his epistemology plays a determinative role.[12] It is a truism that one's epistemology will significantly affect one's system of philosophy. The present discussion of Hick's epistemology focuses on its ramifications for the shape of his theodicy hypothesis.

Hick does not seek to defend theism as an explanatory hypothesis in the fashion of natural theology. He sympathizes with those who believe this to be "a fundamentally misconceived programme, because it substitutes philosophical inference for religious experience."[13] He maintains that the judgment that the existence of God is not philosophically demonstrable "agrees both with the contemporary philosophical understanding of the nature and limits of logical proof and with the biblical understanding of our knowledge of God."[14] In other words, there are both philosophical and theological reasons for contesting the validity of theistic proofs, though he believes that the philosophical reasons are more compelling.[15] Note that his assertion entails the de jure denial of even the possibility of ever formulating a universally valid proof for the existence of God. It is in principle impossible ever to demonstrate, either by a priori or by a posteriori methods, the truth of the proposition that God exists. This is because a priori reasoning "is confined to the realm of concepts" and a posteriori reasoning "would have to include a premise begging the very question at issue."[16] Thus, his judgment about the failure of natural theology is quite general. It is particularly interesting to note the conviction that "one main reason" why "we cannot share the hope of the older schools of natural theology of inferring the existence of God from the evidences of nature . . . is precisely the fact of evil in its many forms."[17]

Despite Hick's general opposition to natural theology, he warns against the denial that theistic belief is rational. "The theist cannot hope to prove that God exists; but despite this it may nevertheless be possible for him to show it to be wholly reasonable for him to believe that God exists."[18] What he thinks is positively defensible is "the theist's right, given his distinctively religious experience, to be certain that God exists."[19] Theistic belief is positively rational on "experiential rather than inferential" grounds.[20] Hick's defense of the rationality of religious belief is based on its analogy with an individual's experience of the external physical world. Religious experience may be regarded as veridical in the same way and to the same degree that experience of the physical world is naturally regarded as veridical.[21]

While one individual's experience of God may not compel belief for another person, it is at least rational for the one who has firsthand experience of God's presence to persist in religious belief and to act in accordance with it.

As one might expect, Hick does not attempt to construct a theodicy for the purpose of creating faith. Instead, he construes theodicy as a defensive tactic. Its purpose is "only to preserve an already existing faith from being overcome by this dark mystery."[22] Basic to this "relatively modest and defensive" posture is his conviction, noted above, that all attempts on the part of natural theology to demonstrate the existence of God ultimately fail. It must not go unnoticed that Hick, far from associating theodicy with rational argumentation for the existence of God, understands the positive case for belief in God only in terms of the unique components of an individual's personal religious experience: "For us today the live question is whether [evil] renders impossible a rational belief in God: meaning by this, not a belief in God that has been arrived at by rational argument . . . , but one that has arisen in a rational individual in response to some compelling element in his experience, and decisively illuminates and is illuminated by his experience as a whole."[23]

Teleology

Hick first articulates the problem of evil in the interrogative mode: "Can the presence of evil in the world be reconciled with the existence of a God who is unlimited both in goodness and in power?"[24] This he understands as "a problem equally for the believer and for the non-believer" in that it "sets up an acute internal tension to disturb [the believer's] faith and to lay upon it a perpetual burden of doubt," while it "stands as a major obstacle to religious commitment" for the nonbeliever.[25]

Moreover, he observes that evil is a special problem for the Christian belief system since "the problem of evil does not attach itself as a threat to any and every concept of deity."[26] The dual affirmation, typical of most Christian thinkers, of God's infinite goodness and power presents an inescapable challenge for Christianity.[27] Hence, Hick narrates the difficulty of the problem of evil in terms reminiscent of those used to describe it in Chapter 1 of the present volume.

Like most fundamental questions of philosophy, the problem of evil can be formulated quite simply and forthrightly: "If God is perfectly good, He must want to abolish all evil; if He is unlimitedly powerful, He must be able to abolish all evil: but evil exists; therefore either God is not perfectly good or He is not unlimitedly powerful."[28] With this account of the nature of the problem of evil before us, we come to the starting point of Hick's theodicy.

Hick's theodicy is essentially teleological; that is, he attempts to reconcile the existence of God with the presence of evil in the world by appealing to the hypothesis of a divine purpose that ultimately justifies both the existence and the amount of evil in the world. For him it is the task of theodicy to frame "a hypothesis or 'picture' in which evil can be seen as ultimately serving a good and justifying purpose."[29] He therefore concludes that the sense in which "this world is good, or good enough, or the best possible" depends upon the purpose God had in creating it.[30] It is all-important to postulate the correct purpose at the outset.

His basic postulate in this regard is that of "soul-making" in the divine economy. Soul-making denotes the "divine purpose to make finite persons who have a genuine autonomy and freedom in relation to their creator and who are therefore capable of entering into personal relationship with him."[31] A proper conception of the divine purpose for creation provides the logical starting point for formulating a valid theodicy. Since this purpose is identified as one of soul-making, Hick's theodicy is frequently called the "soul-making theodicy."[32] This view, that "man is in process of becoming the perfected being whom God is seeking to create," is both "developmental and teleological."[33] Hick attempts to analyze both moral and natural evil in terms of this conception of the divine purpose for humans.[34]

The developmental nature of the soul-making process provides the key to understanding the origin of moral evil. Since "personal life is essentially free and self-directing," it "cannot be perfected by divine fiat."[35] It would be impossible, even for divine omnipotence, to create individuals in an already freely perfected state. Hence, human beings begin as "relatively free and autonomous persons" who by virtue of their freedom are subjected to a "hazardous adventure" designed to lead them to ultimate perfection in their relationship with their Creator.[36] Human goodness is "slowly built up through personal histories of moral effort" as temptations are faced in the physical environment, thus allowing individuals to decide for themselves how they will act.[37] The value judgment implied here is that a greater goodness is achieved if persons are perfected gradually as they encounter opportunities for moral failure than would be possible if they were "created *ab initio* in a state either of innocence or of virtue."[38]

Hick asserts that if God's purpose in creation is soul-making, then "that aim will naturally determine the kind of world that He has created."[39] Hence, the manner in which his theodicy accounts for natural evil is "integrally bound up with its account of the origin of moral evil."[40] Natural evil is regarded as a means of providing those environmental conditions that would be most instrumental to God's purpose of soul-making. In view of God's purpose to perfect and mature free moral persons, it would not be expedient for him to place them in a "hedonistic paradise" devoid of all physical evils. Rather, the realization of God's purpose requires an environment "in which moral beings may be fashioned, through their own free insights and responses, into 'children of God.' "[41] Thus, natural evil plays an important role in the progressive denouement of God's soul-making purpose: "The fact of an objective world within which one has to learn to live, on penalty of pain or death, is also basic to the development of one's moral nature . . . [since] a world in which there can be no pain or suffering would also be one in which there can be no moral choices and hence no possibility of moral growth and development."[42]

Anthropology

This summary account of the teleological focus of Hick's theodicy assumes certain things about the philosophical anthropology that he explicates in his theodicy. Two notions are especially germane to his overall theodicy: his conception of the creation of human persons in two stages and his idea of epistemic distance as a necessary condition for human freedom.

Hick wishes to test his theodicy hypothesis for systematic consistency against the "data . . . of the world, . . . revealed by scientific enquiry."[43] Presupposing the veridicality of the evolutionary account of human origins, Hick suggests that "in the light of modern anthropological knowledge some form of two-stage conception of the creation of man has become an almost unavoidable Christian tenet."[44] The first stage alluded to here corresponds directly to the popular account of humanity's evolutionary emergence out of lower forms of life. With the emergence of *Homo sapiens,* the first stage of human evolution is consummated with "the development of man as a rational and responsible person capable of personal relationship with the personal Infinite who has created him."[45]

By postulating a second stage, involving the individual's "sudden or gradual spiritualization as a child of God," Hick parts company with strictly naturalistic evolutionary thinkers. This second phase in the creative process corresponds to humanity's present condition, which features the exercise of relative autonomy with respect to the Creator as individual human beings progress toward moral perfection. The very environment from which humanity has emerged furnishes the ideal conditions for this "hazardous adventure in individual freedom."[46] This analysis of the physical solidarity of the human species with its environment informs Hick's understanding of the nature of human freedom.

It is his contention that if human persons lived in the immediate presence of God, personal freedom regarding moral choices would be absolutely precluded, for such persons could not help but adjust their wills to that of God. Ergo, as a prerequisite for engaging them in the soul-making process, it was necessary for God to create individuals at an epistemic distance from himself: "But man has been brought into being at an epistemic distance from God through his emergence as part of an autonomous world in which God is not overwhelmingly evident. . . . In such a world man is not compelled to know God but is at the same time free to come to know him by faith."[47]

Hick's notion of epistemic distance also helps account for the origin of moral evil, since persons are accordingly "inevitably morally immature and imperfect."[48] *Homo sapiens* emerges with a natural propensity for self-centeredness, the result of being created at an epistemic distance from God in an environment that is often hostile to human personal existence and comfort. Nevertheless, since this circumstance guarantees the genuine freedom of human persons, all is in accordance with God's purposes.

Eschatology

Hick is convinced that "a theodicy that starts in this way must be eschatological in its ultimate bearings."[49] It is not enough to postulate a divine purpose for allowing evil, or to account for the origin of both moral and natural evil, if the divine purpose of soul-making does not eventually come to fruition.

Since it is rather obvious that virtually no one is fully perfected in this life, it stands to reason that God's purpose of soul-making must ultimately be realized in an afterlife if it is ever to be finally realized at all. "In short, the fulfillment of the divine purpose, as it is postulated in the Irenaean [soul-making] type of theodicy, presupposes each person's survival, in some form of bodily death, and further living and growing towards that end-state."[50]

Furthermore, the eschatological fulfillment of God's purpose must include the universal perfection of *all* human beings whom God has created. "If the justification of evil within the creative process lies in the limitless and eternal good of the end-state to which it leads, then the completeness of the justification must depend upon the completeness, or universality, of the salvation achieved."[51] Hick inflexibly asserts that an acceptable theodicy cannot countenance the literal reality of a hell, for such a place, if it existed, would represent a failure on God's part to bring all individuals into the perfection of full humanity, which is his purpose *ex hypothesi.* Such an eternal residue of evil would fail to justify God's ultimate purposes in creation.[52]

Hick's theodicy therefore requires an eschatological realization of the divine purpose of soul-making. The process effecting such fulfillment is personal in that it is carried out in each individual's experience, and it is universal in that every individual must eventually be brought to human perfection. In addition to postulating an afterlife, these criteria for the realization of God's purpose of soul-making raise further questions about the precise nature of the afterlife in which such absolute and comprehensive fulfillment will take place. Hick sketches an approach to these matters along the following lines: "The person-making process begins for each individual at his birth, making much or little progress as the case may be in this life, and continues in another life *or lives* in another world *or worlds*—perhaps in ways such as I have tried to consider in *Death and Eternal Life*—until it eventually reaches its completion in the infinite good of the common life of humanity within the life of God [italics added]."[53] Although this theme is not developed in Hick's main text on theodicy, *Evil and the God of Love,* it is a very important component in his total system of theodicy since he is led by certain considerations to postulate a kind of modified reincarnationism.

We must look elsewhere, to his book *Death and Eternal Life,* for a more detailed treatment of this element of his theodicy.[54] His discussion there "is intended as a Christian contribution to a global theology of death, exploring both the differences and the deeper convergences of insight on this subject between Christianity, Hinduism, and Buddhism."[55] In this book, Hick rejects both the traditional Christian scheme of "eternal-heaven-or-hell" and "alternative schemes of eastern thought" with their "repeated earthly reincarnations."[56] Instead, he proposes a third, hybrid, possibility, "namely that of a series of lives, each bounded by something analogous to birth and death, lived in other worlds in spaces other than that in which we now are."[57]

This creative hypothesis comes into clearer focus when it is understood that "it differs from the western tradition in postulating many lives instead of only one, and from the eastern tradition in postulating many spheres of incarnate existence instead of only one."[58] Given the eschatological justification of evil in Hick's theodicy, his utilization of reincarnationist notions is also germane to his work on the problem of evil.

Christian Theodicy as "True Myth"

Since the publication of his book *Evil and the God of Love,* Hick has made one particularly significant modification. He now makes quite explicit his view that historically situated religious traditions (including his own Christian tradition) are fundamentally mythological. All of the great religious traditions of the world represent authentic responses to transcendent reality, and yet none of the descriptions of the Transcendent embodied in the various religious traditions of the world is *literally* true. Ultimate Reality is variously conceived by the differing traditions because it is variously manifested in the religious experience of culturally and geographically conditioned peoples.

The Ultimate itself is what Hick, in the spirit of Kant, calls "the Real *an sich,*" or simply "the Real"; the phenomena of religious experience correspond to "the Real as variously experienced-and-thought by different human communities."[59] Since the Real cannot be worshiped as it is in itself but only as it is experienced in some existing religious tradition or other (as Brahman in Hinduism, as Jehovah in Judaism, as Allah in Islam, and so forth), it is nevertheless appropriate for individuals to identify religiously with some particular tradition.

Hick now includes a surprising array of "gods," from the collection of gods represented as such in the innumerable religious traditions around the world, within the range of theism. Any deity broadly conceived as personal qualifies as theistic for Hick. Since the quality of religious experience is what determines one's particular religious beliefs, and there are many varieties of religious experience in the world, there is a corresponding luxuriance of, to say nothing of mutual incompatibility among, conceptions of the Ultimate. Not only is the resulting conception of the nature of God extremely thin, it also happens that each religious interpretation of the Real is equally justified. This hypothesis has a leveling effect not only among religious perspectives but also between these and nonreligious interpretations of Reality, so that the various *"personae* and *impersonae* of the Real"* are all thought to be viable theoretical accounts of the Ultimate, whether that be God or the Absolute: "The gods and the absolutes . . . are different modes of the presence of the same ultimate transcendent Reality."[60]

According to Hick, an adequate interpretation of religion must account both for the realization that one's own tradition must not be literally true, and for the plausibility of thinking that religious Reality is not a mere projection. A major feature of Hick's "religious interpretation of religion" is the suggestion that the concrete beliefs (both historical and transhistorical) embodied in particular religious traditions can be understood as "mythologically true." They are not literally true since they do not represent the Real (or aspects of the Real) as it is in itself. But they are true in the sense that they represent appropriate religious responses to the Real, where what is appropriate is measured primarily in terms of moral–soteriological criteria.

One might think that theodicy would be a superfluous concern from this point of view. Nevertheless, in conversation Hick has assured me that his pluralist thesis neither removes the need for an Irenaean theodicy nor alters its basic contours. And, indeed, the outline of this approach to the problem of evil appears in the Gifford Lectures more or less unchanged, though much abbreviated.[61]

All of this does, however, lead Hick to provide a new gloss on the enterprise of theodicy. Viewed in the context of religious pluralism, theodicies are now viewed as examples of mythological responses to the experience of pain and suffering within the larger context of religious experience. These responses are inevitably couched in terms of the larger conceptual frameworks embodied in particular religious traditions. So, for example (and by his own admission), Hick's Irenaean type of theodicy

> is mythological in the sense that the language in which it speaks about the Real, as a personal being carrying out intentions through time, cannot apply to the ultimate transcendent Reality in itself. But such a theodicy nevertheless constitutes a true myth in so far as the practical attitudes which it tends to evoke amid the evils of human life are appropriate to our present existence in relation to the Real. . . . Experiencing life's baffling mixture of good and evil in terms of this myth, we may be helped to live in hope, trusting in the ultimate sovereignty of God's love.
>
> This theodicy may be—and indeed I believe it is—mythologically true. That is to say, it may be the case that seeking to bring good out of evil, both through one's own personal bearing of suffering and mutual caring in face of disasters, and by cherishing an ultimate hope beyond this life, is appropriate to the actual character of our situation in the presence of the Real.[62]

So while Hick no longer thinks (if indeed he ever did) that the definite features of his own soul-making theodicy, set within the Christian thought world, are literally true (or even could be literally true), he still thinks that they are "mythologically true." And within religious contexts, such a pragmatic view of truth is the only kind of truth that really matters. The Irenaean theodicy is, for him, a coherent hypothesis that helps him make sense of the mystery of human experience within a broadly Christian framework. Neither that hypothesis nor the framework in which it is embedded is finally regarded as literally true. But he can speak provisionally from within his own religious tradition as if the Christian framework and its associated theodicy hypothesis were literally true.[63]

Summary

That this brief exposition of Hick's theodicy is responsible and accurate may be seen from the following summary by Hick himself. The "main features" of his theodicy include

> the creation of man, through the processes of natural evolution, at an epistemic distance from God, giving him a basic freedom in relation to his Creator; and man's consequent self-centredness as an animal organism seeking survival within a harsh and challenging world which is however an environment in which he can develop, as a morally and spiritually immature creature, towards his ultimate perfection; this development beginning in the present life and continuing far beyond it.[64]

Thus, in the final analysis, "the ultimate responsibility for the existence of evil belongs to the Creator."[65]

COMPARISON WITH THE AUGUSTINIAN TRADITION

With this preliminary exposition of Hick's theodicy in place, and given his professed interest in supplanting the Augustinian tradition, it is salutary to conclude this chapter with some comparisons that Hick himself makes between these two approaches to theodicy.

Points of Contrast

Hick enumerates six main points of contrast between the Augustinian tradition and his own alternative theodicy.[66] First, in the Augustinian tradition, human persons are morally culpable beings who are ultimately responsible for the existence of evil; in contrast, Hick believes that evil was inevitable in God's created universe and that God is therefore ultimately responsible. Second, the Augustinian tradition conceives of the nature of evil in terms of the philosophical notion of nonbeing, whereas the tradition to which Hick subscribes adopts no particular philosophical framework regarding the nature of evil and addresses the matter solely on theological grounds. Third, in the Augustinian tradition, the dynamics of the divine–human relationship are peripheral; in Hick's system these dynamics govern the very structure of theodicy. Fourth, the Augustinian tradition looks back at the past in an attempt to causally *explain* the existence of evil; by a subtle change in emphasis, the soul-making theodicy looks toward the future in an attempt to ultimately *justify* the existence of evil. Fifth, the Augustinian appeal to the doctrines of the fall and of original sin to account for the origin of evil in the world is rejected in Hick's theodicy. Finally, whereas the Augustinian tradition includes the doctrine of hell in its formulation of a theodicy, the alternative tradition that Hick embraces regards this doctrine as ultimately incompatible with the aims of Christian theodicy. A seventh difference could also be added: the Augustinian tradition in no way countenances, much less requires, the modified reincarnationist theme present in Hick's system.

Points of Hidden Agreement

In addition to these differences, Hick cites six points of "hidden agreement," or tendencies toward convergence.[67] First, both systems proclaim "the unqualified and unlimited goodness of God's creation as a whole," the Augustinian tradition by means of the notion of "aesthetic perfection" in God's present universe, the soul-making approach by means of an eschatological realization of the process intended for humanity's moral perfection. Second, both acknowledge God's ultimate responsibility for evil, the Augustinian tradition implicitly, the alternative tradition explicitly. Third, the theme of "O felix culpa" appears in both theodicies in that both envision the use of evil by God for good purposes. Fourth, both admit certain logical limits to the concept of divine omnipotence, although the Augustinian tradition has a tendency to overextend these limits, whereas the soul-making theodicy is more modest about them.

A logical limit upon divine omnipotence does not constitute any real constraint upon the exercise of divine power, for it only prohibits the conception that omnipotence entails that God can perform any task whatsoever, whether or not it is logically incoherent. God cannot create a square circle or a finite stick with only one end. The inability to do these things is not due to a failure in power but to the logical impossibility of such states of affairs. As Aquinas put it, "Whatever can have the nature of being is counted among the possibles, and God is called almighty with respect to these. Whatever implies contradiction does not fall within the scope of omnipotence, for it cannot begin to look possible. It is more appropriate to say that such things cannot be done, rather than that God cannot do them."[68]

When Hick suggests that his own theodicy proposal is more modest about the logical limitations upon divine omnipotence, he means that it is logically impossible for God to have created ex nihilo freely perfected creatures. He supposes that this is inconsistent with the Augustinian tradition, so he disagrees with Augustinians about what it is logically possible for God to do.

Fifth, although the Augustinian tradition generally affirms the existence of the devil and demons in constructing a theodicy, whereas the alternative theodicy developed by Hick does not require them, they are admissible in both views. Furthermore, their existence does not seem to be formally essential to either type of theodicy. The role of a doctrine of Satan in explaining certain evils depends upon one's view of biblical revelation. Hick allows that the notion of a personal devil with minions who act in his service has permanent value as a vivid symbol of gratuitous evils perpetrated in society. Nevertheless, in contrast to Augustinian thinkers, he is doubtful about appealing to the reality of demons to explain the existence of some evils.

Lastly, both views allow for divine purposes other than the soul-making purpose central to Hick's system, although the Augustinian tradition has customarily placed greater emphasis on these other purposes. Hick does not state here what these other purposes might be, but he acknowledges that the Irenaean thinker should be willing to learn from the Augustinian in this regard.

Criticisms of the Augustinian Tradition

Let us turn now to several specific criticisms that Hick levels against the Augustinian perspective. Three primary objections motivate his effort to construct anew a theodicy for today. These need to be brought out briefly but explicitly.

First, to assign the intrusion of evil into the world to the operation of free will on the part of human agents, as the Augustinian tradition does, "amounts to a sheer self-contradiction." In Hick's view, it is inconceivable that creatures with entirely good wills should ever become sinful. "To say that they do is to postulate the self-creation of evil *ex nihilo!*"[69] It is entirely unsatisfactory to attribute the origin of moral evil to creaturely free will in an effort to absolve God from responsibility for evil, for evil would already have to characterize the moral condition of such creatures for them to act on an evil impulse. This does not absolve God, since he will have created them with the very flaw that explains their capacity to sin, making him the ultimate source of evil in any case. A theodicy with this sort of starting point "collapses into radical incoherence."[70]

Second, the Augustinian doctrine of evil as privation does not adequately characterize the true nature of evil in human experience. In particular, since evil is "positive and powerful," this doctrine is not sufficient to describe it as a loss or lack of goodness. "Empirically, it is not merely the absence of something else but a reality with its own distinctive and often terrifying quality and power."[71] Hick's objection has to do with a reductionist tendency in the Augustinian tradition when defining evil. The doctrine of privation, though metaphysically sound in a certain qualified sense, does not do justice as an empirical description of evil in human experience. This description fails to capture that peculiar aspect of evil that "impinges deleteriously upon the realm of the personal" in terms of real pain and suffering, which are positive realities, that is, "emphatic and intrusive realities of experience." Furthermore, far from corrupting into nothingness, an evil will often intensifies into "a very positive and terrible moral evil."[72] Moral evils therefore cannot be described as mere "privations of their corresponding moral goods."[73]

Third, under Plotinian influence, Augustinian theodicy tends to view the love of God "in metaphysical rather than personal terms." God's policy during all of his creative activity centered around an abstract principle of plenitude. The divine purpose that governed the formation of the universe had to do with the realization of an extravagant harmony of the effulgence of being. "It is not so much the love of the personal Infinite for finite persons, as the inexhaustible creative divine fecundity, expressed in the granting of being to a dependent universe with its innumerable grades of creatures."[74] Thus, God's love is not primarily expressed in terms of personal relationship with individual creatures.

This objection is not so much logically incisive as emotively forcible. It depends upon the repugnance felt when confronted with such an impersonal conception of divine love, denoted by the overarching principle of plenitude within the Augustinian tradition. A logical difficulty enters the picture, however, in connection with a certain consequence that ought to obtain in the empirical world but that clearly does not obtain. "The logic of the principle of plenitude demands that there be creatures of every conceivable kind," and yet we witness that a rather large set of possible entities does not exist in the world, though it should on this supposition. Clearly, then, the principle of plenitude fails to describe the actual state of affairs in the empirical world.[75]

These are the chief objections that Hick brings against the Augustinian tradition. In *Evil and the God of Love* he amplifies and illustrates these difficulties in the thinking of a host of illustrious proponents of the Augustianian theodicy. He discusses, for example, the ruminations of such diverse thinkers as the twelfth-century Catholic theologian Hugh of Saint Victor; St. Thomas Aquinas; the contemporary Thomist Charles Journet; Protestant reformer John'Calvin; twentieth-century dialectical theologian Karl Barth, with his doctrine of *das Nichtige;* and, from the eighteenth century, Archbishop William King and Gottfried Leibniz.[76]

This concludes the preliminary exposition of the main features of John Hick's theodicy. Every effort has been made to remain descriptive up to this point. In Part III our attention will turn to a critique of the particulars of Hick's proposal (his theodicy proper) with a view to defending the adequacy of the Augustinian tradition, which his theodicy is meant to supplant. But first we must consider background epistemological issues. In particular, we need to investigate the possible structure of evidence that would positively justify belief in God. That is the task of Part II.

PART II
RELIGIOUS
EPISTEMOLOGY

4

The Value of Natural Theology

While no effort has been made to identify all the differences between John Hick's theodicy and the Augustinian tradition, a sufficiently detailed exposition has been carried out in Part I to illustrate the tension that exists between them. What follows is a critical evaluation of the particulars of Hick's theodicy and its challenge to the Augustinian tradition. These will be treated seriatim following the expository outline from Chapter 3, in which the main features of his position were analyzed under four general and inclusive headings: epistemology, teleology, anthropology, and eschatology. This division reflects the order and logical relationship of the chief elements in Hick's system of theodicy.

THE NEED TO ADDRESS HICK'S RELIGIOUS
EPISTEMOLOGY

This inquiry into the particulars of Hick's program begins with certain epistemological considerations that are integral to his motivation for formulating a theodicy as he does. He has worked out a sophisticated epistemology of religious belief in his first book, *Faith and Knowledge*.[1] While a detailed analysis of his entire epistemology would call for a separate volume, any responsible evaluation of his position on theodicy cannot fail to address important aspects of his epistemological point of departure.

There are at least three reasons why it is imperative to begin this evaluation with an appraisal of Hick's religious epistemology. First, one's epistemological stance is ineluctably programmatic for one's overall philosophical outlook. In matters regarding the justification of religious belief epistemology is unquestionably fundamental. Since the problem of evil is enjoined as a threat to such justification, it is inevitable that epistemological presuppositions will significantly determine the shape of one's theodicy. Hick's emphasis upon our epistemic situation appears again and again. Most recently it has guided his work on the problem of religious pluralism.[2]

Hick himself traces his development as a philosopher of religion back to his seminal work on religious epistemology in *Faith and Knowledge*. He remarks that, having written his first book, he never expected to write another.

> I thought that I had said all that I had to say. But presently the theodicy issue, the question whether the reality of suffering and wickedness are compatible with the reality of a loving God, was insistently demanding a response; and the result was another book, *Evil and the God of Love*. . . . This built upon the epistemology developed in *Faith and Knowledge*, particularly in the notion of "epistemic distance" and in the notion of faith as a fundamental expression of human freedom.[3]

So, in his formulation of a theodicy, Hick has not only worked from a carefully devised epistemological base, he has done so consciously and deliberately. Inquiry into the particulars of his theodicy hypothesis therefore invites a preliminary scrutiny of relevant features of his epistemological commitments.

Second, Hick's dismissal of all theistic arguments for the existence of God reveals an early important distinction between his approach to constructing a theodicy and this task as conceived by adherents to the Augustinian tradition. The validity of his repudiation of natural theology ultimately depends upon the acceptability of his own epistemological principles.

Third, it is unlikely that Hick would have conceived of the task of theodicy as he does if his epistemological orientation did not oblige him to do so. As I hope to show in the next chapter, his central epistemological notion of rational belief is particularly vulnerable to the argument from evil, and the structure of his theodicy is largely determined by a difficulty arising within his religious epistemology.

HICK'S OPPOSITION TO NATURAL THEOLOGY

In his book *Arguments for the Existence of God*, Hick seeks to demonstrate how "the major theistic arguments are all open to serious philosophical objections," as well as to theological objections "ranging from a complete lack of concern for them to a positive repudiation of them as being religiously irrelevant or even harmful."[4] His analysis leads him to conclude that natural theology is "a fundamentally misconceived programme."[5] There is no question that his "own conclusion concerning the theistic proofs is negative."[6]

Nevertheless, although Hick is resolute in his avowal that "none of these arguments actually proves the reality of God," he further maintains, somewhat unexpectedly, that theistic arguments "serve an important purpose. They show the explanatory power of the concept of God by formulating fundamental questions to which the existence of God would constitute an intellectually satisfying answer."[7] Thus, Hick would like to allow a limited role for natural theology: "Its office is not to prove the existence of God, or even to show it to be probable, but to establish both the possibility of divine existence and the importance (that is, the explanatory power) of this possibility. I believe that reason *can* ascertain that there *may* be a God and that this is a genuinely important possibility."[8]

Natural theology as traditionally conceived has, of course, been much more ambitious than this. Since Hick's leaner version of natural theology is so severely discontinuous with the actual practice of natural theology historically, it does not seem appropriate to regard Hick as a natural theologian in the *sensus receptus*. Natural theology is not normally defined in terms of allowing just *any* role for theistic argumentation, however limited it may be. A sine qua non of natural theology has always been the conviction that theistic arguments do more than establish the interesting possibility of the existence of God. Indeed, if natural theology exhibits the explanatory power of the hypothesis that God exists, as Hick suggests in the above quote, then ipso facto it establishes the relative probability of the truth of this hypothesis; the stronger the explanatory power, the greater the probability.

In his deposition against natural theology Hick adduces a series of both theological and philosophical criticisms.

Theological Criticisms of Natural Theology

Hick summons three theological criticisms of natural theology. First, he notes that the biblical person of faith, the religious believer, finds no necessity in appealing to theistic proof since such a person does not "think of God as an inferred entity but as an experienced reality."[9] He apparently has in mind the widespread notion that religious persons seldom believe in God on the basis of rational evidence.

Next, he protests that "the God whose existence each of the traditional theistic proofs professes to establish is only an abstraction from and a pale shadow of the living God who is the putative object of biblical faith."[10] This is the age-old bifurcation between the God of the philosophers and the God of Abraham, Isaac, and Jacob. It is one thing to demonstrate the existence of a necessary Being; it is something else to place one's faith in an august personal God of Judeo–Christian proportions.

Lastly, theistic proof may be regarded as "a form of coercion and would as such be incompatible with God's evident intention to treat his human creatures as free and responsible persons."[11] That is, proof of the existence of God would *compel* belief in God, an eventuality that would seem to forestall the believer's exercise of freedom. Thus the discursive nature of philosophical inquiry into the grounds for religious belief is almost too rigorous for its own good.

Evaluation of Hick's Theological Criticisms

These three pronouncements from the theological constituency merit some response. With his admirable penchant for objectivity, Hick himself acknowledges that these theological reasons for rejecting theistic arguments are far more tenuous than the philosophical objections and that "theologians who reject natural theology would therefore do well to do so primarily on philosophical rather than on theological grounds."[12] One can only wish that Hick would explain what *he* thinks is tenuous about considerations of this kind, or even what exactly he means by distinguishing them from properly philosophical grounds—his third theological reason for barring dependence on theistic proof evokes certain important questions about the nature of proof.

In response to the first religiously oriented protest, there does not appear to be any logical difficulty inherent in identifying God both as an inferred reality—or an inferable entity—and as a religiously worthy object of worship. Hick presents us with a false dilemma; one might be justified in concluding that the "inferred entity" of theistic argument corresponds to the "experienced reality" of biblical faith and that such an argument provides corroborative evidence of the objective existence of the putative "experienced reality." Aspects of the religious experience of God may even encourage the propensity to link the experienced reality with the inferred reality. Theistic arguments are supposed to be helpful in exhibiting the relation of identity between experienced reality and objective reality, which is an epistemological requirement if one is to believe with integrity. It only begs the question to state in advance of these considerations that as philosophers we are not dealing with the same entity that we are as religious believers.

Hick's real contention is not that the identification of God as a religiously experienced reality and God as a philosophically inferred entity results in a certain kind of *logical* confusion; his claim is a *factual* one. He simply says that religious believers do not think of God as an inferred entity. But surely this is mistaken, for there are several counterexamples among the biblical writers. For instance, the Psalmist observes how the heavens proclaim the glory of God.[13] The apostle Paul considered certain facts about the divine nature—"his eternal power and deity"—to be inferable from "the things that have been made."[14]

A moment's reflection will reveal that indeed most of our judgments concerning matters of fact, and not just religious experiences, include an element of inference. Our relationships with people and experiences of various other kinds depend upon our making appropriate inferences. When I hear a voice that sounds like that of my wife, I infer, however immediately and perhaps erroneously, that it is my wife speaking. Thus, even in cases of experienced reality there is no basis for insisting that inference plays no part. The requirement that inference be excluded from an analysis of experience is a silent but unwarranted assumption in Hick's objection.

His second religious criticism of theistic proof is unconvincing as well. Many features of human experience admit of different kinds of analysis, and reputed experiences of God are no exception. A philosophical description of God's nature—potentially "very strong and exalted"[15]—and the biblical–theological portrayal of his character are by no means necessarily mutually exclusive. They may in fact be mutually informative about the nature and character of God, yielding a more profound theological, even devotional, understanding when taken together. Many who believe in God on the strength of some sort of alleged encounter with God tend to seek further rational understanding about the nature of God. This is precisely the impulse that gives rise to the general project of theology, or philosophical theology. And there is no reason why philosophical inquiry into such matters should ignore the possibility of arguments for the existence of God.

Indeed, there may be aspects of the divine nature that are lost to typical religious experience of God but that are epistemically accessible using philosophical principles. To deny this is to presume to know something about God that is not normally a component of profound religious experience; so where does the notion of privileged access to God via religious experience come from if not a peculiar turn in ratiocination about the divine nature? Faith seeks understanding, when it comes to the existence of God no less than when it comes to aspects of his nature and of his ways with human persons.

Furthermore, the God of the philosophers is more than a mere abstraction. Theistic arguments are construed by natural theologians themselves as positively evincing the concrete existence of God, not just the conceptual coherence of the idea of God. (Natural theologians are no more obliged to think of God as a kind of Platonic form than Hick is to think of God as an atomic fact of human experience.) The God of the philosophers is not an abstraction *simpliciter*. Clearly, if the philosophers' conception of God is merely an abstraction, then the proposition that God exists is meaningless when uttered by them, for the object of such an abstraction could not exist. To suggest that a particular argument for the existence of God treats God as an abstraction does not even touch the natural theologian's claim that this argument demonstrates the existence of God or rationally supports belief in God.

It might be suggested that an adequate deflection of Hick's specific objection here would have to show, not that there is a logical possibility of identity, but that the God actually demonstrated by traditional arguments is in fact the God worshiped in the religious context. But suppose at least one argument, constructed along more or less traditional lines, effectively demonstrates either that God exists or that it is more rational to believe that God exists. If one insists that there may yet be no identity between this God of the philosophers and the God of biblical faith, then which one shall we say exists? Both are *ex hypothesi* strictly monotheistic conceptions, so it is impossible for both to exist if they differ.

Furthermore, how can it be an argument against the existence of the God of philosophers to assert simply that this God either is not essentially continuous with or is positively discontinuous with the God of Abraham, Isaac, and Jacob? What are we to do with a successful argument for the existence of God vis-à-vis the religious believer's claim to know God through revelation? Hick's criticism is raised as an objection to theistic arguments. But it is not enough to say that we know philosophical arguments to be defective simply because their conclusion does not give us the God worshiped in the religious context. There is still the matter of showing that these arguments fail to demonstrate the existence of a God that competes with the Judeo–Christian God of revealed theology.

If we do not accept the view that identity holds between the God of religious awareness and the God of philosophical inquiry we are left with something like the following choice: embrace the God of religious awareness and defy the probative force of any argument for the existence of an alternative God, or assent to the inferred entity and surrender the veridicality of experienced reality. What is to prevent us, as rational persons, from bringing our interpretation of experience into conformity with the conception of God at the end of a theistic argument if this argument is a truly successful argument for the existence of God? Perhaps interpretations of religious experience are more malleable than the conclusions of philosophical arguments. Why not seek to harmonize the monotheistic results of these distinct avenues of cognitive access to God?

To speak of distinct avenues of epistemological access to God is perhaps a bit misleading. It is theoretically perilous to omit ratiocination from an analysis of human experience. No argument for the existence of God, however abstract, is effected in total abstraction from human experience (except perhaps the ontological argument). In any case, the God of philosophy is the God of *some* experience by virtue of being the result of philosophical inquiry, which is a mode of experience.

It is a rather simple matter to describe a possible procedure for demonstrating the identity between the God of religious awareness and the God of philosophical inquiry. There is no need to be severely technical. The following argument identifies the main steps involved in one fairly straightforward strategy. If

1. The God worshiped in the religious context exists as represented in the religious experience, and this God is experientially represented as the only God there is;

and if

2. The God of theistic argumentation exists, and it is a sine qua non of such theistic argumentation that there is only one God;

then,

3. There is only one God, revealed in both religious experience and philosophical argument.

What is straightforward about this strategy is not the degree of difficulty in establishing the premises of this meta-argument but the validity of the argument. Admittedly, not all reputed experiences of the divine are amenable to such an analysis, for one might not be led through experience to conceive of God as a unitary Being. A successful argument for the existence of one God would be genuinely problematic for cases of this kind. When both experience and philosophy generate a properly theistic conception of the divine (that is, a strictly monotheistic conception), however, then the path to identity is short and direct.

Any difficulty encountered in showing the de facto identity between the God of Abraham, Isaac, and Jacob and the God of natural theology is a difficulty as well for all religious experiences of God as an object or person worthy of worship. The problem of identity transfers to all separable encounters with God, not only to experiences of God by different individuals, but also to distinct experiences of God by the same individual. If the attributes predicated of God are the same between the inferred entity and the religiously worthy object of worship, then we are well on our way to considering the inferred reality of natural theology to be identifiable with the God worshiped in the religious context. One task of theistic argumentation is to show that corresponding to the God allegedly encountered and worshiped in the context of religious experience is the objective reality of the God so worshiped. What ensures their de facto identity is the impossibility of dualism concerning God together with the absence of any discernible difference in how the nature of God is characterized, a difference that would preclude their identity.

Furthermore, theistic arguments support belief in the objective reality of the attributes predicated about God by those who experience God in personal relationship. The dynamics of personal relationship make it possible for persons to experience God as having attributes that cannot be properly predicated of him. God becomes different things to different people in virtue of differences in their "experiencing-as." Philosophical inquiry sometimes attests to and sometimes disconfirms what the religious believer thinks may be predicable about God based on religious experience. But the data of experience will always be relevant to philosophical judgments about the existence and nature of God.

There are, of course, degrees of abstraction, and Hick does not make clear what degree of abstraction he is willing to permit. Some criterion is needed here to justify his judgment that the God of the philosophers is an unacceptable abstraction, for Hick himself must abstract in his development of a systematic philosophy of religion. Even the stipulation that God is known only in concrete experience must appeal to some level of abstraction when it comes to comparing experienced entities as experienced. Only if these fall under some shared concept of "God" can they be regarded as experiences of the same reality. That is, to answer questions of identity across experiences of objects or persons we must have recourse to a measure of abstract judgment. Reflecting upon and describing our experience(s) of God implicates us in the act of abstraction about God. The very accusation itself that God is a mere abstraction in the philosopher's quiver of arguments and syllogisms is intelligible only in virtue of the power of abstraction. To suggest that God is not an abstraction is to use the term "God" in some generalized sense, and thus it resembles the philosophical use of the term in traditional arguments for the existence of God. Armed with abstraction the philosopher is not thereby also religiously threatening.

Something similar obtains when we compare common-sense knowledge with theoretical science. Whereas commonsense knowledge is largely concerned with the significance of facts for human values, "theoretical science deliberately neglects the immediate values of things, so that the statements of science often appear to be only tenuously relevant to the familiar events of daily life."[16] Hence, the language of science is generally more abstract than that of common sense. However, as Ernest Nagel points out, "It would be an obvious error to suppose that common-sense knowledge does not involve the use of abstract conceptions. Everyone who believes that man is a mortal creature certainly employs the abstract notions of humanity and mortality. The conceptions of science do not differ from those of common sense merely in being abstract."[17]

No doubt what H. D. Lewis calls "the need for enlivened personal apprehension of God" is real.[18] But this is not excluded by natural theology. If Hick means only that so-called abstract treatments of the question of God's existence (i.e., the classical arguments of natural theology) are not enough to furnish us with a fully satisfactory knowledge of God for religious purposes, so much is true, of course. Even this agreement, however, does not entail agreement about the precise nature of the *relation* between the God of the philosophers and the God of Abraham, Isaac, and Jacob. To put it another way, the relation between religiously adequate and distinctly philosophical conceptions of God may be variously conceived. It is nevertheless fruitful to recognize that the being inferred in some theistic arguments may be identifiable with that one we call (perhaps on the basis of religious experience) God. (The reader will recall that this is expressly what Aquinas claims on behalf of each of his five ways.) In virtue of these various considerations, Hick's second objection on religious grounds comes to nothing.

Finally, with respect to the third theological objection that Hick deploys against the viability of theistic argument, it is neither the purpose nor the expected result of theistic arguments to "coerce" belief in God. Rather, these arguments are designed to lead persons to the belief *that* God exists. At most, theistic arguments may demonstrate that it is reasonable to believe *in* God or that one should believe in God. But they do not, indeed they cannot, coerce commitment to God.[19] This is consistent with the crucial distinction between identifying God as a philosophically inferred reality and worshiping him in a fiduciary act of commitment. The rational methodology of philosophical analysis inherent in theistic argumentation is neither coercive at the level of valuation nor inimical to the ultimate commitment of faith.[20] One's freedom remains no less intact when one's intellect is confronted with a sound theistic argument.

Surely it is possible to persist in unbelief regarding some proposition even when all the evidence supports the proposition. To be sure, such a skeptical posture is palpably foolish—one biblical writer expressed the opinion that "the fool has said in his heart there is no God"[21]—but foolishness of this kind is not excluded by even the strongest possible evidence. It is the genuine freedom of human persons that guarantees the possibility of resisting, even suppressing, the manifest truth. The result is then folly of the most loathsome magnitude, and sometimes even moral culpability.

Hick's resistance to the idea of compelled belief in God misses the mark. It is not that belief of this kind is the result of an imposition on human freedom. The problem goes deeper. Compelled belief is a contradiction in terms, for belief contains a voluntary element either directly or indirectly. We can be made to *act* in a way that conflicts with our deepest internal commitments; the act does not necessarily abrogate the commitment. Nietzsche once proclaimed, "If one were to *prove* this God of the Christians to us, we should be even less able to believe in him."[22] It is always possible to resist the persuasive effect of a philosophical argument.

Allowing that belief includes a component of free choice at least indirectly does not commit one to accepting doxastic voluntarism, a controversial philosophical doctrine. This is not to say that doxastic voluntarism is not defensible. It is often thought that when one has a belief, the state of mind constituted by having that belief is somehow determined by evidence that to one seems favorable to the truth of that belief. As A. C. Ewing puts it, "I cannot hold a belief against what seems to me true."[23] Now this is supposed to show that holding a belief is not a function of any sort of free choice (on the precise occasion of beginning to hold it). But I do not think it shows this at all. It only establishes at most a correlation between holding a belief and thinking that the proposition that is the object of that belief is true. It does not make clear what that correlation is. These may just be two ways of referring to the same mental act. The freedom to believe what one wills is not thereby analyzed away. It still remains an open question whether the proposition's seeming true to me is at all up to me. The mental event of "seeing x as true" (or "seeing that x is true") can be described either passively or actively with respect to the believing subject. To rest the case against doxastic voluntarism on a passive description of this mental act is to leave the relevant question unanswered. One thing doxastic voluntarism has going for it is that there being doxastic decision principles would seem to depend upon this doctrine being true, and it might be difficult to get a regulative theory of knowledge without some such set of principles.

In the final analysis, it is puzzling that Hick would appeal to the notion of coercive proof to inveigh against the project of natural theology. His own account of human freedom, central to his theodicy hypothesis, contains either the same seeds of its own destruction or the resources needed to meet this very objection. In Part III I discuss his view of human freedom.

Philosophical Criticisms of Natural Theology

Hick's philosophical case against traditional theistic argumentation is basically twofold. The two paths of philosophical opposition to theistic arguments parallel the two broad ways in which theistic arguments have traditionally been attempted: the a priori and the a posteriori.

With regard to the a priori method of theistic argumentation, Hick concludes that "it is impossible to demonstrate the reality of God by *a priori* reasoning, since such reasoning is confined to the realm of concepts."[24] The only a priori argument, which "operates from a basis which is logically prior to and independent of experience,"[25] is the so-called ontological argument in its various forms. Since Hick is an empiricist, it is not surprising that he dismisses this type of theistic argument. Indeed, his criticisms seem legitimate. It is even possible to extend Hick's criticism of the ontological argument for the existence of God. The ontological argument certainly does not prove the actual existence of God or of a necessary Being. For this argument is vulnerable to the possibility of conceiving of the nonexistence of God, or even of the nonexistence of anything at all. As long as this possibility is conceivable, the argument fails. It is logically possible that nothing ever existed, including God. Hence, the argument fails to prove that God exists.

Hick is likewise certain, however, that all a posteriori arguments for the existence of God are philosophically objectionable. This is because a posteriori reasoning "would have to include a premise begging the very question at issue."[26] At stake here are the cosmological and teleological attempts to demonstrate the existence of God.

Hick's difficulty with the cosmological argument hangs on the question of the intelligibility of the universe. Proponents of the cosmological argument must prove that the universe is intelligible before they can argue from contingent effects to a first Cause identifiable as a necessary Being. After all, the universe might be an unintelligible brute fact with no cause at all. Hick can think of no reasons that could compel one to grasp one or the other of the two horns of this dilemma: "Either there is a First Cause or the universe is ultimately unintelligible." Thus, the natural theologian cannot meet the preliminary requirement: "This inability to exclude the possibility of an unintelligible universe prevents the cosmological argument from operating for the skeptic as a proof of God's existence—and the skeptic is, after all, the only person who needs such a proof."[27]

The force of the teleological argument is believed by Hick to be severely attenuated by David Hume's "classic critique" of this argument in his *Dialogues Concerning Natural Religion.* The cumulative effect of Hume's criticisms is to establish a distinction between the minimal conclusion of the design argument and the more magnanimous conclusion sought by Christian theists, of an infinitely wise, good, and powerful God.[28]

Since philosophical objections to natural theology tend to be tied to specific versions of theistic argument, I will save until later my response to Hick's philosophical critique of natural theology. My own view of the possibility of natural theology is much more optimistic than is Hick's, and in Chapters 6 and 7 I argue for this possibility. But first I wish to discuss two other matters. First, what is the significance of natural theology for dealing with the problem of evil? I develop an answer to this question in the final section of this chapter. Second, what alternative account of the rationality of religious belief does Hick offer, and how adequate is it? That is the subject of Chapter 5.

THE SIGNIFICANCE OF NATURAL THEOLOGY
FOR THEODICY

Here I wish to discuss the significance any *successful* natural theology must have for dealing with the problem of evil. In my exposition of the theodicy tradition of St. Augustine, St. Thomas Aquinas, and Gottfried Leibniz, I gave some indication of their preference for addressing the question of God's existence prior to and independently of any consideration of the reality of evil. It could not be more evident that Hick diverges from the Augustinian tradition on this point. This is important to note since the degree of one's confidence in theistic argumentation greatly influences one's conception of the task of framing a theodicy and of the permutations of a theodicy adequate to the situation.

Natural Theology in the Augustinian Tradition

One must bear in mind that in speaking of the Augustinian tradition, reference is to a general strategy discernible within the tradition. While it is certainly true that Augustine, Aquinas, and Leibniz all had comparable regard for theistic argumentation, each devised his own way of expressing what he believed to be a valid argument or combination of arguments for the existence of God. Their commitment to theistic argument is so central to their shared strategy in formulating a theodicy that any defense of the tradition should include this same optimistic outlook regarding the possibility of natural theology. That is, membership in the Augustinian tradition of theodicy depends minimally upon at least a general endorsement of the endeavor of natural theologians to demonstrate that belief in God is rational. However, membership in the tradition obviously does not require commitment to each of the distinct methods of theistic argumentation devised by Augustine, Aquinas, Leibniz, and others. It is very unlikely that one could escape inconsistency if one sought to harmonize every argument for God's existence proposed by some prominent adherent to the Augustinian tradition of theodicy. At any rate, it is not enough that members of the tradition exhibit a policy of openness to theistic argument. True fidelity to the tradition also depends upon how one conceives of the relevance of such theistic argument for the construction of a satisfactory theodicy.

There are bound to be misgivings about this claim, for it has seemed to many that advocacy of the so-called free-will defense is sufficient to secure a seat among one's Augustinian peers. If the thesis advanced here is correct, then any free-will defender who does not also embrace the natural theologian's view—of the possibility of natural theology *and* of its constructive role in theodicy—does not stand squarely within the tradition of Augustine.

Alvin Plantinga is one highly celebrated philosopher who fits this description. While he has contributed significantly to the articulation of a free-will defense, he does not relate this necessary condition of a bona fide Augustinian theodicy to the equally essential regard for theistic argumentation discernible within the tradition. Plantinga does, however, point out that the atheologian who wants to show that evil makes theism improbable "must show that [theism] is improbable with respect to the relevant body of total evidence, whatever exactly that is. To do this, he would be obliged to consider all the sorts of reasons natural theologians have invoked *in favor of* theistic belief."[29]

Still, Plantinga has been known to reject both fideism and natural theology in favor of what he calls the "proper basicality" of belief in

God. (Belief in God is said to be held in the basic way when it is not based on propositional evidence, and such belief in God is thought to be proper if it violates no epistemic requirements.) And while Plantinga's verdict on the possibility and value of natural theology appears to be undergoing a welcome transformation, his tendency is to subordinate the warranting function of natural theology to the justification that accrues when belief in God is accepted in the basic way.[30]

In contrast, Augustinian theodicists have traditionally appealed to the program of natural theology as an essential first step in formulating a theodicy. For them this step is noneliminable. Hence, failure to include it, whether deliberately or inadvertently, as a prolegomenon to theodicy proper is methodologically suspect from an Augustinian point of view. So even a champion of the free-will defense of the stature of Plantinga, who resists the use of natural theology for certain traditional purposes, departs from the tradition in a nontrivial way. But the implications are even more far-reaching than this, for one could be both a proponent of the free-will defense and an advocate of theistic argumentation and still not meet all conditions for membership within the tradition if one stopped short of relating theistic argumentation to the articulation of a theodicy.

Theodicy or Defense?

It is now widely accepted, at least among theists, that there is a nontrivial distinction between a defense and a theodicy. Moreover, it seems to be just as widely assumed that these are the only philosophically interesting alternatives open to the theist for responding to the problem of evil. I think that this distinction between theodicy and defense deserves further analysis as the line of demarcation between the two is not as clear as the literature implies.

A defense is supposed to show that no contradiction can be made out between the existence of God and the existence of evil. But this does not show that God actually has a justifying reason for permitting evil. A theodicy, it is often thought, is supposed to show what justifying reasons God actually has for permitting evil. But theodicies are not generally convincing to nontheists impressed by the reality of evil. So where does this leave matters? Are we at an impasse? I do not think so, *if we have recourse to natural theology.* I propose that the theist should appeal directly to the resources of natural theology in response to the challenge from evil.

Let us suppose that natural theology succeeds to the point of showing that theism is superior to its alternatives and that it is therefore either probably true, or most rational, or both. Would the resulting case for theism constitute a defense or a theodicy? That is, when the natural theologian comes to the problem of evil with the knowledge of God in the background, how do things stand with respect to the problem of evil?

While some philosophers have tried to formulate the problem of evil as generally as possible, so as to include both the logical and the evidential challenges from evil, the differences between these two types of challenge must be kept in mind if we are to know what counts as an adequate response to the problem of evil. The logical problem of evil asks, Is it logically *possible* that God and evil coexist? Any answer to this problem must show that the existence of God is compatible with the fact of evil in the world. This form of the problem does not demand a theodicy so much as a defense, although a theodicy would encompass a defense.

The evidential problem of evil asks, Is it evidentially *plausible* that God and evil coexist? This objection has the following form: God must have a morally sufficient reason for allowing any evil that he allows; but there is much evil in the world for which we can imagine no morally sufficient reason, such that it is highly unlikely that God exists. Here, it is often thought, nothing less than a theodicy will do, for this problem remains even if and after the logical form of the objection can be answered. I think it is a mistake to conclude that the evidential form of the objection necessitates the formulation of a theodicy, if by theodicy one means a specification of the actual reasons God has for permitting evil.

How do things stand with respect to the logical or deductive problem of evil if one addresses this problem against the background of natural theology? A demonstration of the existence of God would entail either that evil is not a reality or that the reality of evil is compatible with the existence of God. Even if natural theology demonstrates only that it is highly likely that God exists, this may undercut the suspicion that God and evil are incompatible. Very good evidence for the existence of God places a greater burden of proof upon the atheologian to actually demonstrate a contradiction between the propositions that God exists and that evil is a reality.

What about the evidential or inductive problem of evil? Here the natural theologian concludes that, against all appearances, the amount of evil we witness in this world is justified. So the actual worry picked out by *all* atheistically motivated formulations of the problem of evil is severely attenuated. All this without ever specifying what is or what might be the actual reason God has for permitting evil.

The overall result is a strategy that amounts to more than a defense on the one hand and to less than a theodicy on the other. For this strategy shows both that there is (or probably is) no contradiction in the theistic set and that we can plausibly assume that God has a justifying reason for allowing even those evils for which we cannot divine a reason. A mere defense achieves the first result, though in a different way, but not the second result. For a defense, the question of whether God actually has a justifying reason for permitting evil is left open. But the strategy I have developed here does address this question without specifying the precise nature of God's justifying reason. That God has a justifying reason would be evident, perhaps without any intimations about what that reason is.

Admittedly, an element of real mystery would remain, even when the atheistic problem of evil had been answered. But the natural theologian's resolution of the problem of evil is not purchased *with* an appeal to mystery. At worst it only *ends in* mystery about that which is no problem for the existence of God: namely, the specific reason God has for permitting evil.

There is room for speculation about the mystery surrounding God's actual reasons for permitting evil. But failure to identify the actual reasons God has for permitting evil will touch the natural theologian's conclusion—God exists—*not at all.* The natural theologian will remain confident that there is a Being of great power and goodness who created and sustains the universe and who has, with moral justification, permitted whatever evils there are in the universe. Whatever positive warrant there is for theistic belief may embolden the theist to formulate whatever theodicy she can utilizing the principles at her disposal. She would be well advised, however, not to put more stock in her theodicy hypothesis than her principles and the evidence allow.

The Testimony of Others

A number of theists have thought it worthwhile to address the question of God's existence first, independently of any consideration of the reality of evil. If his existence can first be reasonably affirmed on independent grounds, then the prospect of solving the problem of evil will be most promising. For instance, Keith Yandell writes: "If *N* has any reason to think theism true, then *N* has reason to think that what theism entails is true, and theism entails that God has a morally sufficient reason for permitting whatever evils he permits."[31] Brian Davies has us suppose that if "one had very good reason for believing that God exists . . . [then] one would also have reason for denying that evil makes it unlikely that God exists since one would already have good reason that God does exist." He further observes that this circumstance effectively requires the nontheist "to start engaging with the believer's reasons for believing in the existence of God."[32]

Theists who are sympathetic with natural theology are not the only ones to recognize the important relationship between a successful natural theology and the task of theodicy. M. B. Ahern, who apparently does not think that theistic argumentation can succeed, at least acknowledges that "if God's existence were proved independently, it would follow that actual evil is in fact justified even if we do not know which good justifies it."[33] According to Nelson Pike, Hume seems to admit the same: "As Philo himself has suggested, when the existence of God is accepted prior to any rational consideration of the status of evil in the world, the traditional problem of evil reduces to a noncrucial perplexity of relatively minor importance."[34]

Many skeptics and agnostics seem willing to grant this possibility on the strength of their conviction that no theistic argument can ever succeed. Michael Scriven, an avowed atheist, agrees that "it is not an absolute *contradiction* to assert that God exists and that there is inexplicable pain and evil. It is just that unless there are really impregnable proofs that God exists, the existence of inexplicable evil *virtually* precludes it."[35] Wallace I. Matson concurs when he says of the cosmological argument that if it were valid it "would prove the existence of God and would entail as a strict corollary that this is the best of all possible worlds."[36]

William Rowe, an atheist who describes the strategy we are considering as a special application of "the G. E. Moore shift," thinks that it is the best approach for a theist to follow in rejecting the idea that there is gratuitous evil in the world.[37] Michael Martin, another atheist, apparently agrees that "an essential part of any argument for the nonexistence of God is the refutation of arguments for the existence of God" since "arguments for the existence of God may tend to confirm theism more than evil disconfirms it."[38]

Of course, some atheists are reluctant to concede the point being made here. H. J. McCloskey, for example, will not permit a cop-out on theodicy via the arguments for God's existence, though it is difficult to imagine how evil could count against the existence of an omnibenevolent and all-powerful God if such a Being were known to exist on independent grounds.[39] But even McCloskey is guarded about exacting a detailed theodicy from the theist in the justification of religious belief. He acknowledges that "the possible arguments for the existence of God are unlimited in number, hence until all possible arguments are refuted, and until it is shown that any (some) or actual evil is logically incompatible with the existence of God, it will remain possible that both propositions: God exists; Evil exists: will be true."[40]

Who Needs a Theodicy?

Proponents of the Augustinian tradition do not presume to construct a complete theodicy strictly on the strength of theistic arguments. The task of theistic argumentation is merely preliminary and contributes only a part—though clearly a nontrivial part—to the overall task of framing a theodicy. If we were to conclude that "the evidence for the existence of evil *and* the evidence for the existence of God are irrefutable," that "*both* clearly exist," then a problem of evil remains, though not in its original guise.[41] Under these conditions, evil does not create an insuperable problem for the existence of God. Rather, evil presents a problem for our understanding of *how* both can exist, not *whether* both do exist.

One should not, of course, pay one's respects to the program of natural theology merely for the sake of admission into the Augustinian tradition of theodicy. The only proper incentive for embracing this theodicy tradition is a sense of the promise that such a program holds for constructing an adequate theodicy. The proposal here is that the theist should begin formulating the particulars of a theodicy only *after* first developing a positive case for the existence of God on the basis of theistic argumentation. This is in keeping with the spirit of the Augustinian tradition, according to which it is in the very nature of theodicy to begin with the existence of God and attempt to account for the existence of evil accordingly. It is evil that then needs explaining, not God.[42] In the final analysis, this is all that theodicy ever amounts to.

The logic behind this contention becomes apparent when we consider who it is that demands a justification of the ways of God to finite persons. Aristotle observed that the end and object of all persuasive discourse is determined by the intended audience.[43] Theodicy is normally construed as an effort to justify the ways of God to those who regard evil as a defeater of the proposition that God exists. Theodicy, then, is a defeater of a defeater. The general task, if it be possible, is to demonstrate that belief in God is rational. In the absence of theistic argumentation, the theodicist offers the atheist what the atheist does not seek, namely, an answer to the question of how to reconcile two existential verities—God and evil. (Little wonder that standard attempts to theodicize are so often met with insipid responses on the part of nonbelievers.) But the atheist repudiates the existence of God, and so this challenge calls directly for an effort to positively evince support for the truth of the proposition in question, the proposition that God exists. This is the task of theistic argumentation. The theist will have deflected the specific objection to the existence of God on the basis of evil *without even the most cursory analysis of evil* if the theist has produced a compelling argument for the existence of God on independent grounds.

Understood in this way, theodicy is a residual exercise, perhaps more needful for the religious believer than for the atheist. It is most likely that any theodicy will be lost upon the atheist who persists in demanding a positive reason to believe that God exists when evil is prima facie evidence that God does not exist. If the theist rests the case for the existence of God upon positive arguments for the existence of God, the atheist might well reply, "Yes, but then there is the matter of evil in the world." The trouble is that falling back on the argument from evil in this way, though common enough, does not answer the positive arguments advanced by the theist. These require separate attention. But from the point of view of the theist, these arguments, if successful, have quite definite ramifications for the argument from evil. Ralph Barton Perry once suggested that "proverbial difficulties easily become logical difficulties."[44] Similarly, the oft-repeated argument from evil may seem an imposing threat to the existence of God even after the proposition that God exists has been well supported philosophically; this may be because the argument from evil has achieved a kind of legendary status through constant repetition. Not enough has been made of the possibility of answering the problem of evil in principle by means of theistic argumentation. The problem of evil may turn out to be a nonstarter as an argument for the nonexistence of God. This is a result worth considering even if the traditional arguments do not initially *appear* successful.

Careful (even painstaking) attention to theistic argumentation is an investment with important dividends for constructing a sound theodicy. This Augustinian line of defense is most auspicious for several reasons. First, the problem of evil itself will be of a different kind than customarily thought. Rather than counting as a threat to the proposition that God exists, it is regarded as the considerably different problem of our understanding the relationship between two existential facts, God and evil. One may prefer to regard evil as a genuine threat to the existence of God rather than as a threat to our capacity for understanding reality, but one must be prepared to argue for the objective validity of this preference over the other. The Augustinian argues that evil is no threat to the proposition that God exists, for God is reasonably judged to exist on the basis of other considerations. On what basis does the nonbeliever insist that evil cannot be merely a problem for our understanding how there can be both God and evil?

Robert Nozick thinks that the problem of evil is only one of many philosophical problems that can be characterized as ones "of understanding how something is or can be possible."[45] In theodicy, the question is how evil is possible given the existence of God. Since evil is also given, in experience, we know evil is possible because we know it to be actual. So the question of how does not necessarily imply skepticism; it may only betray perplexity. Suppose we find ourselves believing for independent reasons that both

1. God exists,

and

2. There is evil in the world.

It appears that (2) entails not-(1). But *ex hypothesi*, we have both (1) and (2). Our supposition, together with the apparent entailment, suggests that there is perhaps a peculiar relation between (1) and (2) that is not immediately evident. The question, How is evil possible, given the existence of God? (or conversely, How is God possible, given the reality of evil?) is ambiguous. In the skeptical sense the question implies the denial of this possibility. But there is another sense of the question that acknowledges (even if only for the sake of argument) the twin verities of God and evil but is puzzled about the nature of their relation.

Nozick observes that, since philosophical problems typically focus "on the possibility only of some statements on one side of the relation," there remains the question of "what determines in which direction the question is salient."[46] In the controversy over the problem of evil, the possibility of God has customarily been taken to be the salient side of the puzzling relation. But why should this be? Natural theology enters a plea that proposition (1) is not susceptible to this skeptical bias.

Furthermore, since (paraphrasing Nozick) a demonstration of (1) yields the conviction that (1) is true, though it need not give us the understanding of how (1) *can* be true (given the apparent excluder, namely, evil), there is still the independent project of formulating a theodicy. It must be kept in mind that a demonstration of (1) need not even mention the reality of evil. Nevertheless, embedded either in the argument for (1) or in the propositional belief that (1), there may be clues for the theodicist to draw on in coming to the specific task of seeking to understand the relation between (1) and (2). An analysis of this relation is the chief task of theodicy.[47]

If nothing else, there is something intrinsically valuable in working out a theodicy in this context. The believer may not need a theodicy in the sense usually intended. Nevertheless, work on theodicy may lead to the discovery of "deeper explanatory principles,"[48] which may in turn become aids to the believer's devotion to God. Hick, however, cannot in principle regard the formulation of a theodicy as merely an intrinsically worthwhile exercise, for he cannot rely on any argument for the existence of God to remove the problem of evil to a second-order level of inquiry.

A second reason for proceeding in the manner of the Augustinian tradition is that only in the aftermath of demonstrating the independent rationality of belief in God, which includes identifying certain attributes of the divine character, can one ever hope to construct a theodicy that is more than hypothetical speculation. It is one thing to postulate a variety of ways God might employ to defeat evil if God exists; it is much more desirable to have some kind of theistic map to use in navigating the difficult waters of theodicy. We are more likely to be on the path to the proper analysis of evil in God's world if we have some prior specific knowledge about God's existence and character (although the reality of evil certainly may cause us to reflect more deeply about what it means for God to be good). The Augustinian tradition, with its commitment to natural theology, holds out the promise that this is a realistic possibility. Otherwise, the divine nature is too severely underdetermined to allow anyone to know which of a multitude of possible theodicies is the best (i.e., most plausible) or correct one. This is relevant in Hick's case since he now holds to such an attenuated version of theism that one can wonder whether theodicy is at all important to a defense of his religious position.

Third, as many have noted, in redressing challenges to their position, theists characteristically seek to argue from a posture of deep conviction that the core of what they believe is true. They are often criticized for this because such a stance seems to represent an irrational stubbornness of sheer belief and a resistance to the logic of certain objections to theism. But recourse to strong conviction about the existence of God, in response to the challenge of explaining evil, may well be justified by the success of one or more of the arguments for the existence of God. In short, we eviscerate our theodicy when we exclude a detailed theistic argument. Natural theology is a fitting prolegomenon to theodicy. These are confluent endeavors.

CONCLUSION

Naturally, it makes little sense to propose that theodicists begin their task with theistic argumentation without also pointing the way for successfully going about it. In Chapters 6 and 7 I argue for the possibility of natural theology. This includes an effort to sketch a case for ascribing to God such predicates as are especially relevant to the theodicy debate: personality, power, intelligence, and goodness. In Chapter 8 I respond to two difficulties Hick is likely to raise, the first having to do with the possible unintelligibility of the universe, the second associated with his suggestion that the universe is religiously ambiguous.

The discussion up to this point should make it clear why misgivings about Hick's dismissal of natural theology are relevant to a critique of his theodicy. The Augustinian tradition endorses a highly optimistic view of the prospects of theistic argument, for the type of theodicy devised within this tradition is rooted in a commitment to the soundness of some line of argument for the existence of God. Furthermore, the specific features of a viable Augustinian theodicy become at least faintly discernible as implications of the preliminary case for theism are traced out.

If optimism about the possibility of natural theology underwrites optimism about deflecting the traditional problem of evil, we might ask whether the failure to adopt the strategy of natural theology would render alternative accounts of justified belief in God specially vulnerable to the challenge of evil. The answer may depend upon the particular contours of the alternative approach to religious epistemology. In the next chapter I argue that Hick's approach, at least, is vulnerable to the reality of evil in a way that that of natural theology is not. The appeal to natural theology in argumentative theism protects the theodicist against the charge of ad hocness that inevitably characterizes postulational theism. A theodicy strategy that is postulational from beginning to end cannot hope to justify its claims. An investigation of Hick's own approach to the justification of religious belief reveals his susceptibility to this grave deficiency.

5
The Danger of Dismissing Natural Theology

Having just considered the value of natural theology for meeting the challenge of evil, we can now reflect upon the consequences of rejecting natural theology when constructing a viable theodicy. I examine John Hick's approach to the rationality of religious belief and show how this approach is vulnerable to the reality of evil in a way that natural theology is not. I argue that natural theology can be viewed as a research project with a problem-solving capacity that makes possible the grading of theoretical problems and subordinates the problem of evil for theism to more fundamental cosmological problems confronting nontheistic conceptual frameworks.

HICK'S ACCOUNT OF THE RATIONALITY OF RELIGIOUS BELIEF

Hick insists that, given the "systematic religious ambiguity" of the universe, no Christian philosopher can hope to demonstrate with certainty the correctness of the theistic interpretation of reality. This does not mean, however, that no realistic defense of the rationality of religious belief is possible. Indeed, he promises "to argue . . . that it is rational to believe in the reality of God."[1] He means only that any such defense must first acknowledge this situation of cognitive ambiguity and then proceed with appropriate caution and humility. Beginning with this conviction, then, he devises an epistemology of religious belief that ostensibly rescues religious belief from ultimate skepticism while avoiding the pitfalls of natural theology.

Analogy Between Religious Belief and Ordinary Perceptual Belief

Hick's strategy for realizing this objective depends upon an analogy between religious experience that evokes belief in God and ordinary perceptual experience that gives rise to the belief that there is an external world.[2] So strong is the analogy, he thinks, that religious belief is itself a form of what he calls "natural belief." Centuries of philosophical speculation have shown how hopelessly impossible it is to prove that an external world, mediated by the faculties of sensation, even exists. Nevertheless, it is rational—because natural—to believe as we do, and to act upon this belief as we must. The situation with belief in God is much the same. We are no more justified in believing in God than we are in affirming the existence of the external world. On the other hand, things could be worse, for we are at least as justified in believing in God as we are in believing there to be an external world.

The justification of religious belief, then, consists in defending the rationality of such belief. "The question is whether [the believer] is acting rationally in trusting his own experience and in proceeding to live on the basis of it."[3] Hick attempts to demonstrate the rationality of religious belief by comparing the cognitive status of religious experience with that of an ostensibly analogous though rather different level of human experience. "The analogy that I propose is that between the religious person's claim to be conscious of God and any man's claim to be conscious of the physical world as an environment, existing independently of himself, of which he must take account."[4] It is Hick's conviction that experience of the reality of God can be vindicated in much the same way that experience of the physical world as external to oneself can be vindicated. These experiences are analogous, and human experience of external physical reality is paradigmatic for understanding religious experience. In the same way that solipsism is standardly averted, religious experience constitutes grounds for "rational belief" in God's existence.

When the criteria of rationality are fully satisfied, then a particular belief is warranted, whether this be the belief that God exists or the belief that I am presently writing out this sentence on a page that exists apart from my consciousness of it. Notwithstanding important differences that obtain between the belief–experience complex of sensory perception and the parallel belief–experience complex of religious perception, belief in God is to be justified "in basically the same way as our beliefs about 'what there is and how things are' in our total environment: namely, by the impact of that environment upon us, our consciousness of which is our experience of it."[5]

Hick's Criteria for Rational Belief

In his book *An Interpretation of Religion,* Hick specifies two conditions that must be fulfilled for belief in the reality of some entity to be rational. "One is that we have responsibly judged (or reasonably assumed) it to be possible for such an entity to exist. The other is that it seems to be given in our experience in a powerful, persistent and intrusive way which demands belief in its reality."[6] Let us call the first condition, which is quite general, the possibility condition, and the second, the criterion of givenness.

Certain differences of emphasis obtain between this statement of the conditions of rational belief and Hick's earlier accounts. In past discussions Hick has recommended no less than three necessary conditions for rational belief in the reality of some entity that seems to be presented in experience. Let us consider Hick's earlier account of the rationality of religious belief and note how closely it parallels his more recent statements.

On his early account, the conditions for the rationality of religious belief are modeled after those which constitute the rationality of belief that there is an external world. While there are three reasons why belief in an external world is a perfectly "natural belief" (and therefore rational), these reasons do not provide a logical demonstration of the reality of an external world. Each of these criteria for the justification of natural belief in the physical world has a counterpart in the justification of belief in the existence of God.

Two criteria are positive; they consist in "features of our sense experience in virtue of which we all take this view" that there is an external world.[7] The first criterion is "the givenness or the involuntary character" of our experience of the external world as objectively real. The experience arises naturally and spontaneously, and it is as if we cannot help but experience "things" in this way. This is the criterion of givenness, and it appears relatively free from modification in Hick's more recent account of rational belief. We are justified in holding a belief if we are in some strong sense induced to believe as we do, that is, if we cannot but believe: the entity "seems to be given in our experience in a powerful, persistent and intrusive way which demands belief in its reality."[8]

The second feature of sense experience in virtue of which we form the belief in an external world is "the fact that we can and do act successfully in terms of our belief in an external world."[9] Our beliefs about the physical world enable us to function in ways that are more conducive to life than would be expected if these beliefs were false. Let us call this the criterion of fruitfulness.

This second condition found in Hick's earlier account is not expressly mentioned in *An Interpretation of Religion* as one of his two criteria for rational belief, though it may be thought to fall within the scope of his requirement that one responsibly judge or reasonably assume that the existence of an entity is at least possible. The criterion of fruitfulness is applied with particular subtlety when Hick describes his own Irenaean theodicy as a "true myth" when viewed in the context of religious pluralism.[10]

In addition to these two positive criteria of givenness and of fruitfulness, Hick has proposed a third, this time negative, criterion: "The absence of any positive reason to distrust" our perceptual experience.[11] This criterion of justified perceptual belief, formally stated in the earlier accounts, is satisfied when we simply have no reason *not* to believe or to go on believing the reports of our perceptual faculties. Alternatively, when one is confronted with a reason not to persist in some belief, the rationality of this belief is seriously at risk.

This negative criterion also is not expressly mentioned in *An Interpretation of Religion* as one of the two conditions for rational belief. Nevertheless, it too seems to fall within the scope of the possibility condition. The negative criterion is retained, for example, in the remark that *"in the absence of any positive reason to distrust one's experience . . .* it is rational, sane, reasonable for those whose religious experience strongly leads them to do so to believe wholeheartedly in the reality of God."[12] He also writes, "It is a good reason *only if there are no countervailing considerations,* or only to the degree that remains after such considerations have been fully and fairly taken into account."[13] Hick argues that "to believe, *without any positive reason,* that that which persistently appears within our experience has no objective existence, or to fail to adjust our beliefs about our environment in accordance with our seeming experience of it, would border upon insanity."[14]

So in both early and late accounts, Hick reasons that the two positive criteria (the criteria of givenness and of fruitfulness), together with the negative criterion, are applicable to religious beliefs no less than to ordinary perceptual beliefs.

Experiencing-as

Hick suggests that being rational means adopting natural beliefs about the external world since the aforementioned criteria are met; failure to do so is irrational or insane. The very definition of "to be rational" is based on the way we actually do find ourselves believing that there is something beyond our individual selves.

For Hick, religious experience is vindicated by invoking an analogous principle for ascertaining the cognitive nature of the experience. By "religious experience" he does not have in mind any sort of direct awareness of God or mystical awareness of the Transcendent. Rather, religious experience is inclusive of the entire manifold of human experience, "mediating the presence and activity of God."[15] In other words, the religious mind interprets all perceptual experience as having religious significance.[16] In effect, those who have this quality of experience to the greatest degree "could no more help believing in the reality of God than in the reality of the material world and of their human neighbours."[17] The veridical character of this religious experience of God's existence is as indubitable as that of the evidence for an external world supplied by the senses. Hick concludes that the criteria of givenness and fruitfulness are discoverable in religious experience no less than in experience of the physical world. "It therefore seems prima facie, that the religious man *is* entitled to trust his religious experience and to proceed to conduct his life in terms of it."[18] This judgment is found again in his more recent statement: "When someone believes in the existence of God on the basis of compelling religious experience, his or her belief is accordingly a case of rational or reasonable or well-founded belief."[19]

The Coercion Motif

One other feature of Hick's discussion of rational religious belief must be emphasized here. He remarks that for those who undergo some sort of religious experience, this experience *"strongly leads them* to . . . believe wholeheartedly in the reality of God." The experience is said to be "compelling." Indeed, it is so "powerful, persistent and intrusive" that it *"demands* belief" in the reality of God.[20] The coercion motif is a persistent feature in Hick's system of religious epistemology.

EVALUATION OF HICK'S ACCOUNT

I wish now to point out two sets of difficulties with Hick's account of the rationality of religious belief. One set regards his proposed analogy between religious experience and ordinary perception. The other is associated with his negative criterion for rational belief.

Limitations of the Analogy with Ordinary Perception

Hick himself qualifies the analogy between religious experience and ordinary perceptual experience in several important respects. He admits, first of all, that religious experience as he describes it is far from universal, whereas sensory experience is more or less universal. He says of our experience of the material environment that "we cannot help accepting this as the perception of a material world around us in space. . . . And the world which we thus perceive is not plastic to our wishes but presents itself to us as it is, whether we like it or not."[21] The religious consciousness of God at the highest level is, however, forcible in a way that consciousness of the physical world is not. It is, in fact, coercive, and this precisely because it is conscious-ness of God. Thus, religious belief is rational for someone who has this experience. Conversely, failure to believe subsequent to having an experience of this kind is not only not rational but apparently not even possible. Of course, the believer must allow that the agnostic's unbe-lief is also rational inasmuch as the agnostic lacks the experience of God that is its own justification. Consequently, it is possible for one to hold a religious belief rationally even if it is not true. The question then arises whether any experience can really *require* the judgment that God exists if God does not exist.

It is not clear that Hick's account of these matters is adequate. A fundamental difference among the kinds of experience here supposed to be analogous lurks in the shadows of his discussion, making the analogy seem too tenuous to be useful. Hick would be on more solid logical ground with his analogy if he were to press the correspon-dence between religious experience and ordinary experience to a greater degree. A spate of questions intrudes. How can a religious experience be more coercive of belief than experience of the physical world upon which it is predicated? Why does God reveal himself to some persons within the context of their normal experience, thereby compelling belief in him, and not to others? If the manifold of ordinary human experience is the medium of religious experience, why does the atheist or the agnostic—whose experience of the physical world is otherwise very like that of the believer—remain unaware of the divine presence in the same forcible way as the believer?

Hick's analogy begs the question if it fails to specify how these two levels of experience are similar. What he describes is the similarity of their general *effect* on the one who has them. But the effect in the case of religious experience is so privatized that the success of the analogy cannot rest on this observation. There must be a greater correspon-dence between the two kinds of experiences if the analogy is to stand. Hick himself analyzes religious experience in terms of more general experience. All of one's experience of reality is said to mediate awareness of the Transcendent. So in a very important sense, sensory experience is primary, and thus there is only one way to interpret the data; whereas religious experience is either secondary, or even tertiary (because predicated on general experience),[22] or it is merely a different way to interpret the same data as that which the senses apprehend. That is, either the analogy breaks down because it treats of such altogether different experiences, or it dissolves because one and the same datum is experienced and interpreted in different ways simultaneously.

To preserve the validity of the analogy Hick must allow religious experience to be at least as universal as the experience of the physical world and grant that religious experience as such is no more coercive than sensory experience. In pressing the analogy, he might even have invoked the familiar words spoken by the apostle Paul on Mars Hill: "Yet [God] is not far from each one of us, for 'In him we live and move and have our being.' "[23] Of course, strengthening the analogy in this way would entail that the nonbeliever is not finally rational in withholding belief. This consequence calls to mind the apostle's warning that those who persist in unbelief do so without enough warrant to excuse them.[24]

If Hick were to press the correspondence of the analogy in the way I have suggested, he would perhaps be very close to the so-called existentialism of Thomas Aquinas, which formed the basis of his own theistic arguments.[25] Frederick Copleston observes that "St. Thomas expressly teaches that the immediate and proper object of the human intellect in this life is the essence of material things. The fundamental notions and principles which are presupposed by St. Thomas's natural theology are not, according to him, innate, but are apprehended through reflection on and abstraction from our experience of concrete objects."[26] For Aquinas, sensible objects, which are "the first concrete objects the mind knows,"[27] are finite and contingent effects (which can be metaphysically analyzed into existence and essence). These effects provide the basis for inferring the existence of God (for whom alone existence and essence are identical). On the principle of the analogy of being, being which is the primary object of cognition (the first of which is physical being perceived by the senses), a being that transcends sensory experience is known as that which bears a necessary relation to sensory objects precisely at the level of being.[28]

Hick, of course, does not take the Thomistic route in developing his case for rational belief in the existence of God. This avenue is not open to him given his opposition to the whole program of natural theology. For him Aquinas has no logically compelling basis for presupposing the principles employed in natural theology. But for Aquinas these principles are, in the words of Copleston, "apprehended through reflection on and abstraction from our experience of concrete objects."[29] Hick sees no reason for thinking that such principles can yield certain truths about the nature of reality. The principles themselves may be useful to us in interpreting reality, and our use of them may even be involuntary, but they are ultimately suspect in that we cannot be certain that our experience of things as "external objects" has any correspondence in reality. And these are the things from which we professedly apprehend the principles. In the absence of any logical demonstration of the fundamental principles of thought, used, for example, in the cosmological argument by Aquinas, any argument for the existence of God includes "a premise begging the very question at issue."[30] Here, the unsubstantiated premise of all natural theologians is that the principles of logic apply to all of reality. But arguably, those principles upon which Aquinas bases his own argument for the existence of God are as natural for us to believe (in Hick's sense of "natural") as it is for us to believe that there is an external world.

So it appears that Hick's alleged analogy between belief in an external world and belief in God is strained by the fact that belief in an external world is very largely universal, whereas belief in God is apparently much less so. One further difficulty facing Hick's approach, given this state of affairs, is the plausible possibility that having a religious experience, for those who do, depends in some way upon having and applying a relevant set of concepts, which in turn are generated by prior background beliefs one has about the nature of the world.[31] In contrast, if natural theology is possible, then a natural-theology case for the existence of God will provide antecedent warrant for applying distinctly theistic concepts in interpreting the total range of human experience. The "rightness" of interpreting experience religiously will then be underwritten by the deliverances of a successful framework of natural theology.

The Negative Criterion and Religious Experience

It is disappointing to find Hick displaying an obvious willingness to qualify his analogy and yet overlooking the need for even further qualification in light of additional difficulties. Apart from contesting the applicability of the criteria of givenness and fruitfulness to the distinctively religious experience, we might want to ask whether Hick is not mistaken in thinking that the negative criterion is not relevantly violated at the level of religious experience. The foregoing analysis of his religious epistemology serves an important purpose in my evaluation of his theodicy, for I do not think he has paid enough attention to the threat to rational religious belief represented by the fact of evil in human experience.

As I see it, the fact of evil is just the sort of reality that demonstrates that Hick's own negative criterion for the rationality of religious belief is violated. Recall that this criterion consists in "the absence of any positive reason to distrust" our experience of an entity ostensibly given in experience; that is, nothing in our experience compromises the rationality of our belief in the reality of the entity. Naturally, on the analogy devised by Hick to vindicate religious experience, it bears asking: Is there nothing in experience that might stand as a positive reason to distrust the veridicality of religious experience? With this question we are faced with the very strong possibility that Hick's position on the rationality of religious belief is fundamentally inadequate. For as we review the texture of human experience with this question in mind, we are at once confronted with the challenge of evil.

Let us keep in mind that, in the context of exploring his analogy, he conceives of the religious experience as ultimately coercive and, therefore, of the rational belief vindicated by this experience as impervious to doubt. So compelling is this "experience of God" that the believer "is no more inclined to doubt its veridical character than to doubt the evidence of his senses."[32] But how can this be when we consider that evil is a very real part of our experience? Hick himself says in another passage that evil is "a problem equally for the believer and the non-believer." He explains: "In the mind of the latter it stands as a major obstacle to religious commitment, whilst for the former it sets up an acute internal tension to disturb his faith and to lay upon it a perpetual burden of doubt."[33] It seems that evil itself fulfills the conditions needed to bring religious belief into doubt, such that Hick's own negative criterion fails to be satisfied given the total quality of experience. How is religious experience coercive and impervious to doubt for the believer when at the same time evil is said to lay upon the believer's faith "a perpetual burden of doubt"?

Furthermore, in his development of the analogy in question, Hick implies that the chief reason for admitting the "rational" status of the agnostic's position is that religious experience is not universal and so, in the absence of the positive criteria of the givenness and fruitfulness of religious experience, for the agnostic it is rational not to believe. But elsewhere, when he treats theodicy directly, Hick allows that evil might constitute a genuine impediment to religious commitment on the part of the nonbeliever. And what of the possibility that the positive criteria of givenness and fruitfulness are both present in one's experience, *but so is evil,* which represents a positive reason to distrust the otherwise theistic character of one's experience? This, apparently, is what obtains in the case of the believer for whom evil "sets up an acute internal tension to disturb his faith." Evil is a potential defeater of a religious interpretation of experience. What justifies the believer in God in breaking the stalemate between theism and naturalism in favor of the existence and goodness of God? Why is the universe not finally "religiously ambiguous" for the believer if evil is a persistent feature of the believer's own experience?

The reality of evil is just the sort of evidence that should count compellingly against the cognitivity of religious experience as understood by Hick. A further complication ensues: whereas religious experience may be felt by a relative minority of individuals, the experience of evil is universally attested and is therefore "a problem equally for the believer and the non-believer." As one writer puts it, "The messy problem of pain and suffering keeps popping up, regardless of our erudite attempts to explain it away. . . . Like Hercules' battle against the Hydra, all our attempts to chop down agnostic arguments are met with writhing new examples of suffering."[34] Is not the agnostic or the atheist more rational than the believer in judging from the *total quality* of human experience (as understood by Hick) that God does not exist?

It is rather odd, therefore, that for all his concerted effort to treat in various contexts the problem of evil, Hick never discusses the problem in explicit connection with his analogy of religious experience with ordinary sensory experience. Thus, the analogy is misleading. It is only natural that Hick should consider the possibility that evil undermines the justification of religious belief in virtue of its violation of the negative criterion. Hick does not explicitly acknowledge this possibility in the context of his attempt to vindicate religious belief in God apart from theistic argumentation.

In his recent work, Hick does make it clear that he does not allow "the mere fact that in this religiously ambiguous universe a different, naturalistic, epistemic practice is also possible" to count against religious belief.[35] But in the immediate context of this passage he does not say why; he does not argue for this important claim. And yet, this is truly the eye of the storm. He does say that some positive reason to believe in God is a good reason "only if there are no countervailing considerations, *or only to the degree that remains after such considerations have been fully and fairly taken into account.*"[36] When he says this he implies that some criteria are available for deciding whether an account of countervailing factors is full enough to warrant belief in God. But we are never told what these criteria are.

What he says in another context may even lead us to despair of ever knowing what these criteria could be. In explicit connection with the question of theodicy, Hick avows that the balance of experiential evidence can never be decided in favor of one interpretation of reality over another since we live in a religiously ambiguous world.[37] If this is true, how shall we ever know whether mitigating conditions, like the fact of evil in human experience, have been sufficiently taken into account to justify the rationality of belief in God? What exactly is to count as a full enough appreciation of the deleterious ramifications of evil for rational belief in God? It is clear that Hick believes his soul-making theodicy fulfills this requirement. But without some fairly specific guidelines that can be used to judge whether it does so, his claim can only appear to beg the question.

Hick reasons that the argument from evil at most only counterbalances the sum of all positive evidence for the rationality of belief in God. The evidence of evil against the rationality of religious faith does not outweigh the evidence for the rationality of such faith. Nor does the evidence for the rationality of belief in God tip the scale in favor of such belief vis-à-vis the naturalistic belief that God does not exist. This is said to be because the universe is religiously ambiguous. What ensures the basic ambiguity of the universe is the possibility of giving either a theistic or a naturalistic interpretation of the total data of human experience.

Hick agrees that the fact of evil must be factored into the assessment of the total matrix of human experience and taken into account alongside all evidence amenable to a theistic interpretation of reality. He does not, however, allow that evil could ultimately outweigh the theistic hypothesis as long as a coherent account of God and evil can be formulated. He frames his theodicy with precisely this concern in mind. But I submit that when evil is factored into a total appraisal of experience (against the backdrop of Hick's own epistemology of religious belief), it effectively neutralizes the data of experience that once seemed to recommend the rationality of religious belief, lending additional weight to the naturalistic thesis that God does not exist.

Hick, however, argues that the negative evidence represented by the fact of evil cannot be assigned a value greater than that which characterizes the positive evidence for the existence of God. He thinks that any attempt to quantify in favor of one form of evidence against the other must ultimately be arbitrary and subjective. Theism and naturalism are, in effect, equiprobable, so that purely in terms of logic and evidence they are at a standoff.[38] But this view of the matter cannot be sustained, for there is plenty of reason to suppose, judging from the responses of believers and nonbelievers alike, that evil weighs in more heavily than Hick allows given the total quality of human experience—unless, of course, there is good evidence for the existence of God and this evidence is not at all logically attenuated by the reality of evil. For evil is a very real feature in every individual's experience. The unsettling experience of evil is universally attested, whereas the settled conviction that God exists is attested by some and disputed by others. No one denies the felt reality of evil, but many testify that they do not find God mediated to them in their experience.

Furthermore, Hick has remarked that "the fact of evil in its many forms" is at least one of the chief reasons why "we cannot share the hope of the older schools of natural theology of inferring the existence of God from the evidences of nature."[39] That is, the evidences of nature that might be construed in favor of theism are effectively canceled by the evidence of evil. But this too can be misleading, for if the fact of evil forbids the admission of evidence that could support belief in God, then why should it not have the same effect on the evidence derived from the religious quality of human experience? Hick supposes that the reality of evil is problematic for traditional efforts to establish the existence of God while claiming that his own account of rational theistic belief is immune to this difficulty. This looks suspiciously like a form of special pleading. Moreover, his judgment about the bearing of evil on the outcome of natural theology seems to me to be simply false.

Hick would like to think that the reality of evil is problematic for the traditional attempt to justify belief in God in a way that it is not problematic for his own notion of rational belief predicated on coercive religious experience—a type of experience that is involuntary when it occurs but is not universally given. But the "older schools of natural theology" are on more solid footing (in terms of overall strategy) in seeking to justify belief in God independently of the reality of evil and then subsequently addressing the problem of evil in light of the reasonable belief that God exists. If God exists, then there can be no logical problem of evil. It is only a problem for our understanding and for experience when pain is to be endured.

In saying this I do not mean to make light of the gravity of these difficulties. However, *it makes all the difference in the world how one comes to the conclusion that God exists.* If one does so in the traditional way, via theistic argumentation, then evil cannot sabotage the case for God's existence. But if one seeks to justify belief in God's existence as Hick does, by an appeal to the total character and quality of human experience (in which all features of the total fabric of experience are on an evidentially equal footing), then evil—which is an unmistakable feature of everyone's experience—cancels out the prima facie evidence for religious belief. Only some individuals are compelled to interpret experience religiously, whereas all are faced with pain and suffering and injustice—the religious person no less than the nonreligious person.[40]

ON GRADING THEORETICAL PROBLEMS

It may be objected that the Augustinian program of rationally justifying belief in God runs afoul of the same difficulty facing Hick. The a posteriori arguments in particular depend upon the validity of inferring the existence of God from what are thought to be the effects of God's causal agency. This move involves an appeal to our experience of the world. Surely the natural theologian is no more justified than Hick in passing over our experience of evil when listing those aspects of reality that require the kind of explanation that the conception of God answers to.

It can certainly appear that the reality of evil ought to be factored into the equation during our reflections about the possible existence of God. This is partly what David Hume assumes in his *Dialogues Concerning Natural Religion*. But this criticism confuses the features of experienced reality *relevant for theistic argumentation* with the conception of religious experience that Hick has in mind. And it assumes, contrary to fact, that all features of experienced reality are in rough epistemic parity.

In reality, the strategy of natural theology has the greater advantage. The efforts of natural theologians must be measured in terms of their success or failure in demonstrating the rationality of belief in God from the evidences of nature. Natural theologians are not obliged to factor the reality of evil into their preliminary case for the existence of God. To suppose that they are is to confuse the features of experienced reality relevant to theistic argumentation with those relevant to Hick's positive justification of religious belief. And this confusion rests upon a failure to notice the structural differences between two very different approaches to the evidence embedded in experienced reality.

What is particularly relevant in the type of argumentative theism that I sketch in the next two chapters is the virtual certainty that the actual universe, with all of its attendant evils, had a beginning. In Hick's stratagem, the whole continuum of lived experience, including the mystery of evil, is uniformly relevant to the case for theistic belief. And this is precisely the weakness of his analysis. Natural theologians can justify their selective consideration of states of affairs that point to divine causal agency, for these states seem to depend upon the existence of God whether or not this world includes either the possibility or the actuality of evil. The presence of evil in the world does nothing to attenuate the apparent need to explain why there is something rather than nothing in terms of the existence of God. Due consideration of the challenge posed by evil can therefore await the results of prior considerations that confirm or tend to confirm theistic belief. But Hick cannot postpone meaningful engagement with the problem of evil in the wake of confirmed belief in God on the basis of (religious) experience, for this experience is itself inclusive of pain and suffering. He has no similar criterion for justifiable selectivity. Evil poses a serious threat to the rationality of religious belief from the very outset.

The Problem-solving Capacity of Theism

It is helpful to view the philosophy of religion as a kind of problem-solving activity, resembling the scientific enterprise in interesting respects. In his discussion of the problem of scientific progress, Larry Laudan has argued that the goal of science is problem solving: "If problems are the focal point of scientific thought, theories are its end result. Theories matter, they are *cognitively* important, insofar as— and only insofar as—they provide adequate solutions to problems. If problems constitute the questions of science, it is theories which constitute the answers."[41]

Laudan's view that science is essentially a problem-solving activity and his suggestion that all problems are fundamentally "scientific" problems imply that the philosophy of religion can be viewed as an intellectual discipline concerned with solving a certain range of problems and that the method of scientific problem solving is applicable to this range of problems. There is no problem within any intellectual discipline that is not susceptible to this analysis, according to Laudan. Thus, if there is a philosophical problem of evil, it too may be understood in this way.[42]

Another point Laudan makes is that there is needed both a taxonomy of the types of scientific problems and an acceptable method of grading their relative importance. The same can be said of problems in the philosophy of religion. In particular we can ask, for our purposes, how the problem of God's existence as a general question and the problem of evil (including its implications for the existence of God) are to be graded in relation to each other. Moreover, it can be asked whether these are problems of the same type. What counts as a type of problem in the domain of philosophical theology? This concern has logical priority over the concern to identify criteria for solving problems, for a suitable set of criteria for solving a philosophical problem depends upon a proper formulation of the problem. And a proper formulation of the problem must include a consideration of the relation between it and other problems concerned with the same object(s). If there are alternative solutions to the same problem, then degrees of comparative adequacy must be discerned.

Laudan complains that "in assessing the adequacy of any theory, the philosopher of science will usually ask how many facts confirm it, not how important those facts are."[43] This reflects my own concern perfectly. The atheistic hypothesis rests upon the observation that there is evil in the world together with certain assumptions about what this implies for the existence of God. The theistic hypothesis (according to the natural-theology tradition) rests upon more general considerations about the being and character of the universe together with certain assumptions about what this implies for the existence of God. Are the facts relevant to each theory of God's possible relation to the world (or theory of God's possible existence given the fact of evil) *qualitatively* equivalent? Much of the literature in the philosophy of religion leaves the impression that they are and that a final assessment of the adequacy of either theory depends upon a *quantitative* weighting of the evidence on both sides. But this is artificial. The facts are not at all equally significant.

Perhaps to preserve the rationality of belief in God the theist does not need to deny what the atheist takes to be essential about the nature of evil. But can the atheist also affirm what the theist insists is essential about the nature of the universe without also affirming the existence of God? As Laudan puts it, in general the philosopher "will ask how many problems the theory solves, not about the significance of those problems."[44] Natural theology is in the advantageous position of being able to answer both questions satisfactorily. Theism offers solutions to both the problem of God's existence and the problem of evil. Theism also makes suggestions about the relative significance of these problems. It treats the puzzle of the existence of our universe, such as it is, as more fundamental than the puzzle of evil in the universe. In doing so, it is able eventually to respond to both problems. The question is, is this ordering of difficulties justified?

There is a certain logical symmetry between the two questions, If God exists, how is evil possible? and If evil exists, how is the existence of God possible? There is also an important asymmetry. The problem of God's existence is distinct from (because more general than) the problem of evil (which is, nevertheless, conceived as a problem for God's existence). The problem of God's existence is tied not only to the reality of evil but also to questions about the coherence of the concept of God in theism and to questions about the origin and arrangement of the universe. This is made the more evident when we consider that a successful demonstration of the existence of God would be successful whether or not there is evil in the world. We might then ask how these problems are to be weighted relative to each other.

An Anomaly for Naturalism

Laudan observes that "anything about the natural world which strikes us as odd, or otherwise in need of explanation, constitutes an empirical problem."[45] I notice that he does not say "anything 'within' the natural world." Granted, "whether something is regarded as an empirical problem will depend, in part, on the theories we possess."[46] But this is just to say that whether it strikes us as odd that there should even be a universe depends upon the theories we hold. Yet even those who confess that it is reasonable to suppose that the universe is a brute fact often openly admit that this is a mystery (that is, that it strikes one as odd that the universe should be a brute fact). Certainly it strikes many as odd that there should be a physical world at all. This is therefore an empirical problem, in Laudan's terms. I think this is one way to respond to the claim made by many naturalists that the universe as a whole does not require explanation, but only things within the world.

If one wishes to avoid theism, perhaps the best way to respond to the issue I have just raised is to assert that the existence of the universe is not a problem. If it were a problem it would mean that theism and naturalism could be compared in terms of their capacity to solve this problem. If theism could solve this problem and naturalism could not, or if theism could solve it better than naturalism, this would constitute a reason for accepting theism over naturalism. It is increasingly evident that naturalism cannot solve this problem, so rather than conclude that naturalism is not rational, persistent naturalists determine that the existence of the universe is not a problem and that therefore no solution is needed. Is the assertion that the existence of the universe is *not* a genuine problem a matter of faith, or is it a datum of knowledge? And if it is known that the universe is a brute fact, how is it known?

If one answers that the universe is known to be a brute fact in the sense that it follows from the theoretical commitments that naturalists make, then this either begs the question or it is hollow, since theists make conflicting theoretical commitments. If it is an article of faith, then the possibility remains that the problem is genuine. And if the problem is genuine, then there is reason to appeal to the resources of the theory that can best solve the problem. Natural theologians have attempted to show how theism can solve the problem of the existence of the universe.[47]

In other words, it is a virtue of theism that it allows us to think of the existence of the universe as a problem, precisely because theism offers a solution to the problem, whereas naturalism does not. To quote Laudan again: "Unsolved problems generally count as genuine problems only when they are no longer unsolved."[48] And they are no longer unsolved whenever there is at least one theory that solves them. When this is the case and when theories that do not solve them exist, they are for those theories anomalies, and it is incumbent upon the theorist for whom they are anomalous to solve them. There is important work to be done in the area of identifying criteria that can help.

One consideration that may help identify relevant criteria is this: theists have a theory, and so do naturalists. For the theist the origin of the universe is not a problem except as solved. For the naturalist the origin of the universe is not a problem except as anomalous. The naturalist may insist that it is not even an anomalous problem since she acknowledges no problem of explaining the existence of the universe. But the notion of an anomalous problem is transtheoretical while appearing theory-dependent. Perhaps there is no clear answer to the question, Is naturalism the *sort* of theory that should be expected to solve this problem? Naturalists themselves may disagree about whether it is.

Perhaps an illustration from the history of science will help. Laudan describes the episode concerning the polyp observed by Abraham Trembly in 1740. He concludes with this remark: "In short, what transformed the polyp from an idle curiosity into a threatening anomaly for vitalistic biology was the presence of an alternative theory (or, as I shall later call it, an alternative research tradition) which could count the polyp as a solved problem."[49] Analogously, what transforms the origin of the universe from an idle curiosity into a threatening anomaly for naturalism is the presence of an alternative theory (an alternative research tradition in the form of natural theology) that can count the origin of the universe as a solved problem.

Note, this bodes well not just for theism in general but for natural theology in particular. That is, it is a lesson not only for naturalists but for anyone (including the theist) who doubts the capacity of natural theology. It does not hurt any that many scientists continue to hope for something like a complete theory of the universe. As I hope to show in Chapter 6, there is now the possibility of pressing the anomaly of the origin of the universe as decisive for naturalism.

In this section I have been treating the philosophy of religion as if it were analogous to science, in the sense that it too is a problem-solving activity. I have concentrated on the general problem of finding an explanation for the existence of the universe. The significance of this is to show that this problem demands greater cognitive adequacy on the part of any explanation than does the problem of evil. What I mean is, the need to explain the existence of the universe takes precedence over the need to explain the reality of evil. For whatever counts as the best explanation for the existence of the universe is likely to be significant for the possibility of explaining the reality of evil. If a theistic explanation for the former is required, or more rational than its alternatives, then whatever evil is discoverable in the universe must be interpreted in light of that hypothesis. Thus, the significance of evil is relativized to conceptual frameworks formulated in response to more general concerns, such as, Why is there something rather than nothing?

THE POSTULATIONAL CHARACTER OF HICK'S THEODICY

The heart of Hick's entire religious epistemology is his analysis of the cognitive status of experience in general. Hick is an empiricist who understands the cognitive status of human experience in terms of pragmatic necessity.[50]

Hick believes that all knowledge claims are subject to doubt. To be sure, it is reasonable for us to hold some of our "beliefs," because they are grounded in our constitution as individuals living in a physical environment where we are surrounded by other external objects. Solipsism cannot be rejected on the basis of logical demonstration. But since we seem to find ourselves existing in an extended world with numerous physical objects all about us, it is reasonable to refuse solipsism and get on with living. This renunciation of solipsism is the result of a reasonable interpretation of our perception of reality. We postulate that reality as perceived is just what the term denotes: that which is real. This postulate makes a practical difference for us vis-à-vis the alternative of solipsism. So the objectivity of the physical universe is asseverated on the basis of a practical necessity from which we cannot extricate ourselves.

One consequence of this analysis is that the whole cognitive enterprise teeters on rather dubious footing. It is therefore not surprising that the process of extending our knowledge to matters of religious belief yields at least equally dubious results. Nevertheless, because of the practical value of our primary beliefs about the physical world, we have a basis for ascertaining the *reasonableness* (though not necessarily the *truth*) of beliefs that we acquire about other matters. Analyzing the reasonableness of belief in terms of strictly pragmatic criteria, though failing to eradicate all manner of skepticism, does at least encourage moderate optimism about cognitive pursuits: if it is the best we can do, we might as well make the best of it.

The net effect of Hick's epistemology, when applied to religious categories, seems to be a version of what Frederick Ferré calls "postulational theism."[51] Ferré uses this locution in reference to Kierkegaard, but the phrase is apropos of Hick as well. For there are affinities between his method and Kierkegaard's in describing the nature of religious faith. This is nowhere more apparent than in Hick's attempt to formulate a viable theodicy. Hick does not just deny the validity of theistic argumentation; his rejection of all a posteriori arguments for the existence of God is a function of his pragmatic–empiricist epistemology. In his system, belief in God is something of a practical postulate.

Ferré notes that both Kant and Kierkegaard postulate the existence of God out of practical necessity. In this sense they are alike. But they differ in that Kierkegaard's postulate "is not made, like Kant's, a presupposition for thinking consonantly with morality, . . . but on the basis of a passionate leap, rooted in inwardness and prompted by despair."[52] Hick's motivation for postulating the existence of God differs from that of both Kant and Kierkegaard, but he is prompted by practical considerations no less than they are. Moreover, Hick's religious epistemology is on many points explicitly patterned after Kant's general epistemology. This is especially evident in his view that the universe is religiously ambiguous. And this has important ramifications for his conception of the task of theodicy.

Hick rejects all traditional arguments for the existence of God and, in principle, the possibility of *ever* producing a successful theistic argument. Nonetheless, he maintains that the conclusion of these probative attempts, as a proposition *simpliciter,* is true. According to Hick, God does exist. It is a propositional belief whether or not the truth of this belief is, strictly speaking, logically demonstrable. In this respect, Hick appears to be a realist about religious beliefs.[53] Furthermore, although the truth of the propositional belief that God exists is not logically demonstrable, it is rational in that the believer (in a weaker sense) is justified in holding this belief. The rationality of this belief is not a deliverance of philosophical argument but of immediate experience.

Since evil is frequently construed as reliable evidence that God does not exist, however, Hick is compelled to show how the reality of evil is compatible with the existence of a God of love. But much depends on how one comes to believe that there is such a God. I have already suggested that the reality of evil itself violates Hick's own negative criterion for justified belief in God. Hick is therefore obliged to address the problem of evil, and the fact that he has addressed this issue numerous times in a variety of contexts reflects an obvious concern to meet the challenge posed by evil. The focal point of his concern is to show "that the mystery of evil, largely incomprehensible though it remains, does not render irrational a faith that has arisen, not from the inferences of natural theology, but from participation in a stream of religious experience."[54] The task of theodicy therefore has "a negative rather than a positive function. It cannot profess to create faith, but only to preserve an already existing faith from being overcome by this dark mystery."[55]

Hick speaks of belief in the reality of God as "a foundational natural belief" in that it "arises, like perceptual belief, from a natural response of the human mind to its experiences."[56] There is no way for one to check the veridicality of theistic belief that arises in this manner. Belief in God arrived at in this way is neither the result of an inference nor susceptible to verification by means of philosophical argument. But it might seem to be disconfirmed by the experience of evil. Thus, there is a need to meet this challenge. The challenge cannot, however, be met, even initially, by simply pointing to what is the theistic character of experience of some people. For experience is inclusive of evil, and such evil represents a potential defeater of the judgment that God is given in experience. The only way to meet the challenge of evil, then, is to formulate a logically possible explanation for the reality of evil on the assumption that God exists. In the nature of the case, the probability that Hick's theodicy proposal is literally true cannot be assessed, for the evidence might be interpreted according to different assumptions, yielding different conclusions about God and evil and the relationship between the two.

When this sort of method is employed, by whomever, it invites suspicion that the conclusion has first been determined and that the evidence has subsequently been interpreted in favor of the conclusion. Kenneth Surin gives expression to this suspicion: "While theodicists . . . often display remarkable ingenuity in their attempts to establish the logical invulnerability of their conclusions, these conclusions nevertheless give the appearance of resting on precariously makeshift foundations: the arguments advanced by the theodicist in support of her conclusions seem at times to be no more than ad hoc devices designed to prop up a theoretical superstructure already on the verge of collapse."[57] I submit that Surin's insinuation about contemporary theodicies applies with particularly painful relevance to Hick's methodology. Ultimately, the resulting theodicy has no more status as a truth claim than does any other reasonable hypothesis awaiting future verification. Little wonder that M. B. Ahern begins his evaluation of Hick's theodicy with the observation that "there is no way of knowing whether it is true."[58]

Not only can the truth of Hick's theodicy not be verified in the present, because of the oblique circularity of the argument inherent in his thesis, its plausibility cannot hope to ever be firmly established. The plausibility of his theodicy depends upon his case for rational belief in the existence of God. But this case rests upon the quality of human experience, which itself includes an uncomfortable mixture of both confirming and disconfirming features. Is it really rational to believe in the existence of God strictly on the basis of the quality of experience when the scope of experience includes pervasive evil? The reality of evil in human experience threatens the rationality of belief in the existence of God. This is why it is risky to attempt to deal adequately with the problem of evil without employing the resources of natural theology.

Perhaps Hick can at least be credited with meeting the demands of the logical problem of evil, for his postulates have the minimal plausibility of being real possibilities in the event that God does exist. They could be construed as valid interpretations of experience for one who believes in God. Although Hick may not have succeeded in showing that belief in God is rational, he does effectively illustrate the possibility that both God and evil are reconcilable entities, thus ameliorating the logical problem of evil, a problem that rests on an alleged inconsistency in affirming both the existence of God and the reality of evil.[59]

Hick's postulates show that it is at least conceivable to reconcile God and evil in terms of a purpose that God might have for allowing evil into his universe. This teleological theme is the starting point of his theodicy proper and the subject of Chapter 9. But first, since I take the program of natural theology to be crucial to answering the problem of evil, the reader may wish to know how I would state the possibility of natural theology. After all, it is one thing to note how convenient it would be, for the purposes of theodicy, to have recourse to natural theology and how vulnerable theistic belief might be apart from natural theology; it is quite another matter to demonstrate that a successful program of natural theology might be possible.

6

The Possibility of Natural Theology, Part 1: The Argument for a Non-Natural Reality

I have suggested that natural theology and theodicy are confluent endeavors; that natural theology is a fitting prolegomenon to framing a theodicy; and that, in the Augustinian tradition at least, theistic argumentation is even a noneliminable first step in formulating an adequate theodicy. But clearly, natural theology can play no constructive role in theodicy if natural theology itself is not even possible. Thus the problem of evil becomes an occasion for reinvestigating the possibility of natural theology. In this chapter and the next I argue for this possibility. By "possibility" I mean that natural theology stands a reasonable chance of being a going enterprise. And when I speak of natural theology, I have in mind the systematic formulation of reasons to believe that God exists, that he has a particular nature, and that he stands in relation to the world in certain definite ways, without relying directly upon sacred texts or any prophetic tradition. In this chapter and the next I seek to make a contribution to the wider discussion about the rationality of belief in God on the merits of natural theology.

CHARACTERISTICS OF THE ARGUMENT

I wish to clarify at the outset two features of my approach to natural theology.

It Is a Cumulative Argument

It is regrettable that arguments for the existence of God have come to be treated in isolation from one another, often by their exponents as well as by their opponents.[1] I do not suppose that any single argument for the existence of God (as commonly understood) can on its own produce the results needed to carry out the requisite prolegomenon to theodicy. Natural theologians have tended to be open to more than one type of theistic argument. This raises the question of the relationship among those arguments one accepts.

The line of argument presented here is cumulative, but since others have offered cumulative-case arguments that differ in their conception from what I have in mind, some clarification is in order. There are at least two approaches to setting forth a cumulative argument for the existence of God. They are alike in their basic aim to combine aspects of the traditional arguments to produce the greatest persuasive effect on behalf of theism. They differ primarily in how they seek to relate the various subordinate arguments to that end.

Significant differences between the two approaches can be illustrated by the ways in which they each respond to Antony Flew's caveat about the "Ten-leaky-buckets-Tactic." He warns that it will not do

> to recognize that of a whole series of arguments each individually is defective, but then to urge that nevertheless in sum they comprise an impressive case; perhaps adding as a sop to the Cerberus of criticism that this case is addressed to the whole personality and not merely to the philosophical intellect. We have here to insist upon a sometimes tricky distinction: between, on the one hand, the valid principle of the accumulation of evidence, *where every item has at least some weight in its own right;* and, on the other hand, the Ten-leaky-buckets-Tactic, applied to arguments none of which hold water at all. The scholarly and the businesslike procedure is to examine arguments one by one, without pretending—for no better reason than that they have been shown to be mistaken—that clearly and respectably stated contentions must be other than they are.[2]

Simply put, "If one leaky bucket will not hold water that is no reason to think that ten can."[3]

Basil Mitchell and Richard Swinburne are two contemporary philosophers of religion who have adopted cumulative-case arguments for the existence of God. Mitchell regards the evidences for the existence of God as "contributions to a cumulative case" that turns out to be neither deductively certain nor inductively probable in any formal sense, such as we expect of a probability calculus.[4] Still, as a Christian theist, he believes that "theism makes better sense of all the evidence available than does any alternative on offer."[5] This he takes to be the result of a personal judgment about the unique adequacy of theism to explain the relevant bits of evidence taken together. The rationality of this personal judgment in favor of theism does not depend upon any formal decision procedure. The case for theism,

according to him, rests upon the mutual reinforcement of independent considerations that, on their own, are not as compelling as they
are collectively. But it is vital to realize that the different elements in
the theistic scheme do not stand in relation to one another in the
fashion of a chain argument, in which each element is placed in a
logically ordered sequence from beginning to end (with each successive conclusion serving as a premise in the next inference in the
claim). Mitchell takes Flew's warning in stride, though perhaps not
very seriously, when he remarks that it is "no more than a salutary
reminder of possible risks."[6]

Swinburne's cumulative approach differs little from Mitchell's in its
general conception.[7] Swinburne's contribution to the case for theism
lies in his careful and provocative use of confirmation theory to
recommend the rationality of belief in God. Moreover, more emphatically than Mitchell, Swinburne concludes his inductive analysis with
the judgment that the existence of God is indeed highly probable, and
not merely rational. Those familiar with the details of Swinburne's
argument will recognize, however, that this is the assessment he gives
only *after* adducing the peculiar evidence of religious experience.[8] He
responds to Flew by pointing out, in a footnote, that "if you put three
weak arguments together you may often get a strong one, perhaps
even a deductively valid one. . . . Clearly if you jam ten leaky buckets
together in such a way that holes in the bottom of each bucket are
squashed close together to solid parts of the bottoms of neighboring
buckets, you will get a container that holds water."[9] One may wonder,
however, how many times the experiment with leaky buckets will
have to be performed to get these assured results. A single container
made up of so many leaky buckets can be expected, at best, only to
retard the leak and to render it nearly imperceptible. It will not
prevent gradual drainage. In the final analysis, arguments that resem-
ble leaky buckets squashed together will probably not be very satisfying in the long run either.

Fortunately, the notion of a cumulative case for theism can be
conceived in a more satisfactory manner. The approach adopted here
is not to be confused with that of either Mitchell or Swinburne. It is a
genuine alternative to their way of relating the elements of theistic
argument. Nevertheless, what I have in mind can be described as a
cumulative case for the existence and nature of God. The emphasis is
not merely upon a steady accretion of plausibility on behalf of theism
but also upon the filling out of the specific content of theism as this is
required by a wide range of phenomena calling for explanation. One
begins with a very general phenomenon, such as the existence of a
temporally finite universe, and infers the existence of a non-natural

reality as the best explanation of this phenomenon. Further investigation into particular features of this spatiotemporal world subsequently yields an increasingly precise conception of the non-natural reality causally responsible for the space–time world.

On this approach one can welcome Flew's invitation to consider the independent merits of each successive step in the argument. Three reasonable assumptions protect against zealous overstatement at any one stage of this line of argument for the existence of God. In the first place, it does not seem to me to be possible to argue effectively for the existence of God and yet remain entirely agnostic about the nature of God. If the existence of any object depends upon its having the properties that it does, then our knowledge that any particular object exists suggests that we know at least certain of its properties. By extension, at least a limited knowledge of God's nature must, it seems, be included in the knowledge that God exists.

Second, the nature of God cannot be cognitively apprehended in its inexhaustible totality at all, much less from any single datum of being. Thus, while any knowledge that God exists must include some insight into the attributes of God, since God is infinite no human knowledge of the divine nature can ever be complete.

Finally, I assume that once the existence of God is exhibited, together with certain minimal aspects of the nature of God, then the presumption is subsequently in favor of thinking always and evermore about the rest of reality in terms of its relation to the divine reality. If we conclude finally that theism is true, we must give some consideration, and with appropriate humility, to the universal significance of this truth. If we discover ours to be a world "with God in it," as Richard Purtill puts it, then this should make a difference of considerable magnitude in our further reflections about every feature of the world.[10]

As John E. Smith has rightly observed, "No complete idea of God is possible apart from considering the structure of the world and even of cultural–historical existence. . . . The nature of God is given throughout the full range of finite being, and such being must be consulted at every level if we are to be clear about the meaning of the divine attributes."[11] This confidence that the divine nature is given throughout the whole range of finite existence rests upon the prior conviction that the very existence of this finite world system depends causally upon the existence of God. The first order of business, then, is to argue for this conviction.

Part of what it means for the argument presented here to be cumulative is that the argument proceeds from the general to the particular. That is, it begins with very general considerations that require explanation. And the explanation given at this initial stage is correspondingly general. Thereafter the argument proceeds by seeking explanations for other more particular features of this world, with the result that our conception of the general explanation posited at the first stage of the argument becomes more and more complete. The particular phenomena relevant for learning more about the character of God might be inexhaustibly manifold, so that we might always be learning about his nature.

This point cannot be overemphasized, for it may be that theistic arguments used in isolation from one another will not adequately support the weight of a natural theologian's intuitions about theodicy. Michael Tooley complains that "virtually none of the arguments in support of the existence of God provides any grounds for concluding that there is an omnipotent, omniscient, *and morally perfect* person"; thus, the positive evidence for the existence of God that comes from the traditional arguments is not very relevant to the argument from evil. He apparently means that none of the traditional arguments yields a sufficiently rich conception of God to "overturn the problem of evil."[12] But this is misleading, for the prospects of natural theology for meeting the challenge of evil greatly depend upon how theistic arguments are individuated and how they are related to one another in a total case for the existence and nature of God.

Tooley's criticism falters, for although he raises a question about how the total evidence for God's existence might outweigh the evidence from evil for the nonexistence of God, his specific objection to this possibility is entirely irrelevant. His objection depends upon individuating theistic arguments in much the way that they are individuated in freshman philosophy textbooks and treating those arguments in isolation. To illustrate, he concludes that since the cosmological argument, in its best-known versions, supports a conclusion that "involves" no claims about the moral character of the being in question, the cosmological argument cannot "serve to undercut the argument from evil."[13] Tooley generalizes this difficulty for various other traditional theistic arguments, but only by treating them in isolation as well. He does not consider how the arguments might be combined in a single framework of evidence for the existence of God, a framework that does relevantly subordinate the negative evidence from evil. And in particular he does not even mention the class of moral arguments for the existence of God, which should have the most direct bearing upon his question.

Indeed, it is significant that Tooley qualifies his negative judgment concerning natural theology by saying only that "*virtually* none of the arguments" achieves the requisite result. This leaves open the possibility that some extant theistic argument or set of arguments *does* "involve" the assignment to God of moral predicates that become relevant for the purposes of a theodicy.

Moreover, Tooley does not clarify what he means by "involve." This word can be used to cover a fairly broad range of degrees of implication. For example, one lesson that we can learn from so-called perfect-being theology is that some surprisingly strong entailment relations might exist between attributes traditionally ascribed to God. Certain great-making properties, such as omnipotence and omniscience, may entail divine goodness.[14]

Finally, Tooley does not reach a completely negative judgment about the prospects for natural theology, for he grants, if only for the sake of argument, that theistic arguments could be successful in yielding a God of more limited (particularly nonmoral) proportions. But this would constitute a significant move in the direction of theism and away from any form of naturalism.

Philosophers of religion will not begin to address the problem of evil adequately until they have paid closer attention to the *structure* of positive evidence for the existence of God.

The line of argument I offer here is cumulative in another sense: the theistic conclusion comes to enjoy greater support as more and more features of reality are found to be best explained theistically. In this respect it is similar to the approaches of Mitchell and Swinburne. The more numerous the phenomena best explained in terms of a theistic hypothesis, the greater the confirmation of that theistic hypothesis, where confirmation is understood in terms of increased explanatory power.

It Is an Inference to the Best Explanation

Often the traditional arguments, both a priori and a posteriori, have been construed as deductive in nature.[15] It is arguable whether they have always been intended as thoroughly deductive arguments by their most influential proponents. In any case, the argument I present here is not to be mistaken for a strict deductive argument for the existence of God. The plausibility of certain of its premises depends upon the inductive strength of various inferences. Like any other argument that proceeds by way of inference to the best explanation, this argument gets its force from considerations of the comparative explanatory power of alternative hypotheses. I do not think that this is any great liability, for given the nature of the evidence for the hypothesis that God exists, there are not many plausible alternatives to that inference.

It is not necessary to think of demonstration as requiring strict logical necessity at every stage of an argument for the existence of God. Nor is it essential to a proper conception of natural theology that it proceed in strictly deductive fashion so that it yields absolutely certain results every step of the way. I wish to emphasize this because of vagueness that occurs in certain writers. For example, William Abraham observes that Swinburne's work in the philosophy of religion can be read "as a massive restatement of classical natural theology," only to remark a moment later that the probabilistic logic of Swinburne's position represents "a crucial discontinuity with natural theology."[16]

Another Christian philosopher, Ronald Nash, first defines natural theology as "an attempt to discover arguments that will prove or otherwise provide warrant for belief in God without appealing to special revelation" and notes that it is a major assumption of natural theology that "belief in God is *not* properly basic."[17] Nash himself thinks, along with Alvin Plantinga, that belief in God is properly basic for certain people. One therefore infers that Nash may not be a natural theologian. But after recasting his original definition of natural theology, he concludes that natural theology is not entirely useless in the justification of theism.[18] An appeal to the proper basicality of belief in God is, as he puts it, the task of "negative apologetics," whereas the procedure of natural theology involves one in "positive apologetics." Thus, Reformed epistemology (as "negative apologetics" is more commonly called) and natural theology may be viewed as complementary approaches to exhibiting the justification of belief in God.

Like Nash and other Reformed epistemologists I believe that the rationality of belief in God does not require coercive proofs for God's existence. I am not convinced, however, that the rationality of belief in God can be tied to the proper basicality of belief in God. I am inclined to think that *evidence* is always relevant to the rationality of belief in God, whether or not one who is justified in believing in God is ever aware of a good *argument* for the existence of God. I take it that many who believe in God are justified in so believing without being able to state an argument for the existence of God (and indeed without being able even to recognize a good argument for the existence of God when they see one). It does not follow, however, that belief in God must for them be properly basic. They simply have evidence from which they quite rightly infer the existence of God, though they cannot formulate their decision procedure formally.

The conception of demonstration I have in mind, while plenty ambitious, needs to be qualified. The idea is that, in the absence of meaningful alternatives to the theistic explanation of relevant phenomena, the case for the existence of God has the character of being demonstrative without being deductively certain.[19] Or, if one does not like this use of the term "demonstrative," when the best explanation is not only best but is also the only explanation at one's disposal, then *a fortiori* that is the explanation that one ought to accept. To do otherwise—where doing otherwise consists in opting either for some largely ad hoc hypothesis or for some merely logically possible hypothesis—would be possible but certainly not rational. Indeed, it is only even psychologically possible for one who performs this type of noetic act in bad faith.

In the absence of agreement about whether a particular deductive argument succeeds, certain principles of rationality inform the rational person about what ought to be believed anyway. As J. L. Mackie puts it, "It is absurd to try to confine our knowledge and belief to matters which are conclusively established by sound deductive arguments. The demand for certainty will inevitably be disappointed, leaving scepticism in command of almost every issue."[20] The rational person should be willing to accept propositions or sets of propositions that provide the best explanation of certain states of affairs.

Sometimes reasonable thinkers do not acquiesce to theism in the face of what many theists think is the greater rationality of theism. When this happens we should not discount the *possibility* that the reason is a matter of personal distaste for the conclusion. Such distaste, when it is a reason for rejecting theistic arguments, cannot be founded on any objective moral or even aesthetic considerations without begging significant questions in favor of theism.

On this account of demonstration, all that a successful argument for the existence of God requires is that the candidate argument show that it is more reasonable to affirm the existence of God than not to. In short, my claim is that inference to the best explanation can result in powerful justification for the conclusion that God exists.[21] This means, among other things, that the approach of natural theology is *methodologically* philosophical. From the standpoint of the *intentionality* of this project, the approach is, of course, theological. Hence the name "natural theology" for this sort of intellectual exercise.

In *The Miracle of Theism*, Mackie treats theism as a hypothesis that can be tested for its degree of explanatory power. I have followed him in this, for I believe it is a useful approach to reconnoitering the rationality of belief in God. Some theists, however, have doubts about the wisdom of this approach. Plantinga, for example, has objected to this whole line of inquiry (regardless of the outcome) by calling into question the propriety of treating theism as a hypothesis. He does not think that theism is "relevantly *like* a scientific hypothesis."[22]

Can theism function as a hypothesis? The answer to this question depends upon what we take to be the necessary and sufficient conditions for determining what a hypothesis is. Plantinga defines a scientific hypothesis as "a theory designed to explain some body of evidence, and acceptable to the degree that it explains that evidence."[23]

To say that theism is a hypothesis is not to say that theism is *no more than* a hypothesis. I suggest that a hypothesis is more like a proposition or set of propositions that, whatever other role it might play, is considered with an eye to its explanatory power. It is a supposition with possible explanatory power. Furthermore, even if theism is defensible along other lines, the propositions embodied in theism and offered for belief may be examined for their possible explanatory power as well. When they are, theism is treated as a hypothesis, and this seems to be unproblematic.

Unless Plantinga thinks that the set of propositions referred to by the term "theism" explains nothing, he should have no problem thinking of theism as a hypothesis. Certainly he believes that God created the universe, and this belief of his is a nontrivial part of his theism. But does he really think that the existence of God, who created the universe, has no explanatory relevance for there being a universe? Even Plantinga must have moments when he finds it inevitable to regard theism as explanatory and therefore in some measure as a hypothesis.

It does not seem entirely consistent to say, as Plantinga does, both that "theism is not relevantly like a hypothesis" and that "there are *many* good theistic arguments."[24] He has suggested that even if natural theology is not needed to meet the evidentialist objection to theistic belief—because there are alternative, nonevidentialist ways for belief in God to be warranted—natural theology may contribute to the warrant for theistic belief (by "increasing warrant," as he says). But then it would seem that natural theology does, in its role of adding warrant to the theistic belief, treat theism rather like a scientific hypothesis. Plantinga even acknowledges that "good theistic arguments could play the role of *confirming* . . . my belief in God."[25] So it seems that Plantinga should accept that theism can function as a hypothesis after all.

Whether a set of propositions is a hypothesis does not depend upon its degree of explanatory power. A disconfirmed hypothesis may still be thought of as a hypothesis, though it would not be a very good one. If theism were decisively disconfirmed by the evidence, one would not be justified in believing in God, however basic this belief might seem. If only hypotheses can be disconfirmed, and theism is not a hypothesis, then of course theism cannot be disconfirmed, not because it is true, but because it is not the sort of thing that can be disconfirmed. A hypothesis may come to be neglected when it is disconfirmed. Even when a new paradigm has gained ascendency, anachronistic hypotheses are still hypotheses. They just happen to be discredited hypotheses.

So theism is a hypothesis. Indeed, its status as a hypothesis is secure just as long as somebody—anybody—entertains the possibility that its constitutive propositions have explanatory power. How good a hypothesis it is depends upon its measure of explanatory power in comparison with alternative hypotheses.

THE ARGUMENT FOR A NON-NATURAL REALITY

In the remainder of this chapter I argue for the existence of a non-natural, self-subsistent reality. In the next chapter I explain why I think we should be prepared to ascribe personality, intelligence, power, and goodness to this Being. I use "God" to designate the entity having these specific properties.

The initial stage in this argument begins with a recognition of the apparent empirical certainty of an origin for the universe. This is followed by a brief philosophical argument for an absolute beginning of the universe. I then suggest that the hypothesis of a non-naturalistic explanation for this state of affairs, in terms of the causal activity of a self-subsistent Being, ought to be adopted. The prudence of accepting such a hypothesis is disclosed by the complete lack of any naturalistic explanation for the origin of the universe. The scarcity of alternative hypotheses is a matter of fact that could in principle be overcome by the adequate formulation of some empirically reliable hypothesis not yet envisioned by scientists. Thus, one other reason for thinking that the theistic hypothesis must remain the best explanation is mentioned: that a non-naturalistic explanation may yet be more desirable than a naturalistic one given certain non-natural features of reality, such as the existence of consciousness. That is, even if, contrary to fact, there exists a naturalistic explanation for the beginning of the universe, a non-naturalistic explanation might still be more adequate given certain other features of the universe.

Empirical Evidence for an Origin of the Universe

Many scientists today are very sure about certain general features of the structure, order, and development of the universe. (By "universe" I mean the familiar array of galaxies, stars, and other entities that make up physical reality. I am not referring to "all that exists.") There is considerable confidence among practitioners of scientific cosmology that it is now possible to formulate the basic sequence of the development of our universe from primitive elements and to assign reasonably accurate ages to the various objects of the cosmos. Some version of the big bang cosmology is by far the model of choice among astrophysicists for describing the origin of the universe. Thus, according to current scientific theory, the universe had a beginning.

This is virtually an empirical certainty. "In the beginning there was an explosion," says one Harvard astrophysicist, Steven Weinberg.[26] Robert Jastrow, director of the Mt. Wilson Institute in California, has this to say: "Most remarkable of all, astronomers have found proof that the Universe sprang into existence abruptly, in a sudden moment of creation, as the Bible said it did," and "the astronomical and biblical accounts of Genesis are alike in one essential respect. There was a beginning, and all things in the Universe can be traced back to it."[27]

Phenomenal advances in observational astronomy during this century have made it more and more difficult to consistently think of the universe as infinite in duration. The by now routine observation of the redshift of distant galaxies is powerful evidence that the universe is expanding. This is thought to imply a primeval state of the universe of infinite density, a conclusion independently supported by the discovery of background radiation. Not only is the universe expanding, but the rate of its expansion continues to decelerate over time. The net effect of this accretion of evidence is to suggest that the universe originated in the remote but nevertheless finite past, approximately 16 to 20 billion years ago.

Scientists refer to the big bang as a "singularity." Paul Davies explains:

> The first instant of the big bang, where space was infinitely shrunken, represents a boundary or edge in time at which space ceases to exist. Physicists call such a boundary a *singularity*.[28]
>
> The essential feature of a singularity is that it is rather like an edge or boundary to spacetime and hence, one supposes, to the physical universe. An example of a singularity is the infinitely dense, infinitely compact state that marked the beginning of the big bang. . . . The existence of a boundary to spacetime suggests that natural physical processes cannot be continued beyond such a thing. In a fundamental sense a singularity represents, according to this view, the outer limits of the natural universe. At a singularity, matter may enter or leave the physical world, and influences may emanate therefrom that are totally beyond the power of physical science to predict, even in principle. A singularity is the nearest thing that science has found to a supernatural agent.[29]

Davies concludes with this cryptic remark: "There is no unanimous agreement among physicists about the status of spacetime singularities, or even about the precise state of the primeval universe."[30]

The significance of calling the big bang a singularity is that the big bang represents an event that cannot be regarded as the natural outcome of prior physical conditions and natural laws. Now this might mean one of two things. Either the universe originated from nothing, or the universe emerged from an eternally quiescent state, a state in which no events had occurred.

Some take the notion of a singularity to mean the former. An infinitesimally small and infinitely dense starting point for the universe suggests that there was nothing from which the universe originated.[31] This is not just a loose way of speaking for some theorists. The primeval state of the universe is a state of literal nothingness. It is a state in which there is no matter, no energy to be converted into matter, and no physical laws according to which the universe might "happen." Thus, our universe has an absolute beginning. It is not just that there is a beginning of the present order of nature. Scientists aware of (and unhappy with) these implications have attempted to supplant the big bang account with steady-state theories, oscillating models, vacuum fluctuation models, and the like. A good deal of the impetus for this sort of research seems to be tied to the point that otherwise the universe originated from nothing.

Others think of the big bang singularity as a transition from primeval physical stuff. On this view, the big bang is still the first event of the universe. There is, thus, an absolute beginning of the present order of nature, while that from which it begins has no beginning. The eventless state "prior" to the big bang is sometimes called the quiescent universe. As one philosopher has put it, "It is possible that there is a finite temporal series of events in the universe preceded by an eternal quiescent or eventless universe."[32]

So on the first view, the big bang singularity occurs ex nihilo, whereas on the second view it does not. Perhaps it does not finally matter which view one takes, at least for the purposes of arguing to a personal Creator of the universe. For on either view there is a first event that cannot be explained in terms of the operation of natural processes among physical entities. Still, there are problems with the quiescent-universe proposal.

First, to suggest that there is one universe that passes from a previously quiescent state into its present ordered state raises questions about the identity conditions of the universe as it passes from one state to another. In what sense is our universe now the same object as the quiescent universe from which it arose? Specifying identity conditions is particularly difficult when singularities have to be taken into account, for there do not seem to be any laws at work that could account for the change that the physical stuff of the universe undergoes.

Second, William Lane Craig argues that "an eternal, quiescent universe is simply physically impossible." He produces three empirical reasons for this: "(i) Such a universe would have to exist at a temperature of absolute zero, which is physically impossible, (ii) Matter in the early stages of the universe was anything but cold, being collapsed into a volatile fireball with temperatures in excess of billions of degrees Kelvin, and (iii) In a lump of matter frozen (*per impossible*) at absolute zero, no first event could occur."[33]

Third, the naturalist gains nothing by thinking of the present order of the universe arising from an already existing but completely eventless universe. Positing the primordial existence of physical stuff does nothing to explain the existence of the present order of nature if the big bang really is the first event. Craig has even argued that the hypothesis of a quiescent universe actually helps the cause of the theist, since if a quiescent universe is so unstable as to be naturally impossible, the existence of this kind of state of affairs would take "a miracle of the most stupendous proportions conceivable, since it would involve suspension of all the laws of nature."[34]

Whereas some scientists have assiduously resisted a point of origin for the universe, the various theories they have devised to circumvent this conclusion have been moving toward oblivion under the pressure of recent observational data.[35] James S. Trefil writes:

> The picture of a universe that is reborn every hundred billion years is very attractive. The main advantage of an eternally oscillating universe is that the questions of why it all started and where it all came from simply do not have to be asked. The universe always was and always will be.... It is a fascinating thought, but ... I should warn you that there are some serious problems with the oscillating-universe picture.... Our present data seems to favor a quite different type of future.[36]

John Gribbin expresses similar misgivings about the steady-state model in his book *Spacewarps*.[37]

Naturally, physicists have been somewhat reluctant to conclude that the universe began to exist, for this raises the question, What caused the universe to come to be in this way? a question that is, at the same time, unanswerable in principle by the methods of science as it is currently practiced. Nevertheless, some cause is to be sought if we are not to capitulate to mysticism about the nature of the cosmos. Even if the cause of the origin of the physical universe is not directly and empirically accessible, theoreticians fail in their capacity as scientists if they resist the conclusion to which the evidence leads, for the ideal objective of science is to explain all phenomena.

Scientists not disturbed by philosophical problems associated with induction can say with complete candor that it is scientifically verifiable that the universe began to exist. And as long ago as 1948 the philosopher Bertrand Russell remarked, "The net result of this summary view of the astronomical world is that, while it is certainly very large and very ancient, there are grounds—though as yet they are very speculative—for thinking that it is neither infinitely large *nor infinitely old.*"[38]

Philosophical Demonstration of an Origin of the Universe

Still, a few scientists have objected, for ostensibly philosophical reasons, to assigning a beginning point to the universe. Arthur Eddington, for example, remarked in 1931: "Philosophically, the notion of a beginning of the present order of Nature is repugnant to me. . . . I should like to find a genuine loophole."[39] More recently, Sir Fred Hoyle has reiterated the same sentiment on behalf of his own steady-state theory: "This possibility seemed attractive, especially when taken in conjunction with aesthetic objections to the creation of the universe in the remote past. For it seems against the spirit of scientific enquiry to regard observable effects as arising from 'causes unknown to science,' and this in principle is what creation-in-the-past implies."[40]

If a philosophical control on what it is possible to conclude about the origin of the universe is what these scientists desire, then I would invite their attention to philosophical considerations that reinforce the empirical claim that the universe has a beginning. If time has no beginning, but stretches into the infinite past, then an infinity of moments must occur prior to the instantiation of this particular moment. But then there would be no end to the amount of time needed to reach this moment. It would take a limitless amount of time to traverse an infinite sequence of moments. But this is very odd, for it is plain that we have reached this moment in time. This means that the time needed to reach this moment is fully realized. Thus, what has no end has come to an end. This very moment marks the absolute limit upon the amount of time needed to arrive at this moment. But an infinity of moments can have no limit. Furthermore, not only this moment, but any particular moment of the past sets a limit upon the time needed to reach that moment. The universe must have a finite history.[41]

As against this sort of argument, Russell pointed out that "it is not essential to the existence of a collection, or even to knowledge and reasoning concerning it, that we should be able to pass its terms in review one by one." Though one may never complete the task of literally counting the terms in an infinite collection, this does not remove the possibility that such a collection exists. Thus, an infinite series of moments as a class might actually exist.[42]

What Russell did not appreciate, however, was the difference between classes whose members must in principle be literally countable and those whose members may not be countable. If the class in question is the class of all whole numbers, then admittedly the impossibility of ever counting each member of this class is no problem for the existence of the class. This is because whole numbers, though they stand in a certain relation to each other either logically or ontologically (or both), do not *come to be* in any kind of succession. If for a whole number to exist it had to await the coming to be of its immediately previous integer in the number sequence, then the class of numbers existing at the present moment would be finite. Indeed, it would be finite at any moment. The class of numbers is not formed by adding one member after another, however. We sometimes speak of the "ancestral relation" between numbers. But since, in the case of numbers, the ancestral relation is not temporal, the locution can be misleading. Unlike numbers, moments in time come to be in succession, and whether or not they are ever counted, they must be finite in number because they are instantiated one by one. This relation between the members of the class of all past moments in time determines that the class cannot be infinite.

Thus we have good scientific *and* philosophical reasons for thinking that the universe has a beginning. What is salient about this result is that there exists no naturalistic explanation for this state of affairs; that is, there is no explanation in terms of the types of entities we know to make up the physical or natural world. The only alternative to positing a non-natural first cause to explain the origin of the universe is to suggest that the universe might have just emerged spontaneously out of a void, as Anthony Kenny makes clear: "According to the big bang theory, the whole matter of the universe began to exist at a particular time in the remote past. A proponent of such a theory, at least if he is an atheist, must believe that the matter of the universe came from nothing and by nothing."[43] Kenny's remark is a claim about what any atheist who accepts the big bang cosmology (or any other model that entails an origin of the universe) ought to say about a final explanation for the beginning of the universe. But do atheists ever in fact take up the gauntlet thrown down by Kenny?

The Necessity of a Non-Natural Explanation

Mackie, in his *Miracle of Theism*, reasons that "a sheer origination of things, undetermined by anything," is possible, however improbable it may seem to us. We do not know a priori, he says, that "there could not have been a sheer unexplained beginning of things" having no physical antecedents.[44]

Two things are worth noting about this point. First, Mackie never actually commits himself to the view that the material universe has an absolute but uncaused beginning. At times he even seems agitated by the scientific confirmation of an absolute beginning of the universe. Thus, he is willing to say that to the extent that a sheer unexplained beginning of things seems improbable, this very improbability "should cast doubt on the interpretation of the big bang as an absolute beginning of the material universe." In other words, he would rather wait it out for some future internally self-explanatory naturalistic model of cosmology than allow that the universe began to exist: "We should infer that it must have had *some* physical antecedents."[45] It is, however, not always prudent to withhold judgment until further evidence becomes available, and it is not very intellectually honest to stubbornly withhold judgment on the mere wish that further evidence should one day become available. Moreover, it has already been argued that there are also good *philosophical* reasons for thinking that the universe had a beginning. If this is right, then Mackie's dream will never be realized.

Second, Mackie nevertheless expresses supreme confidence that it is a genuine possibility that the universe might have just popped into existence willy-nilly. "We have no good ground for an *a priori* certainty that there could not have been a sheer unexplained beginning of things."[46] But several problems accrue to this claim. First, whether we have a priori certainty or not is beside the point. The notion of a "sheer unexplained beginning of things" is quite obviously counterintuitive. We do not know of anything else at all that has come to be from nothing. All events that we now know of have had antecedent causes, or at least so we have thought. Even David Hume, who cast doubt on the epistemic certainty of the principle of causality, wrote to a friend, "I never asserted so absurd a proposition as that anything might arise without a cause: I only maintain'd, that our

Certainty of the Falsehood of that Proposition proceeded neither from Intuition nor Demonstration; but from another Source."[47] Mackie would do well to take to heart a bit of advice from David Lewis, who is, to be sure, a surprising authority to invoke in this regard.

> It is pointless to build a theory, however nicely systematised it might be, that would be unreasonable to believe. . . . A worthwhile theory must be credible, and a credible theory must be conservative. It cannot gain, and it cannot deserve, credence if it disagrees with too much of what we thought before. . . . Common sense has no absolute authority in philosophy. . . . It's just that theoretical conservatism is the only sensible policy for theorists of limited powers. . . . Part of this conservatism is reluctance to accept theories that fly in the face of common sense. The proper test, I suggest, is a simple maxim of honesty: never put forward a philosophical theory that you yourself cannot believe in your least philosophical and most commonsensical moments.[48]

For that matter, to regard the principle of causality as exceptionable in the way Mackie recommends is to undermine the whole enterprise of science. For science is deeply committed to the assumption that every event that it investigates (and thus every coming to be of anything) must have a cause. Indeed, the extraordinary fruitfulness of science, which accounts in large measure for its immense prestige, has depended to a great extent upon its commitment to this very assumption. Mackie knows this and is cautious about qualifying the universality of the principle of causality, for he suggests that the principle probably still has universal application *within* the world.

> In so far as our reliance on such principles is epistemically justified, it is so *a posteriori*, by the degree of success we have had in interpreting the world with their help. And in any case these principles of causation, symmetry, and so on refer to how the world works; we are extrapolating far beyond their so far fruitful use when we postulate a principle of sufficient reason and apply it to *the world as a whole*. Even if, *within the world*, everything seemed to have a sufficient reason, that is, a cause in accordance with some regularity, with like causes producing like effects, this would give us little ground for expecting *the world as a whole*, or its basic causal laws themselves, to have a sufficient reason of some sort.[49]

Mackie obviously believes that seeking explanations may not have to go beyond finding explanations for phenomena within the world. But this looks like an arbitrary decision about where to draw the line in terms of expecting an explanation. The attempt evokes the suspicion that it is done to save a metaphysical theory. The theory it seeks to save is atheism, and the move amounts to little more than special pleading. Mackie restricts the scope of application for the principle of causality without arguing for the restriction. While it may be true that "we have no right to assume that the universe will comply with our intellectual preferences,"[50] we also have no alternative as rational beings but to think about the world as if it is a rational place. Even less do we have a right to assume that the universe does not comply with one or another of the basic principles of rationality. And the universal assignation of the principle of causality seems intuitively more rational and less arbitrary than Mackie's restriction. It makes more sense to seek causes for all events properly so called, whether or not they occur within the universe. The coming to be of the universe, as an event, calls for causal explanation. In any case, it seems psychologically defeatist to be satisfied with ultimate explanations that are not really ultimate.

Mackie also draws attention to the practical limits of seeking ultimate explanations for phenomena:

> The sort of intelligibility that is achieved by successful causal inquiry and scientific explanation is not undermined by its inability to make things intelligible through and through. Any particular explanation starts with premises which state 'brute facts', and although the brutally factual starting-points of one explanation may themselves be further explained by another, the latter in turn will have to start with something that it does not explain, *and so on however far we go.* But there is no need to see this as unsatisfactory.[51]

To insist, however, that every explanation must start with some set of "brute facts" that must in turn be explainable by a prior set of facts is to express a prejudice against the possibility of ultimate explanation. The explanation we seek is not to be confused with giving reasons. It has to do, rather, with locating causes. The issue is not about the soundness of epistemological foundationalism; it is about the possibility of identifying causally ultimate explanations for events of a certain type, namely, "bangs," however large or small.[52]

While all of this is disturbing enough, a further and more significant difficulty intrudes. Mackie reports with all candor that the whole universe might have just sprung into existence out of nothing. (We can be sure that none of its current parts or any of its present states as a whole appeared in this mysterious fashion.) His confidence that there is no rational necessity to posit a first cause of the universe depends upon the assumption that the spontaneous eruption of the universe into existence is a genuine possibility. But Mackie takes no care to explain what it is that constitutes this as a meaningful possibility. (This, perhaps, is one reason why he never quite comes out endorsing this hypothesis as *the* "explanation" of choice.) Again, Mackie resorts to special pleading, for he thinks that belief in the self-subsistent being of God involves the theist in "sheer mystery."[53] But unless the universe is an effect of some adequate cause, the first state of the universe must be a self-subsistent Being, and thus no less sheer a mystery. If there must be a self-subsistent Being in any case, it must be the sort of thing that could subsist on its own.

There is no reason to think that the universe itself is this sort of thing and every reason to think that it is not. In contrast to Mackie's supposition that the universe might have just popped into existence out of nothing, the hypothesis of a self-subsistent Being responsible for bringing the world into existence is far less mysterious. This hypothesis constitutes a genuine explanation, whereas the Mackie hypothesis is not any sort of explanation and thus is not really a hypothesis at all. Mackie's claim is entirely lacking in explanatory power.

Mackie asserts that "there is *a priori* no good reason why a sheer origination of things, not determined by anything, should be unacceptable, whereas the existence of a god with the power to create something out of nothing is acceptable."[54] But the point carries little weight. For one thing, reasons for accepting one hypothesis over another might be perfectly good without their being a priori in nature. Even Mackie thinks this is true: "It is absurd to try to confine our knowledge and belief to matters which are conclusively established by sound deductive arguments. The demand for certainty will inevitably be disappointed, leaving scepticism in command of almost every issue." He recognizes that "we therefore have to rely on nondeductive arguments."[55] Furthermore, there are, it turns out, demonstrably good reasons for preferring the hypothesis of theism over Mackie's rival hypothesis. These reasons have to do with the dubious status of Mackie's claim as a hypothesis. Mackie concedes that the theistic hypothesis is at least "vaguely explanatory."[56] I submit that his counterproposal is not even remotely explanatory.

Could our universe have sprung into existence from an absolute void? It certainly could not unless it did so in response to conditions determined by the void. But any void constituted by such conditions, whatever they may be, is not then a true void. About the only recourse Mackie has to ward off the cogency of this objection is to appeal to the possibility that the universe is just some sort of brute fact, that it did just spring into existence out of nothing. But recall, he does not profess that this is the case.

More important, he involves himself in an inconsistency with his own principles about what ought to be believed. In the introduction to his book he allows that the weight of evidence must count on behalf of the best explanation. As he says, "Whether there is a god or not . . . must be examined either by deductive reasoning or, if that yields no decision, by arguments to the best explanation; for in such a context nothing else can have any coherent bearing on this issue."[57] He does not seem to think that deductive reasoning will settle the issue either way. We are left with inferences to the best explanation. But part of what it would mean for the universe to be a bare fact would be that no evidence could support this contention. Nothing answering to the nature of an explanation is involved in the proposal that the universe might be a bare fact. It is not enough, even for Mackie's purposes (which are evidential), to plead that the "brutally factual" existence of the universe is at least a logical possibility. That sort of judgment has nothing to do with evidence and cannot, therefore, have anything to do with the pattern of argument known as inference to a best explanation.

Mackie's suggestion that it is logically possible that the universe is just a brute fact with no explanation at all does not mean that there are logical grounds for judging that the universe actually is a brute fact; it only means that logic alone does not give us grounds for saying that the universe is not a brute fact. If there are nonlogical reasons for thinking that the universe is not a brute fact, then Mackie's claim is entirely innocuous.

So even on Mackie's own principles it is overwhelmingly more rational to believe that there is a God than that there is not. But most important, I do not think that it makes much sense to insist that the universe could have just popped into existence. For to say that this could have happened is to imply that prior to the beginning of the universe there existed determinate conditions such that a universe like ours might come to be. But who could know this without also knowing what constitutes this as a possibility? It is not enough to affirm this as a possibility without saying something about the content of such a possibility. Theists have often been charged with incoherence for affirming the existence of a necessary Being. The atheist's notion of a spontaneous origination of the universe, however, seems to be genuinely incoherent, whereas the inference to the existence of a causally active, self-subsistent Being seems conceptually secure.

Arguments to the only explanation are special cases of arguments to the best explanation. The better the explanation as compared with competing explanations, the stronger the argument. But if the best explanation is the only explanation (or if the explanation is best precisely because it is the only explanation), then the argument is about as strong as it could be and still be an argument in terms of best explanation. It is perhaps the strongest type of a posteriori argument.

Such an argument would not be strictly deductive for at least two reasons. First, it might not be possible to produce a sound deductive argument that rational persons ought to accept arguments that proceed as inferences to the best explanation. Second, while no alternative explanation than the one on offer for some particular state of affairs may be available when the argument is initially formulated, some such explanation might emerge later whose merits would bear comparison with the heretofore uniquely available explanation. So one does not reject the theistic hypothesis on pain of logical contradiction. Nevertheless, one risks legitimate censure for rejecting the theistic hypothesis while yet failing to provide a plausible alternative to that hypothesis. So while the argument proposed here is admittedly provisional, its provisional status does not undermine the greater rationality of accepting the conclusion until it is disconfirmed.

Even if an alternative hypothesis could be formulated empirically to account for the origin of the physical universe naturalistically, the theistic hypothesis may yet be a better explanation. The problem of consciousness has persisted throughout the history of philosophy, and it shows few signs of relenting to reductionistic accounts. As William Pepperell Montague observed, "The alternative to mere mechanistic determination is not some unknown thing concocted *ad hoc* to help us out of a difficulty. Surely, mind is a *vera causa* if ever there was one."[58] What it is natural to believe, as attested by the majority of human subjects, ought to be taken into consideration whenever the principle of parsimony is applied. The simplest theory ought to make sense of ordinary beliefs. Prima facie evidence can serve as a needful control on what Ockham's razor can accomplish.

If mind is a nonmaterial substance or a form of energy that can cause events in the physical world, as it seems most natural to believe (almost everyone outside the world of professional philosophy *does* believe it), then there are reasons for grounding this possibility in suitable conditions present at the beginning of the universe. Due consideration of this matter may also lead one to infer the existence of some non-natural, self-subsistent Being that could not only bring minds into existence and join them to bodies as psychophysical unities but also have reasons for doing so. If the physical universe is all there is, then some kind of reductionism of mind to matter is needed to explain the phenomena of consciousness, such as the so-called phenomenal properties. But if consciousness proves to be impossible to explain in this reductionistic manner, then there is more to the universe than the merely physical. And whatever this more is, it seems it would have to cooperate with whatever processes account for physical reality.

The point is, if the universe had a beginning, and it turns out that the world is a complex interaction of both mental and physical events, then even if all physical events are ultimately explainable in terms of some primeval physical state, there will be a residual need to locate the explanation of mental events in some non-natural reality that at least coexists with the most primitive physical state from which our material universe has evolved.[59]

The fact remains that only one explanation is readily available and that is the explanation given in the hypothesis of a self-subsistent Being. Now an explanation of some state of affairs might be the only explanation for one of two reasons. In the first place, it might be the only empirically available explanation, despite the conceivability of other logically possible explanations. In the second place, it might be the only logically possible explanation a priori. I do not think it matters much which sense we decide upon in the case of positing God as the only explanation for the existence of our universe. While there are individuals who think that the sheer coming to be of the universe out of nothing is a logically possible explanation, I confess that I cannot see how this could count as any sort of explanation. While it is logically possible that the universe emerged out of a void, taking note of this logical possibility does nothing to explain the existence of the universe. It does nothing to subsume it under more encompassing principles. The notion of "things coming from nothing" does not have the makings of a principle of explanation.

We must distinguish between a logically possible event or state of affairs and a logically possible explanation. We can allow that Mackie identifies or describes a logically possible event, but we cannot then say that this amounts to giving a logically possible explanation. Noting the logical possibility that the universe, though it has a beginning, has no cause explains nothing. Philosophers since Hume have been quick to point out that it is possible to conceive of alternative scenarios without contradiction.[60] But they have seldom appreciated how little this accomplishes. The theistic hypothesis is not only logically possible but explanatory as well. Any merely logical possibility must fail to be explanatory in the sense required. For there is no criterion for comparing the relative probability of competing logical possibilities *as logical possibilities*. Only by thinking of them as having, in addition to logical possibility, a different sort of possibility as well can we begin to think of one as more probable than another.

It might be useful to conclude by noting one reason why traditional arguments for the existence of God fell into disfavor in the modern period. In the nineteenth century the advance of science seemed to many to undercut the explanatory value of the various versions of cosmological and teleological arguments for the existence of God. In retrospect, this dismissal of the arguments appears to have been premature. Even in those "halcyon days" of science (if there ever was such a period), the arguments were not as superfluous as they were thought by some to be. Indeed, these arguments have always had persuasive proponents. But today in particular there is reason to believe that these arguments deserve a new lease on life, and this partly *because of* developments in science.

7
The Possibility of Natural Theology, Part 2: Personality, Power, and Providence

An assumption is often made in connection with theistic arguments and philosophical elaborations of the divine nature. This assumption is that it is one thing to establish that God exists and something else altogether to determine what can be said about the nature of God. But this surely is a mistake, both in terms of the logic of the claim and in terms of the effect it has had on recent discussions in philosophical theology. The truth is, there can be no sense to the claim to have shown that God exists unless some particular idea of God emerges in the process of such a demonstration.

This, however, is not the only difficulty that has arisen within the ambit of discussions about the attributes of God and the relation of these discussions to the question of God's existence. Today there is much less philosophy of religion (in the traditional sense) being done by philosophers and much more philosophical theology. A whole movement has emerged whose chief preoccupation is the harmonization of seemingly conflicting claims about the divine nature. Having so much effort devoted to this type of concern is a mixed blessing. While current work in philosophical theology addresses a genuine need, I believe it leads to unfortunate consequences when this work is not conducted in an atmosphere of sympathy for natural theology.

In the first place, the grounds for belief in God tend to get overlooked. Consequently, the theist is tempted to adopt a strictly defensive posture, that of showing that theistic belief is at least rationally consistent and internally coherent, though perhaps not positively more rational than its alternatives. A second drawback of this tendency to confine discussion to issues in philosophical theology is that it can easily degenerate into a fine intramural discussion that alienates those who do not believe in God but who are interested in the wider issues of the philosophy of religion. At best, the type of theological project that prevails can be fully engaging only for religious thinkers with different ideas about the divine nature. Certain developments, I think, have borne this out, and it is to be hoped that the trend does not result in the general reduction of the philosophy of religion to these refined concerns. Lastly, the current preoccupation with philosophical theology neglects the prospects of a natural theology not only to justify belief in God but also to say something meaningful and specific about the nature of God, as well as about how the details of God's nature ought to be understood in relation to each other.

One sometimes gets the impression that certain theists have in mind that, by ignoring the question of God's existence long enough and limiting the philosophical focus to questions about the nature of God within the context of belief in God, perhaps nontheists will surrender their opposition at the level of existence questions and accept a new definition of the set of problems for religious belief. However, there are still many theists as well as nontheists who concern themselves with traditional issues of natural theology. Often this is due to an awareness that how one judges that it is rational to believe in God has significant bearing upon subsequent problems associated with understanding the nature of God. In this chapter we take an inventory of attributes that we might be justified in ascribing to the non-natural reality argued for in Chapter 6. Only those attributes that are most directly pertinent to the formulation of a theistic prolegomenon to theodicy are considered here.

THIS REALITY IS PERSONAL

As Richard Swinburne notes, "All important *a posteriori* arguments for the existence of God have a common characteristic. They all purport to be arguments to an explanation of the phenomena described in the premisses in terms of *the action of an agent* who intentionally brought about those phenomena."[1] In other words, they are not only arguments to the existence of some non-natural reality but also arguments that this reality is personal.

One can, as J. L. Mackie does, express the hope that a naturalistic explanation for the origin of the universe will be found. But this is a baseless hope. A baseless hope is one for which there is no reason to think it might be true. The only reason on offer for grounding Mackie's hope is that science has been impressively successful in the past. But alas, it has only been successful at providing naturalistic explanations for events that are themselves naturalistic because they happen within the world. But the event for which we seek an explanation is not within the world. Mackie's opinion that explanations should be sought only for events that occur within the world is partly right. He is right to think that strictly naturalistic explanations obtain only with respect to (certain) events occurring within the world. His mistake is in thinking that the universe as a whole does not require explanation. For it is no less apparent that the origin of the universe needs an explanation than it is that this event has no naturalistic explanation.

The Notion of "Personal Explanation"

Of the events that happen within the world, some are not "naturalistic." These are events that can be explained only in terms of the exercise of free will by personal agents.[2] These explanations, which are distinguishable from normal scientific explanations in that they are non-natural, could be called "personal explanations," following Swinburne.[3] So there is precedent for thinking that an event might have an explanation that is non-natural. Indeed, it may be the only hypothesis with any real power to explain certain events. Obviously, it is this sort of explanation that I have appealed to in accounting for the origin of the universe.

The chief difficulties with the doctrine of free will have not been associated with any incoherence inherent in the notion of free will itself. Opponents of the doctrine more commonly suggest either that free will is not really needed to explain anything or that free will is inconsistent with some other deterministic doctrine that it is more rational to believe. In the case of explaining the beginning of the universe, however, we have personal agency that is both free and remarkably powerful. Whatever caused the universe to come into existence ex nihilo must have had amazing power to determine fundamental conditions, conditions that are the basis, really, of all our scientific successes (if that is what they are). Whatever success we have enjoyed in describing the world in a way that lends itself to confident predictions and to generating useful technology we owe first to the orderly arrangement of conditions determined by the First Cause.

It is somewhat of an irony that individuals can hesitate to assign personhood to that which caused the universe when some would assign personhood of a sort to the universe itself, so long as they have thought that it is itself eternal and uncreated. Charles Darwin wrote in the Introduction to his *On the Origin of Species*, "It is difficult to avoid personifying nature."[4] C. S. Lewis thought that "the unbeliever is always apt to make a kind of religion of his aesthetic experiences."[5]

For many, pondering the universe is the ultimate aesthetic experience, and descriptions of this experience are often so lofty as to attain the heights of religious adulation. Carl Sagan, for example, extols the "deep mystery" of the universe as something "wonderful" and "awesome."

> We are, in the most profound sense, children of the Cosmos. The Sun warms us and feeds us and permits us to see. It fecundated the Earth. It is powerful beyond human experience. Birds greet the sunrise with an audible ecstasy. . . . Our ancestors worshiped the Sun, and they were far from foolish. And yet the Sun is an ordinary, even a mediocre star. If we must worship a power greater than ourselves, does it not make sense to revere the Sun and stars? Hidden within every astronomical investigation, sometimes so deeply buried that the researcher himself is unaware of its presence, lies a kernel of awe.[6]

There is in any encounter with self-subsistent Being a very natural if not irresistible urge to admire what one encounters. Little wonder that Stephen Hawking equates having a unified theory of the universe, "the ultimate triumph of human reason," with knowing the mind of God.[7] Still, some research physicists speak somewhat equivocally about the awful specter of living in such a universe as ours must be if God did not have a hand in its coming to be.

> It is very hard to realize that [the earth] is just a tiny part of an overwhelmingly hostile universe. It is even harder to realize that this present universe has evolved from an unspeakably unfamiliar early condition, and faces a future extinction of endless cold or intolerable heat. The more the universe seems comprehensible, the more it also seems pointless. . . . [And yet the] effort to understand the universe is one of the very few things that lifts human life a little above the level of farce, and gives it some of the grace of tragedy.[8]

It is, I allow, very tempting to render homage to self-subsistent Being wherever it is thought to be found. This is not an argument that the cause of the universe is personal. It is, however, a telling observation about how willing some thinkers are to allow the evidence to take them where it leads, whether or not that is where they wish to end up.

The Doctrine of Agent Causation

What sort of cause is needed to explain the origin of the universe? The chain of causes and effects is not infinite. It has a beginning. The usual sort of cause will not do as an explanation for the origination of the universe, for if it were of the usual sort, this cause would itself be determined by antecedent conditions, and these conditions would be determined by other antecedent conditions, and so forth, ad infinitum. Indeed, strict determinism would seem to require an infinity of causes. So if the universe has a First Cause, it seems this cause must be an agent acting freely (that is, in a self-determining fashion). If the universe is caused, but not caused in virtue of some infinite set of antecedent conditions (which it could not be), then we must infer agent causation as the only possible alternative. If this agent acted for a purpose, then this agent is rational as well as free. Furthermore, our own capacity to make judgments about this agent's rationality is itself conditioned by factors determined by this very agent. We seem, therefore, not to be in any position to doubt the intelligence of this Being.

This explanation for the beginning of the universe is not stated in terms of the laws of nature and of certain antecedent conditions that necessitated its coming to be. Such a description would not seem to be available to us by the very nature of the case. In other words, we cannot provide a covering-law explanation for this particular event since it is a first event. Prior to the beginning of the universe—with "prior" used in an ontological rather than a temporal sense—there are no empirical states of affairs of which any law of nature could be a description, and no initial conditions of any empirical sort. If there were, then, according to a covering-law model, we could deduce that the universe would have begun as it did. (Incidentally, on a covering-law model of explanation, no alteration in initial conditions or in the early pattern of the development of the universe could have resulted in there being precisely *this* universe.)

Apparently, then, we are dealing with an event that cannot be fully explained under a covering-law model. Still, it is an event that calls for explanation. And since science seeks to explain all phenomena (and in this sense finding an explanation for the origin of the universe *is* an empirical problem), it must do so here. Thus, science, if it is to have an explanation for this event, must look beyond a covering-law explanation. Depending on what one takes to be the defining characteristics of scientific practice, appealing to other types of explanation may be scientific or it may not. I myself see no reason why the requisite explanation should be regarded as other than scientific.

If the explanation we appeal to does not involve any reference to initial conditions and natural laws that would necessitate the origin of the universe, we have no reason for thinking that the universe (and not just this universe but any universe) necessarily had to come about. In the absence of a covering-law explanation, which would in any case be inadequate to explain this event, it seems we are provided with considerable incentive to think of the beginning of the universe in terms of some type of agent causation. For on no model other than the covering-law model would it be necessary that the universe came to be. So the non-natural reality causally responsible for the origin of the universe is personal and intelligent.

Thomas Reid maintained that "it is very probable that the very conception or idea of active power, and of efficient causes, is derived from our voluntary exertions in producing effects; and that, if we were not conscious of such exertion, we should have no conception at all of a cause, or of active power, and consequently no conviction of the necessity of a cause of every change which we observe in nature."[9] This remark parallels Roderick Chisholm's suggestion that the notion of agent causation is clearer than the notion of causation by an event: "It is only by understanding our own causal efficacy, as agents, that we grasp the concept of *cause* at all."[10]

Chisholm doubts that we can preserve human responsibility if we accept either determinism or indeterminism. If either our actions are caused by other events or other states of affairs, or our actions are not caused at all, then we are not responsible. He then argues from the assumption that humans are responsible for many of their actions to the doctrine of agent causation as a way of going between the horns of the metaphysical dilemma concerning human freedom. To protect human responsibility there must be a cause and that cause must not be some other set of events or states of affairs. It must, he concludes, be the agent himself.[11]

This circumstance parallels the one I have described concerning the origin of the universe. Analogous to Chisholm's interest in protecting human responsibility is our desire to explain the origin of the universe. And as Chisholm has argued that determinism does not preserve responsibility, I have argued that covering-law explanations cannot account for the origin of the universe. The causes that I have suggested cannot explain the event known as the big bang are of the same general kind as those that Chisholm concludes cannot account for events for which we are responsible; these implausible causes are themselves either events or states of affairs. He calls event–event causation or state–state causation "transeunt causation."[12]

I have pointed out that nothing in the set of physical conditions and natural laws prior to the big bang implies that there will eventually be a big bang. This is because the big bang is the first event, even if there is matter or energy before the big bang. If the big bang is the first event in the history of the universe, then there is no earlier physical event or state that can bring it about. In similar fashion, Chisholm notes that "no set of statements about a man's desires, beliefs, and stimulus situation at any time implies any statement telling us what the man will try, set out, or undertake to do at that time."[13] Whether it is a big bang or some action for which a human being is to be held responsible, the datum to be explained cannot be explained by appeal to prior events or states.

In one sense, this judgment is even more secure with respect to the big bang than it is with respect to human action. For Chisholm's inference requires the assumption that humans are responsible. One way around Chisholm's claim that there is something we might call agent causation would be to drop the notion of responsibility. There is no similar assumption that one might dispense with in the case of the big bang.

Notice I have indicated that the primary impetus behind Chisholm's doctrine of agent causation is his interest in preserving human responsibility. So far I have only hinted (in quoting Reid) at the added support this doctrine is thought to receive from our own introspective states. Chisholm and others have argued that the notion of agent causation receives independent confirmation from the way our own actions appear to us. We seem to ourselves to be self-determining beings, the originators of much of our behavior. As Richard Taylor puts it:

> This conception fits what people take themselves to be; namely, beings who act, or who are agents, rather than things that are merely acted upon, and whose behavior is simply the causal consequence of conditions that they have not wrought. When I believe that I have done something, I do believe that it was I who caused it to be done, I who made something happen, and not merely something within me, such as one of my own subjective states, which is not identical with myself. If I believe that something not identical with myself was the cause of my behavior—some event wholly external to myself, for instance, or even one internal to myself, such as a nerve impulse, volition, or whatnot—then I cannot regard that behavior as being an act of mine, unless I further believe that I was the cause of that external or internal event.[14]

Taylor is willing to allow that "we certainly do not know that a human being is anything more than an assemblage of physical things and processes that act in accordance with those laws that describe the behavior of all other physical things and processes."[15] In contrast, however, I note that we do think we know that the universe has an absolute beginning; the origin of the universe is clearly radically different from that of the coming to be of any other physical object we think we understand. So some special metaphysics of causation, other than that which Chisholm calls "transeunt causation," does seem to be required. Ready at hand is a theory that has been devised to explain the appearance of self-determining behavior among humans, namely, agent causation. There is, then, precedent for assigning agent causation as the explanation for the beginning of a causal sequence such as the coming to be of the universe.

In Defense of Agent Causation

As a theory deployed to explain human behavior, the doctrine of agent causation has been the subject of severe evaluation. For instance, Daniel Dennett regards the attempt as an example of "obscure and panicky metaphysics."[16] Even Taylor, who adopts the theory of agency we are discussing, acknowledges that this conception of activity involves some "rather strange metaphysical notions that are not applied elsewhere in nature."[17] Chisholm remarks without alarm that his solution to the problem of human freedom depends upon making "somewhat far-reaching assumptions about the self or the agent."[18] All this is freely admitted by proponents of the view. But I point out that, whether or not human behavior is ultimately reducible to normal scientific patterns of explanation, the beginning of the universe apparently is not. Any metaphysics of causation that does justice to this circumstance can be expected to constitute a radical departure from the standard theories about causal relations that obtain between strictly physical processes and events.

One might wonder why, if some special metaphysics of causation is needed to account for the big bang, one should appeal to the doctrine of agent causation. Why not adopt an entirely unique metaphysics of causation specially formulated to account for first events and call it "first-cause causation"? Why invoke the notion of an agent?[19] My response has three parts.

First, this question is particularly relevant if agent causation is so obscure as to make no sense at all. Then any metaphysics of causation will be at least as good as the proposed "theory" of agent causation. But the doctrine of agent causation is not obscure in the sense that nobody knows at all what it means. Indeed, part of what it means is that there are non-reductive factors in causation. So agent causation is a species of first-cause causation. Any metaphysics of agent causation will be a metaphysics of first-cause causation. Now I say agent causation is a species of first-cause causation without knowing whether there are any other species. The choices available to metaphysicians are few, to be sure.

We must be careful not to confuse the possibility of isolating a concept with the task of conceptual analysis. A particular concept may be irreducible or unanalyzable. It does not follow that it is illicit to form a concept that cannot be submitted to rigorous analysis. We may have any number of concepts that, upon inspection, turn out to be unanalyzable. It would be imprudent to judge in advance that such concepts are necessarily empty.

In any case, the metaphysical theory of agent causation is more illuminating—more explanatorily powerful—than the postulate of some radically peculiar nonpersonal instance of first-cause causation. Appealing to agent causation to explain the first event called the big bang is more illuminating because this event is relevantly analogous to other events (namely, those caused through the exercise of human freedom) that are somewhat better understood by us in terms of agent causation. Thus, the doctrine of agent causation conforms to one important criterion of a good metaphysical theory.

Second, the doctrine of agent causation is not really a newfangled conception of possible causes. The intuition that receives formal attention by Chisholm and Taylor has been around as long as there have been human beings who have thought of themselves as originators of some of their actions. The makings of a metaphysical theory of agent causation can be found in Aristotle, Suarez, Thomas Reid, C. A. Cambell, and others. The history of philosophy has yet to see the intimations of an alternative theory of first-cause causation. Even Aristotle's Unmoved Mover was characterized as Pure-Thought-Thinking-Itself. One would think that a Being who engages in such rational deliberation must be personal in some sense.

Third, any doctrine of causation is bound to be obscure. Even the one we normally appeal to in science to explain ordinary events and states of affairs is obscure, and that theory is inadequate in any case to explain the event of the big bang. The doctrine of agent causation is at least as plausible as any other theory of causation on offer, including transeunt causation. An alternative *metaphysics* of first-cause causation must provide at least a partial specification of what this alternative theory would look like. If the "metaphysical obscurity" of the doctrine of agent causation is a reason not to accept the doctrine, then any metaphysics of causation that is even more obscure must suffer the same fate.

To illustrate, Dennett, who resists Chisholm's doctrine of agent causation, recognizes the need to provide an alternative account that is recognizably more plausible than the one he rejects. He does not simply report his distaste for Chisholm's view. The task of one whole chapter in his book on free will is to describe a naturalistic account of the self or agent that avoids Chisholm's metaphysically mysterious notions about the self: "It is clear that if such a positive account is to be given, it will have to declare the intuitions that support Chisholm's vision of the self as an unmoved mover to be a sort of cognitive illusion. If such a declaration is to be anything better than theory-driven name-calling, it will have to be supported by a convincing diagnosis of the cause of this illusion."[20] The same holds for any proposal that agent causation, as a species of first-cause causation, is too weird to be taken seriously. If some species of first-cause causation is needed to explain some phenomenon (such as the big bang), then anyone who is unhappy with agent causation has the responsibility to formulate a more adequate account of the relevant kind of causation.

Explaining Regularities of Succession

There is more to be said in favor of assigning personal agency to the First Cause of the universe. Perhaps all regularities of succession discoverable in the natural world have as their ultimate explanation some sort of personal agency. This claim has been advanced by Swinburne. I now want to explore this point.

Whatever caused the present universe to come into existence, whether ex nihilo or *ex materia,* must have had amazing power to organize the stuff of the universe and to establish an orderly arrangement of conditions that are fundamental to the entire scientific investigation of the universe. Now this orderly arrangement of conditions includes all the laws of nature, which are, I assume, a proper subset of all regularities of succession. Besides the laws of nature known to us, there seem to be regularities of succession that are not due to the operation of normal scientific laws. This is why I say that the laws of nature are a *proper subset* of the set of all regularities of succession. Regularities of succession that have not yet been satisfactorily explained in terms of natural laws include phenomena normally attributed to the free choices of rational agents.

The reasons why I assume that there are such regularities are, first, that the prima facie evidence for there being free choice in connection with rational deliberation is weighty indeed, and second, that the reducibility of such phenomena to normal scientific explanation has yet to be established. For the time being there is, at best, only the possibility that human behavior that appears to be free is not free after all.

Rational agents produce regularities of succession easily and often. Humans cause such regularities of succession as the arrangement of a course syllabus that sets out topics and assignments for each class period, and, to use examples cited by Swinburne, "the notes of a song sung by a singer or the movements of a dancer's body when he performs a dance in time with the accompanying instrument."[21]

Based on the assumption that humans cause some regularities of succession, Swinburne has postulated that all regularities of succession have a similar cause: "An agent produces the celestial harmony like a man who sings a song."[22] The reasons that I think make this postulate worth endorsing have to do with implications of the big bang cosmology, which proposes a transition from a state either of total equilibrium or of nothing at all to a state in which the laws of nature operate with impressive and advantageous regularity.

Even *before* invoking analogies with human purposive behavior resulting in regularities of succession, there already seems to be a need for some non-natural cause to explain the origin of a universe marked by the operation of regularities subsumable under scientific law. Even if it is not plausible to think that humans produce regularities of succession through rational deliberation and free choice, we need an explanation for there being the regularities that we actually do find.

The operation of natural laws in a universe that did not itself result from the operation of any natural laws is not even an anomaly, for it can never be explained in terms of the antecedent operation of natural laws if there were no such laws. Thus, a peculiar non-natural cause seems to be in evidence given the existence and structure of the universe. A further clue concerning the nature of this cause comes from the sphere of human action. Swinburne argues by analogy for the existence of a powerful personal agent as the explanation for there being regularities in nature. I employ the argument as a way of emphasizing the plausibility of assigning the property of personal agency to a non-natural reality we have other reasons to think exists.

Swinburne thinks this type of analogical argument has the added advantage of making the "explanation of empirical matters more simple and coherent," thus tending to confirm the conclusion of the argument from analogy.

> For if the conclusion is true, if a very powerful non-embodied rational agent is responsible for the operation of the laws of nature, then normal scientific explanation would prove to be personal explanation. That is, explanation of some phenomenon in terms of the operation of a natural law would ultimately be an explanation in terms of the operation of an agent. Hence (given an initial arrangement of matter) the principles of explanation of phenomena would have been reduced from two to one.[23]

Incidentally, it is in this context that Swinburne comments on another principle of explanation, namely, *entia non sunt multiplicanda praeter necessitatem*—"do not add a god to your ontology unless you have to." Now whether we have to add a god to our ontology is, of course, an important question. Without developing further a case that we should add a god to our ontology given the explicanda of natural laws, we should acknowledge that developing such a case in further detail is necessary for the argument to succeed. Any further elaboration of this line of argument would take us too far afield, given the purpose of this book. It would, in any case, require one or more volumes of closer analysis. Here, however, I would like to note that the principle has application when the question is whether to add more than one god to our ontology if one is enough. Perhaps, contrary to David Hume, monotheism is a more likely hypothesis than his polytheistic "committee" because it is a simpler hypothesis that does just as good a job otherwise of explaining the relevant phenomena.

Even Philo (who I assume was speaking for Hume) was undecided about this matter.

> If the whole of natural theology . . . resolves itself into one simple, though somewhat ambiguous, at least undefined proposition, *that the cause or causes of order in the universe probably bear some remote analogy to human intelligence* . . . what can the most inquistive, contemplative, and religious man do more than give a plain, philosophical assent to the proposition, as often as it occurs; and believe that the arguments, on which it is established, exceed the objections which lie against it?[24]

Nevertheless, that Philo was willing to assign intelligence to the cause or causes of the universe indicates that he was impressed with the need to find an adequate explanation for the order in the universe.

THIS REALITY IS POWERFUL

So far I have argued only that the non-natural cause responsible for the existence of the universe is personal. Along the way I have hinted that intelligence and power also belong to this Creator. I wish now to focus briefly on the possibility of assigning great power to this Agent.

Antony Flew calls attention to an important distinction between phenomena counting as evidence and phenomena serving as illustration: when belief can be established on grounds other than the wonders of particular ordered phenomena, "then it might become entirely reasonable to point to them as illustrations of God's independently known qualities."[25] Flew's point is that an instance of what appears to be a "contrivance" cannot be evidence for something like omnipotence. The appearance could be accounted for without referring to omnipotence as a requisite explanation. At best, contrivance is only an illustration of omnipotence once it has been established on independent grounds that God is omnipotent.

The point is well taken. Yet Flew passes this wisdom along without noting a significant extension of it. The attributes of God are not all equally general. Some qualities are contained in the scope, as it were, of other qualities, so that where a more general quality is known to be predicable of God and one can identify a phenomenon in the world that exhibits this quality, it may be possible to infer other more specific qualities from the special features of the phenomenon. So, if we rightly judge (from the fact that there is a temporally finite universe) that God is a person, we may find ourselves discerning other qualities of this person from particular artifacts of his in the universe. Among these qualities it would not be surprising to find intelligence, power, and goodness if order, complexity, and an irresistible compulsion to value persons and actions in terms of right and wrong were exhibited in the world. Now this is what we do seem to find.

The power of God must at the very least be equal to the task of bringing the universe into existence. Doubtless, power of exceeding magnitude, coupled with considerable ingenuity, would be required to "make" a primitive physical object using no preexisting materials of the same type. I am not sure that such an act would demand omnipotence in the Agent, nor am I sure that it would not. But it must be more powerful than anything else we now know of. If all of the lawlike conditions of natural phenomena were determined by God when he initiated the history of the universe, then great indeed is his power. So great, I should think, that miracles involving the manipulation of nature contrary to ordinary regularities cannot be ruled out. For that matter, regularities themselves might well depend upon the ongoing participation of God in the operation of "natural" processes.

THIS REALITY IS MORALLY GOOD

We turn, finally, to consider whether the goodness of God is at all discernible at this stage of the argument. As a free and intelligent Agent the Cause of the universe has met a significant condition for being a moral being. In the interests of exploring this further let us attend briefly to two features of reality that may be seen to support the contention that the Agent who created the universe is also a morally good Being. I have in mind the appearance of certain goods in the world and what George Mavrodes has called "the queerness of morality."

The Appearance of Goods in the World

The appearance of certain goods in the world suggests that God is good. These goods can be described at different levels of generality. I will refer to three classes of goods that other philosophers have taken to support theism. These include the good of human and animal life, the goods associated with personal and social development, and the good of fulfilled promises in contexts of religious experience.

First, the anthropic principle suggests that God is good. In keeping with the line of argument presented so far, it is natural to reflect upon the present state of the universe in an attempt to identify additional properties of the non-natural cause of the universe. If the universe was caused by a personal agent, then we may assume that this agent intended the effect that the agent achieved. If we attend to the specific characteristics of the effect that we call the universe, then we find conditions that would not obtain if the Creator had not acted in the way that he did. One way to approach this investigation is in terms of the anthropic principle.

The anthropic principle derives from the observation that if the conditions of our universe were not what they are, within a very small margin of flexibility, no life of any kind would be in evidence in the universe. In other words, the universe is not only a fit habitat for human and other forms of life but the initial probability of there being such a universe is quite small. George Gale explains:

> Contemporary astrophysicists are investigating the possibility that the existence of life, in particular human life, may set constraints upon the allowable conditions of the early universe. Arguments such as these involve what has come to be called the "Anthropic Principle." Although these efforts differ somewhat from one another in their underlying philosophical spirit, they converge upon one fact: in order for life to exist today, an incredibly restrictive set of demands must be met in the early universe.[26]

The parameters constituting the conditions for the emergence of life are extremely narrow and quite numerous, making it all the more remarkable that there is life at all in the universe. I will describe very briefly just three such parameters to illustrate the general point of the so-called anthropic principle.

First, star formation may proceed at varying degrees of efficiency, depending upon the gravitational force in the universe. A slight increase in the force of gravity would result in all stars being much more massive than our sun, with the effect that planets that would otherwise be able to support life could not do so since their "suns" would burn too rapidly and erratically. Mild decreases in the gravitational force of the universe would prevent the production of suns large enough to maintain life-supporting planets, since none of the heavy elements needed to build such planets would ever be produced.

Second, life would not be possible if the nuclear force holding the particles of atoms together varied slightly. A lesser force would limit all elements in the universe to hydrogen. A greater force would preclude the production of hydrogen and other elements essential to life.

Third, the rate of expansion of the universe is crucial. If the universe expanded more slowly, the types of stars needed to sustain life would not have been produced before the universe collapsed back upon itself. A greater rate of expansion would mean that there would not be any galaxies in the universe, to say nothing of stars. Alan Guth[27] has calculated that the rate of expansion must be within a tolerance of 1 in 10^{55}.

Other parameters for the universe, if there is to be life anywhere at all in the universe, include the entropy level of the universe, the mass of the universe, the stability of the proton, the velocity of light, the distance between stars, and the rate of luminosity increase for stars.[28] George Greenstein, an American astronomer who is not himself a theist, acknowledges that evidence of the kind just described encourages one to think that the universe was "providentially crafted . . . for our benefit."[29]

Other parameters can be cited having to do in particular with the fitness of earth for the habitation of life. The enthusiasm with which some scientists search for extraterrestrial intelligence is motivated in part by the impression that if life-producing conditions are met at all somewhere in the present universe (as they obviously are known to be), then it is likely that they are met elsewhere in the universe. It just does not seem probable that the tiny fraction of space in the universe occupied by our planet would be the only place where there is life if the universe has overcome the improbability of there being life anywhere in the universe. In other words, the probability of life occurring in a universe erupting from a big bang is so low that if life occurs at all it probably has not occurred only in our neighborhood of the universe.

The search for extraterrestrial life is also guided by the parameters known to constitute the necessary conditions for life on earth. That is, since our planet is known to favor the maintenance of life, scientists have directed their search for life elsewhere in the universe to those parts of the universe where similar conditions are present. The relevant parameters for life on the earth include the number of stars in the planetary system; the parent star birthrate and age; the parent star mass, color, and distance from the center of the galaxy; the surface gravity of the planet; the distance of the planet from the parent star; the thickness of the planet's crust; its rotation period; its gravitational interaction with a moon; its magnetic field; its axial tilt; the ratio of reflected light to the total amount reaching the planet's surface; the oxygen-to-nitrogen ratio in its atmosphere; the carbon dioxide and water vapor levels in its atmosphere; the ozone level; and even the level of seismic activity. Given these and other parameters, there are not many stars in the universe with planets capable of sustaining life. Some scientists have marveled that there is any life at all, even on the earth, and have thus concluded that there probably is no life elsewhere in the universe.[30]

Now this fact, that there is life in the universe, together with the probability that life in the universe is limited to our small planet, has been the basis for some versions of the design argument for the *existence* of God. I have already produced a line of argument to a non-natural Being that is personal, intelligent, and very powerful from the need to explain the beginning of the universe. Now I suggest that the existence of life should be attributed to this same Creator. What this adds to our account of the *nature* of this Creator depends upon what we make of our propensity to value life.

If life is a value, a good that *ought* to be recognized by us, then the existence of that good depends upon the Creator. Now it may be that we just happen to value life, and that life has no intrinsic value of its own. In that case there is nothing very special about life such that what becomes of that life should be any cause for denying the goodness of God. The Creator can hardly be blamed for what happens to biological systems if they do not have intrinsic worth. On the other hand, if human and animal life has intrinsic value, then it stands to reason that the Creator is the source not only of life but also of the good associated with life.

A *second* class of goods is referred to in Swinburne's *argument from providence*. Closely related to the anthropic principle as propounded by contemporary astrophysicists is the idea that our world provides human beings with the opportunity to satisfy both their own and others' biological and psychological needs. Swinburne has argued that "the general circumstances of the world are such as to show that a good God is providing for the basic needs of men and animals."[31] He thinks that "the sort of world to which [the laws of nature] give rise is the sort of world [God] has more reason to make than other worlds."[32]

It is desirable that individual agents have a meaningful measure of control over their own destiny. And human beings find themselves existing under conditions that constitute this as a possibility. They learn to act on justified beliefs rather than on mere instinct. They experience deterrent sensations and emotions so that they do not bring great harm to themselves without warning. They are able to form their own character to a great extent; virtue is not foisted upon them, but neither are they strictly determined to turn out morally corrupt. Their "biologically useful" desires extend beyond their basic desires for food, drink, and sleep to include desires to perform various actions and to be in certain situations. On the other hand, their desires are not always so strong that they cannot choose to act on reason. All of these opportunities to influence one's own future are arguably good, even though they are accompanied by the possibility of getting into trouble.[33] Since these kinds of opportunities are desirable, God has a reason for making a world in which they are found.

Swinburne argues that God also has a reason for "making a world in which men have responsibility for the well-being of others. . . . A world in which good things can only be attained by co-operation is one which a God has reason to make—for benefitting each other is a good thing."[34] Humans enjoy the opportunity to provide for the welfare of others in community. Sometimes others benefit as the unintended consequence of individuals seeking their own interests. At other times individuals deliberately cooperate with each other so that each member of the group can achieve his or her own goals. By agreeing to work together, one individual can benefit another and vice versa. But there is also the opportunity for unrequited benefit in our world. The opportunity to confer benefit on others without the assurance of reward is a good thing. Person A can bring benefit to person B, who in turn may benefit person C, whether or not person B is in a position to confer benefit on person A.

Pleasure and enjoyment are gained through cooperation and the companionship it engenders. Friendships develop between individuals united in a common cause, and yet friendship is desirable for its own sake. The fund of knowledge grows as one generation of researchers builds on what a previous generation accomplished. It is possible to plan for the benefit of future generations. Even the suffering of an individual is the occasion for the production of much interpersonal good. The suffering of an AIDS victim gives reason for cooperative research among medical scientists, and this research may lead to the discovery of a cure that can be manufactured and distributed in the form of a drug by others in the cooperative enterprise. In these and other ways humans have the opportunity to confer benefits on one another.

All these goods are possible because of the way our world is arranged. Our world might have been arranged differently so that these goods could not accrue. Even if there are natural laws that are the proximate explanation for there being opportunities of these kinds, the natural laws themselves would not be what they are if God had arranged our world another way.

Mention can be made of a *third* class of goods found in the experiences of some individuals and related to the question of the divine nature. *Religious experience tends to confirm the goodness of God.* There are various types of religious experiences and arguments from religious experience. As J. P. Moreland has pointed out, "Each type of religious experience enters the case for Christian theism in its own way."[35] One form of religious-experience argument that has been developed recently by William Alston is an argument from God's fulfillment of his promises to humans.[36] Alston has argued that the fulfillment of promises recorded in sacred texts and attributed to God is evidence of the work of God in the lives of individuals who believe these promises or who fulfill whatever conditions must be fulfilled to enjoy the blessings of conditional promises.

Conditional promises in particular provide a way of checking up on the validity of a promise. For if a good comes to a person if and only if the person fulfills the conditions specified along with some promise, then that is evidence that these conditions are necessary and sufficient for the realization of such a good. Since the conditions are specified in the context of a promise, then it seems that the alleged source of the promise is vindicated. Furthermore, experiences of this kind are rather difficult to explain naturalistically in terms of one's psychology or in terms of one's digestive processes.

If God exists and is at all concerned about the lives of humans, then it is to be expected that God would do good things for them. God might send benefits their way without announcing his intention to do so. Or he might make a promise, which would involve some form of communication on his part. Moreover, he might have good reasons for providing some goods to his creatures only if they fulfill certain conditions themselves, much like parents often do with their children. Thus he might conditionally agree to produce certain virtues in the life of the believer, or to fortify the mind with confidence and peace during a moment of crisis. So one might argue for the moral goodness of God from the sainthood of certain persons. Sometimes the condition might simply be to *believe* that "he is a rewarder of those who seek him."[37] At other times conditions might include a behavioral component, such as obedience to some command.

At any rate, religious believers often do report that they have experienced answers to prayer in the form of requests granted and that they have been blessed in a variety of ways as an apparent consequence of their devotion to God. And they have been confirmed in their faith in God as a result of these types of experiences. These "coincidences" have seemed to them to call for explanation in terms of the providence of a God.

It may be that they would not have any of the experiences they describe if they did not first believe in God, or if they did not conduct what may be called a "devotional experiment" with genuine sincerity that falls short of believing in God. When Blaise Pascal proposed his now famous Wager, presented as an inducement to bet on God, he did not expect it to be an aid to the person who considered the evidence for or against the existence of God to be decisive. Rather, he considered it prudent to take steps toward belief in God when the proposition that God exists and its contradictory seem equiprobable. He realized that one cannot simply believe a proposition at will. Nevertheless, one can put oneself in a position that can lead to the eventual acquisition of the belief. Sometimes it is prudent to do so. One way to put oneself in a position to come to believe in God, when the evidence suggests that there is at least as much warrant for the proposition that God exists as there is for its contradictory, is to conduct a devotional experiment. This might include consorting with religious believers, participating in religious services, and seeking God in prayer.[38]

Whatever one thinks of Pascal's Wager as presented by Pascal, it does seem to have significance for one who wants to test the hypothesis that the personal Creator of the universe is morally good. For one who already thinks it most rational to believe that a powerful and intelligent personal Creator of the universe exists, such an experiment may help confirm what one would antecedently expect of such a Being: that this Creator is also benevolent.

Another way that one might test the hypothesis of the goodness of God would be to look around for the availability of a revelation from God that explicitly addresses the human condition and speaks to the significance of the reality of evil in the world. Perhaps such a revelation is what one could *expect* if God is good. And if this expectation is satisfied by the revelation claims embodied in one or more of the great religious traditions of the world, then that will tend to confirm, on the one hand, the hypothesis of the goodness of God, and, on the other, the validity of the revelation claims embodied in one or more traditions.

I have already referred to Philo's general conclusion about the success of natural theology at the close of Hume's *Dialogues Concerning Natural Religion.* Philo consented to assigning intelligence to the cause or causes of the universe, indicating that he was impressed with the need to find an adequate explanation for the order of the universe. His next remark suggests that he also believed there is some reason to think this cause is benevolently disposed toward humans: "But believe me, Cleanthes, the most natural sentiment, which a well-disposed mind will feel on this occasion, is a longing desire *and expectation*, that Heaven would be pleased to dissipate, at least alleviate, this profound ignorance, by affording some more particular revelation to mankind, and making discoveries of the nature, attributes, and operations of the *divine* object of our Faith."[39] Without explicitly mentioning the moral attributes of God as part of what can be reasonably inferred from order in the universe, Philo judges that a well-disposed mind should expect divine aid concerning matters that remain a mystery. But why is it proper for a well-disposed mind to entertain such an expectation? Philo seemed to think that the order of nature makes this expectation reasonable. While he was minimally theistic in his general conclusion, he was not thoroughly agnostic about the divine nature. If he was, he would not have felt justified in making this latter remark. There are in the order of nature intimations that the Creator is benevolent, and these are strong enough to warrant the expectation that the one responsible for our existence will seek to make meaningful contact with humans who seek to know this reality better. So, at least, Philo concluded.

If one is justified in believing that there is a powerful and intelligent personal Creator of the universe (the argument from the beginning of the universe), who has constituted the universe, the earth's solar system, and human persons in a way that is remarkably conducive to the maintenance of life (the argument based on the anthropic principle) and to the realization of human personal and social goods (the argument from providence), and this leads one to seek God for goods that God would surely be capable of sending one's way if God wanted to, and these goods are realized in apparent response to one's appeal to God (the argument from fulfilled promises), then there is reason to believe in the goodness of God.

So far I have argued that the goodness of God may be evident from the appearance of certain goods in this world that it seems most reasonable to suppose has a non-natural personal cause. Independent support for the goodness of God comes from a consideration of the nature of morality. I consider this next.

The Queerness of Morality

The queerness of morality suggests that moral obligation is rooted in a non-natural personal reality. Many have held the view that morality is somehow dependent upon religion. This view is attractive to me in part because of the independent evidence for the existence of a personal Creator. If persons are centers of consciousness for whom values are significant, then I assume that the Creator too has values of his own. I also assume that some of these are evident in what he has created.

It is not feasible here to enumerate all possible nonreligious worldviews in which morality is thought to have some hold. My view is that the most common nonreligious views of the world have difficulty accounting for morality. George Mavrodes has attempted to portray the odd status that morality would have in one particularly common nonreligious view of the world, a view he calls "Russellian" because it is supposed to be a generalized version of Bertrand Russell's view. He then contrasts the odd status that morality must have in a Russellian world with the apparent status of morality in the actual world. His suggestion is that to amend a Russellian worldview to remove the queerness of morality and to adopt a view in closer conformity with our intuitions about morality would be to move toward a religious view of morality.[40]

Mavrodes develops his thesis by suggesting that performing our moral obligations will sometimes be counterproductive of the good, at least so far as the good is conceived in a standard, nonreligious view of the world. But this, he thinks, is very strange, in the sense that "we would be living in a crazy world" if we had obligations that would result in the diminution of the good.[41] He suggests that there are two ways to remove this queerness. One is to adopt a religious view of morality; the other is to find some way to analyze judgments about obligations so that the absurdity does not arise. But he concludes that characteristic attempts to remove the difficulty through an analysis of judgments about obligations tend to undercut the notion of "strong obligation" that seems to be in evidence in the actual world.

His chief contention about the nature of morality in the actual world is that it

> seems to require us to hold that certain organisms (namely, human beings) have in addition to their ordinary properties and relations another special relation to certain actions. This relation is that of being "obligated" to perform those actions. And some of those actions are pretty clearly such that they will yield only Russellian losses to the one who performs them. Nevertheless, we are supposed to hold that a person who does not perform an action to which he is thus related is defective in some serious and important way and an adverse judgment is appropriate against him. And that certainly does seem odd.[42]

The question, Why should I be moral? seems to be motivated in part by this sense of the queerness of morality. If it turns out that being moral is not always in the agent's interests, that at times there is nothing in it for the agent, then the queerness of morality intrudes with considerable force. How are we to account for the way in which one's duty would, sometimes at least, seem to override one's interests? Is a world in which this is not accounted for not absurd? Why should anyone adopt the moral point of view as part of a rational life plan if doing so will sometimes mean performing obligations that conflict with one's own interests? It is not clear how it could be reasonable to do so unless morality is deeply rooted in reality. And yet it seems that doing so must somehow be reasonable.

Since the physical universe apparently owes its existence to the action of a non-natural personal Cause, and if moral obligation cannot otherwise be suitably grounded, then what is there to prevent us from assuming that obligation derives from God? If a criterion for the general acceptance of a particular conception of morality is that this conception of morality provide an answer to the question, Why be moral? then a theistic worldview is more plausible than its alternatives. Even a philosophy of immanent purpose, according to which obligation is just an irreducible brute fact about a universe in which non-natural properties somehow exist, does not dispose of the queerness of morality. Nor does such a worldview recognize the existence of a personal Creator of the universe. Once assent to the existence of such a Being is made on independent grounds, there is no necessity to posit the brute factuality of obligation and moral properties. Since obligation is binding on persons, it seems more reasonable to me to hold that obligation is rooted in the intentions of a person—a person with suitable authority to constitute some actions as duties that humans have an obligation to perform.

Furthermore, the queerness of morality is not removed if the effort to remove it ends in claiming that, while morality might be rooted in the reality of God's existence, God might not be a morally good being. The question, How good is God? brings us directly to the task of theodicy. Indeed, the project of clarifying in what sense God is good and filling out the case for the goodness of God goes hand in hand with the task of theodicy. Once the case has been made for the goodness of God along natural-theology lines, the natural theologian may take up the challenge of formulating a plausible account of God's reasons for permitting evil. This involves an attempt to make sense of suffering against the background knowledge provided by natural theology concerning the nature and existence of God.

Another way to exhibit the queerness of morality has direct bearing upon our problem—the problem of evil. If our moral judgments are strictly subjective, then we have no argument from moral objectivism to the essential goodness of God as the requisite ground of such objectivism. If the problem of evil is not pointless, however, it is because it rests upon the possibility of making moral judgments whose truth is not determined by the idiosyncratic preferences of those who make them. Whatever force the problem of evil has depends upon there being some transcendent standard according to which our judgments about what is right and what is wrong are objectively true or false. Feelings of repugnance alone are not enough to warrant disbelief in God. It is a widespread phenomenon that people have wondered whether God is just in permitting any or all evil. But the ground of this worry is necessarily objective, otherwise it has no bearing on the question of God's existence or goodness. On a subjectivist theory of ethics, all it can mean to say on the basis of evil that God is not entirely good is, "I disapprove of God's permission of evil in the world." This, in turn, translates into the following unenlightening statement: "I disapprove of God's permission of those events of which I disapprove."

When atheists indict God for allowing evil they do so with an air of authority that is baseless unless they can appeal to some transcendent (or external) standard of what it would be possible for a morally good God to permit. But if God does exist as the personal, powerful, and purposive Being that our earlier line of argument strongly suggests, then in all likelihood this Being has an ontologically close tie to the implicit standard of morality referred to in the indictment against God. As C. S. Lewis said: "If a Brute and Blackguard made the world, then he also made our minds. If he made our minds, he also made that very standard in them whereby we judge him to be a Brute and Blackguard."[43]

The point is, if values are rooted in reality, and reality is rooted in the being and activity of the non-natural entity described above, then values are rooted in this Being. Alternatively, if values are not rooted in reality, then none of our doubts about the existence of God that depend upon value considerations (as the problem of evil does) can have any effect. God is inevitably and ironically "worshipped with insults."[44] The measure of importance we are entitled to attach to our own value judgments depends upon their degree of objective validity, their tie to some external standard. Any doubts about the existence of an objective morality automatically raises doubts about the probative force of the problem of evil as an objection to theism. "In a word, unless we allow ultimate reality to be moral, we cannot morally condemn it."[45]

It has been notoriously difficult to give an account of why our moral judgments should be regarded as objective. But the failure of meta-ethicists to supply a satisfactory answer to this problem has not prevented most persons, including philosophers, from behaving as if their moral judgments are objectively true. (Thus, if one's behavior is any indication of what one believes, then it is inconsistent for one to deny the objectivity of morality.) And one prominent manifestation of this propensity to act as if morality is objective is the charge that God cannot be good if he creates a world with evil in it. But theism is apparently the only adequate ground for the intelligibility of such a claim. After all, inherent in the argument from evil is an implicit appeal to the absolute objectivity of morality. There is little reason to doubt that this ground is ontologically identifiable with the powerful, purposive, and personal cause of the universe that our earlier argument gives us reason to believe exists.

THEODICY AND THE PURPOSES OF GOD

I should not conclude this discussion of epistemically accessible features of God's nature without calling attention to the independent bearing this has on our ultimate question: How are we to reconcile the existence of God with the existence of evil? If God has brought our universe into existence, there surely is more to this truth than our finite minds can fathom. Recognition of such a reality evokes intellectual humility before the Creator. And this humility ought to characterize our attempts to scrutinize the possible purposes at God's disposal for permitting evil.

Alvin Plantinga is right to protect against the error of presuming that we can intuit the precise reasons God has for each fragment of evil in the world. This is in part why he distinguishes between a theodicy and a defense.[46] Unfortunately, it does little good to make this point unless there are good independent reasons for believing in God. Without the framework of natural theology, I think, Plantinga's proposal comes to little more than an appeal to mystery. What he offers in response to the challenge of evil is too little too late.

Doubtless the theodicist will be helped by any information he can glean from the sorts of considerations briefly touched on in this and the previous chapter. A theodicy involves speculation about the *possible* justifying purposes behind God's permission of evil even if it is never known whether these are God's *actual* purposes. The conclusions reached in a viable natural theology function as controls on what it is plausible to think are God's reasons for permitting evil in the world. Whatever specific formulation of a theodicy proves to be most compelling, given all of the relevant data at our disposal, it must be remembered that theodicy is needed only because it seems appropriate to hold God responsible for the evil that occurs in the universe. And it can be appropriate to take this view only if there are good reasons to think that the universe ought not to have turned out the way it has. Oddly then, natural theology may be seen to provide just the sort of reasons needed to generate a problem of evil.

It may be rational to believe in God even if the actual reasons God has for permitting evil remain unknown to us. But that is true only if theism is well supported, whether or not there is evil in the world. The argument I have outlined in these last two chapters shows that theism may indeed be well supported. It may well be that theology can meaningfully enter into the task of formulating a more detailed theodicy. Revealed (or even speculative) theology may suggest possible reasons God has for permitting evil. The precise point at which speculative theology or revealed theology becomes appropriate depends upon the adequacy of linking the results of natural theology with the practice of speculative or revealed theology. Natural theology may accomplish one or both of two important tasks: it may justify the appeal to revealed religion, or it may invite theological speculation along certain definite lines. It may actually do both jointly, for even revealed theology may take one only so far in explaining the reasons that actually justify the presence of evil in a world created by God.

Some measure of speculation may be inevitable if one insists upon a final explanation of any instance of evil in terms of the actual purposes of God. Depending upon the adequacy of one's natural theology, however, this insistence may be motivated by nothing more than idle curiosity, and it may even be thought to be misplaced curiosity. If natural theology supports the view that some reason does justify God's permission of evil, without specifying what that reason is, then there is no logical necessity to provide any plausible account of possible reasons at all. Still, it is perhaps not quite right to suggest that framing a theodicy adds nothing at all to the adequacy of a theistic hypothesis already well supported by natural theology. In Part III we focus our attention on theodicy proper.

8
Explanation and Religious Ambiguity

In the two preceding chapters I argued for the possibility of natural theology by describing the degree of explanatory power that theism as a hypothesis might be seen to enjoy. I have not, however, remarked at all about specific objections John Hick is likely to make against this particular line of argument. In Chapter 4 I sought to answer each of his general theological objections to natural theology, but I have left until now a discussion of his philosophical complaints about theistic argumentation. Philosophical difficulties with theistic argumentation cannot be easily generalized, for there are many forms of theistic argument. A weakness in one type of theistic argument may not be a weakness in another type. The only philosophical challenges to theistic argument that need concern us, then, are those that can be directed against the argument I have developed in Chapters 6 and 7.

I now want to discuss two specific concerns that Hick in particular is likely to raise in connection with the line of argument I have just presented. The first, the suggestion that the universe might just be ultimately unintelligible, we have already encountered in J. L. Mackie. The second has to do with Hick's notion that the universe is "religiously ambiguous."

THE ALLEGED POSSIBILITY THAT THE UNIVERSE IS ULTIMATELY UNINTELLIGIBLE

Some theists have concluded that "the atheist is entitled . . . to deny that the universe requires explanation, and so long as the matter is left there, the theist's far-ranging claims can rest on nothing more than the abstract consideration that explanation is to be sought wherever possible."[1] Hick obviously concurs, for he believes that the atheist, "having agreed that the universe is either unexplained or is to be explained theistically, . . . would add that there is no reason to adopt the latter alternative. There is no adequate reason here to do other than accept the universe as simply an ultimate inexplicable datum."[2] According to Hick, the theist and the atheist reach an impasse at precisely this point. The cosmological argument poses a dilemma: "Either the existence of the universe, ordered as it is, is explicable by reference to God, or it is not explicable at all but remains a sheer brute fact fruitlessly provoking the question, Why should it be?"[3] Unfortunately, the theist can provide no reason for preferring one horn of the dilemma over the other. On the one hand, Hick does not see why the atheist should have any trouble accepting the disjunction; on the other hand, he does not think the atheist is any less justified in supposing that the universe "is not explicable at all but remains a sheer brute fact." It is equally rational to accept either disjunct. In summarizing the final merits of the cosmological argument, he writes:

> This, it seems to me, is where the cosmological argument leaves us. It points very clearly to the possibility of God as the ground of the ultimate intelligibility of the universe in which we find ourselves, and of ourselves as part of it. But in doing this it does not constitute a demonstration of God's existence. It leaves us with the alternatives that the universe is an inexplicable brute fact, or that its existence with the structure that it has is intelligible in the only way in which it could ever finally be intelligible to us, namely through its dependence upon a reality that is ultimate in the order of mind.[4]

My response to this appraisal of the type of argument I set forth begins with an observation. Hick at least seems to agree that no naturalistic explanation for the existence of the universe is possible. Unlike J. L. Mackie and Antony Flew, he thinks the choice is clear. Either the universe is explicable or it is not. If it is explicable, then the universe is caused by "an eternal, self-existent creative Mind." If it is not explicable, then it is "simply an ultimate inexplicable datum."[5] As far as he is concerned, this is not a false dilemma. If an explanation for the existence of the universe is to be sought at all, it must be found only in a self-subsistent non-natural reality. (Hick even adds that this reality must be "of the same order as conscious mind.")[6] Only the theist offers a bona fide explanation.

Of course, for both Mackie and Flew this is a false dilemma, for they do not think that either the theistic hypothesis of divine creation or the naturalistic assumption of a brutally factual universe is a de jure

terminus to the process of explanation. Flew insists, in explicit response to Hick:

> No reason whatever has yet been given for considering that God
> would be an inherently more intelligible ultimate than—say—the
> most fundamental laws of energy and stuff; much less for postulating
> the actual existence of such a further and extraordinary entity,
> instead of somehow contenting yourself with the idea that the world
> we know is—in the vertical dimension—not dependent on anything
> else, and that it is also, in some state or other, probably eternal and
> without beginning.[7]

In other words, to posit the existence of God to explain the existence of
the universe is no better an explanation than to posit the eternal
self-subsistent existence of the world. They are at least on a par as
possible explanations. Indeed, Flew takes the naturalistic explanation
to be more reasonable since he thinks that the idea of God is "infested
with acute logical difficulties," its object being "peculiarly mysterious
and resistant to inquiry."[8]

As we have already seen, Mackie declaims that the notion of
creation "is only vaguely explanatory," and that this notion therefore
fares no better than the suggestion that there might have just been "a
sheer unexplained beginning of things."[9] Thus, he sees no reason at
all why it should be more likely that God exists uncaused than that the
universe exists uncaused. On either account, there is always an
irreducibly unexplained element in our total picture of reality.

I have already responded to the atheistic position directly. Here I
call attention to the fact that Hick seems to abide by my own claim that
the argument at least shows that the only genuine explanation for the
existence of the universe must be given in terms of divine causality.
This seeming agreement between myself and Hick is ultimately
doubtful, however, for we do not share a common view of the notion of
intelligibility that functions in any true explanation.

Hick adopts a kind of Humean account of intelligibility where our
propensity to seek an explanation for the existence of the universe is a
"very natural prejudice built into our nature," comparable to such
"natural beliefs" as those we have about the existence of phenomenal
objects.[10] The intelligibility of the universe is therefore ultimately
subjective, so that even if we insist on giving an explanation for the
existence of the universe and we are led to do so only in terms of
divine creation, this explanation will be intelligible "in the only way in
which it could ever be intelligible *to us.*" But if this is the only account
of intelligible explanation Hick can accept, I do not see why alternative hypotheses, including that of a brutally factual universe, should

be any less intelligible. If we are to believe proponents of these hypotheses, we must allow that to them these hypotheses are intelligible. If the criteria of intelligibility are subjective, then Hick's cosmological principle imposes a false dilemma. Anything can count as an explanation as long as it seems intelligible to the inquirer. But then meaningful debate is ruled out. On the other hand, if the criteria of intelligibility (or rationality) are objective, then there will be conditions that make some explanations superior to others whether or not this superiority of explanations is recognized by anyone. Since it can be shown on Mackie's own principles that it may be irrational not to believe in God, we can be confident that certain nontrivial standards of rationality are shared by theists and nontheists such that meaningful debate can occur between them.[11]

When Hick speaks of the "inability to exclude the possibility of an unintelligible universe,"[12] we are confronted at once with the same suggestion we noted in connection with Mackie. The sheer unexplainable existence of the universe is supposed to be possible. But what sort of possibility is this? Perhaps it is a logical possibility. But is that enough to constitute it as a rational alternative to the theistic hypothesis? Certainly not. There is nothing in Hick's suggestion to distinguish it from Mackie's, and this has been answered already.

It might be objected that I have missed the point of Hick's criticism. Perhaps he wants to say only that it really is not clear that one horn of the dilemma is more rational than the other. One may be within one's epistemic rights, as it were, either to posit the beginning of the universe out of nothing and for no reason at all or to seek a causal explanation for the beginning of the universe. Now obviously, Hick and I disagree about when it is rational to stop seeking a terminus of explanation. I want to say that it is premature to locate the terminus of explanation where the naturalist does with the suggestion that the universe might have just popped willy-nilly into existence. We should look further than this for explanation. But is this the sort of claim that one could give an argument for, or are we simply at an impasse?

Hick seems to think that we are simply at an impasse here. No reasons could be given (at least none that could be decisive) for suggesting either that this is the place to stop in seeking explanation or that we should go on seeking a further explanation at this point. Others, however, have argued that it is reasonable to suppose that further explanation is both possible and fruitful.[13]

There are a number of rational incentives for going further in seeking an explanation. First, further explanation, in terms of the existence of God, does seem possible. If this is possible then what reason can there be for not pursuing this possibility? To refuse an explanation on the grounds that some state of affairs *might* simply be a brute fact when at the same time a potentially quite fruitful explanation suggests itself is not a very scientific attitude. There is no antecedent probability for the beginning of the universe if it is the ultimate brute fact that thinkers like Mackie take it (possibly) to be. Thus, even a modicum of antecedent probability for the beginning of the universe on the theistic hypothesis is more than there would be without the theistic hypothesis (that is, if the universe were a brute fact). Moreover, as I suggested in Chapter 5 and argued in Chapter 6, since the theistic hypothesis has explanatory power whereas the naturalistic assertion does not, the beginning of the universe is an anomaly for naturalism.

Second, if one wishes to avoid the project of seeking an explanation for the existence of the universe, it certainly is convenient to drive a wedge between the being of the world and the operation of the world, or between the world itself as a whole and features of the world or objects within the world. But when we consider that with the beginning of the universe we have to do with an event, it is not so clear why the requirement to seek an explanation ends when we contemplate this particular event. As an event, the beginning of the universe is still the kind of thing that scientists generally seek to explain (and have enjoyed some success at explaining). Indeed, if the beginning of the universe were not a thing of this same kind, then it would not be appropriate even to refer to it as an event.

Furthermore, under some descriptions, the universe will be sufficiently unique to seem, perhaps, not to require any explanation of itself. But under other descriptions, it will seem to require whatever sort of explanation is required for objects that fall under that description. Importantly, the argument I have proposed does not seek an explanation for the universe as a whole but for a particular event, namely, the event of the beginning of the universe. The event for which we ought to seek an explanation is just one event (namely, the first) in a series of temporally related events that together constitute our universe.

David Hume thought he had squelched the need for explaining the existence of the universe as a whole. "Did I show you the particular causes of each individual in a collection of twenty particles of matter, I should think it very unreasonable, should you afterwords ask me, what was the cause of the whole twenty. This is sufficiently explained in explaining the cause of the parts."[14] But suppose, as I have argued, that the relevant collection of entities requiring explanation is the temporal series of events that make up the universe. We are then seeking an explanation for each event in the series (and not the series as a whole), just as Hume requires. But an explanation for each event in this series must include an explanation for the *first* event in the series. Having an explanation for every other event does nothing to explain the first event. If all events have causes, or if it is rational to think that all events have causes, then it is rational to think that the first event has a cause as well. Why should we make an exception in the case of the first event in a series?

Even if we were to seek an explanation for the universe as a whole, it would not follow that this object must fall under some strictly unique description such that, on that description, it might not (or would not) itself require explanation. The universe as a whole has properties that many of the objects within the universe have. As Richard Swinburne puts it, "The objection fails totally to make any crucial distinction between the universe and other objects; and so it fails in its attempt to prevent at the outset a rational inquiry into the issue of whether the universe has some origin outside itself."[15]

Third, if one wishes to avoid the task of providing a further explanation for the beginning of the universe, then it seems that there is a burden of proof on one to show that this is not only not necessary but not possible. Mackie's argument (and Hick's similar argument) at best shows only that if there is, in the very nature of the case, no explanation for there being a universe, then we cannot be expected to locate one. They have not, however, demonstrated that in the very nature of the case there is no explanation for there being a universe. Without a demonstration of this claim it must at least remain an open question whether there is in fact some explanation for the beginning of the universe. And as long as this is an open question it will be appropriate to consider possible explanations for the beginning of the universe. It is not *necessary* that the sheer existence of the universe itself is the terminus of explanation.

Fourth, it is simply not true that the theistic hypothesis is no less mysterious than the postulate of the brute factuality of the universe itself. God and the universe are not relevantly similar types of postulates. The God postulated by theism is a personal being with the capacity to initiate a causal series. One reason why some have thought that the postulate of God's existence is at least as mysterious as the postulate of the brute factuality of the universe may be that, as materalists, they have not allowed "personal explanations" to play explanatory roles. But nonmaterialists who believe that some phenomena at least have explanations in terms of agent causation might be more comfortable with the greater explanatory power of the theistic hypothesis in comparison with the supposition that the universe is a brute fact. And it is not impossible that many who forbid any reference to "personal explanation" do so to avoid taking a theistic viewpoint.

It is significant that many atheists do not see the need for any further explanation for the universe. They evidently do not consider any explanation, properly speaking, to be possible. If one is not possible it cannot be required. But what happens when it becomes apparent that an explanation is possible? If the possible explanation of the universe can be given in terms of a personal Being (God), then even if it were, contrary to fact, appropriate to seek further for an explanation for the being of God, at least the existence of God would have enough explanatory power to make it more rational to believe that there is a God than that there is not. As Swinburne puts it, "For the theist, explanation stops at what, intuitively, is the most natural kind of stopping-place for explanation—the choice of an agent. If regress ever stops, where it stops is the ultimate source of the diversity of things."[16]

Finally, I have not pretended to demonstrate the existence of God. Rather, I have argued that the rational person should conclude that there is a God. Hick agrees that the cosmological argument, in seeking an intelligible cause of the universe, "says something that is true concerning our cognitive situation." Still, he thinks that the argument "does not compel us to believe that there is a God." His support for this claim comes down to this: "One may opt instead to accept the universe as a sheer unexplained fact. One can say with Bertrand Russell, 'The universe is just there, and that's all.' For it could be that the stronger plausibility of theism only holds relatively to our human minds, and indeed only to some human minds, and may be no more than an illusion to which they are subject."[17] But this view is entirely consistent with my argument. Even if it is merely a feature of our cognitive situation that we seek for further explanation of the beginning of the universe in terms of some cause, that is still a constraint on what it is rational for us to believe. Even if we do not know that some version of the principle of sufficient reason holds objectively and universally, we at least ought to form our beliefs on the supposition that it does.[18] (What, in any case, would an *argument* that it does not—or even may not—look like?)

THE ALLEGED RELIGIOUS AMBIGUITY OF THE UNIVERSE

Hick has an additional reason for thinking that there lies an irreducible impasse between the path of the theist and the path of the atheist, for he argues that the universe is "religiously ambiguous."[19] He means that the universe may be interpreted either naturalistically or theistically. Thus, the atheist is within his epistemic rights if he judges from the total evidence of his own experience that God does not exist.

> The situation seems to be this. Of the immense number and variety of apparently relevant considerations some, taken by themselves, point in one direction and some in the other. One group can fairly be said to count as at least prima facie evidence for the existence of God. For not only do believers urge these particular considerations as supporting their own position but disbelievers concurrently treat them as points requiring special explanation. And likewise there are other considerations which taken by themselves constitute at least prima facie antitheistic evidences. These are matters which non-believers emphasise and in which the believer, on the other hand, sees a challenge to his faith which he feels obliged to try to meet.[20]

Hick's view is that naturalistic and non-naturalistic interpretations of the same experiential facts have the tendency to cancel each other out. He does not, however, take seriously the difference in level of generality between the prima facie theistic evidence and the prima facie antitheistic evidence. Due to the nature of the most general sort of evidence available, the natural theologian maintains that God must exist whether or not there is evil in the world, precisely because there is a world in which evil could exist. In contrast, Hick insists that some aspects of the universe are prima facie evidence that theism is true, while other aspects are prima facie evidence that naturalism is true. That is, certain items of experience "fall more naturally on one or the other side of the balance sheet."[21] Nevertheless, both the prima facie theistic evidence and the prima facie naturalistic evidence can be interpreted by their opposing frameworks. Thus, we are told, neither framework is favored over the other by the sum total of the evidence.

The bearing this has upon my argument is plain. If Hick is correct, the naturalistic hypothesis ought to be able to give some explanation for the origin of the universe even if the fact that the universe has a beginning is prima facie evidence for the theistic worldview. But as I have shown, it is unable to do this. The fact, if it is one, that the universe had a beginning is more than just prima facie evidence that God exists. The beginning of the universe is positively unexplainable apart from the hypothesis of divine creation. And since the coming to be of the universe is the most general sort of empirical phenomenon that calls for explanation, it matters not whether other features of human experience could be interpreted naturalistically. There is reason to think that the whole framework of physical reality and the pattern of human experience are ontologically dependent upon the causal activity of God. Even the so-called prima facie evidence that

God does not exist, such as the reality of evil, may not erode whatever success natural theology enjoys after the fullest possible case has been made.

Furthermore, there is reason to doubt that evil really is the prima facie evidence against God's existence that Hick takes it to be. He notes that "human wickedness and the suffering of all sentient creatures including man are not facts which would be selected by the theist as favourable premises from which to launch his own argument: they are rather difficulties which he must endeavour to meet from the wider resources of theism."[22] The reason why theists do not construct the initial premises of their argument from facts about evil has nothing to do with evil being prima facie evidence that God does not exist. While it may be true that theists are not likely to launch their argument for God's existence from premises about the experience of evil, such premises are not necessarily without positive value in presenting the total case for the existence and nature of God.

Hick states that "no one would be likely to appeal to the fact of distinctively religious experience as positive evidence for atheism, or to the fact of human and animal suffering as positive evidence for theism."[23] But this is arguable. Despite the proliferation of reductionistic accounts of religious experience, probably no one has ever argued from the distinctive quality of religious experience to the nonexistence of God. Likely or not, however, it is a matter of fact that some have interpreted the experience of evil as positive evidence for the truth of theism. Even Alvin Plantinga has recently suggested that there are good theistic arguments from the nature of evil.[24]

There are at least two ways that the presence of evil in human experience can be construed as positive evidence for the existence of God. First, to fault God for permitting the intrusion of evil into the universe requires some objective ground for making the appropriate moral distinctions that encourage skepticism regarding the possibility of God's existence. Thus, the case against God by appeal to evil depends upon a perverse use of moral judgment that can be valid only if God exists.

Second, when we consider the variety of responses humans have made to the reality of evil we discover that, as often as not, they have referred to the existence of God precisely as a way of making sense of their experience of pain and suffering. The circumspect philosopher of religion will have to give some explanation of this propensity. For every individual who defies the reality of God in the midst of personal tragedy there is another who moves toward God in faith, believing that personal pain and suffering have value.[25] C. S. Lewis expressed just this sentiment when he wrote, "God whispers to us in our pleasures, speaks in our conscience, but shouts in our pains: it is His megaphone to rouse a deaf world."[26] Richard Purtill briefly sketches an argument to theism from human indignation against injustice and suffering.[27]

It is therefore not plain whether evil is prima facie evidence that God does not exist. It might be prima facie evidence that God is concerned about the human situation and that he will act on behalf of those who suffer by causing their suffering to redound with otherwise impossible goods. So in at least two respects our contemplation of evil can lead rather unexpectedly to even deeper conviction that God exists. It may not be that evil directly evinces the existence of God. Perhaps the possibility and presence of evil in human experience only insinuates the reality of God. In any case, the possibility of arguing in this way deserves fresh consideration, for it illustrates how the weight of the total evidence, which includes the fact of evil, could positively favor the theistic interpretation of experience over the naturalistic.

The excursus on the possibility of natural theology presented in recent chapters should not distract from the overriding concern of this book, which is to stress the strategic importance of attending to the considerable resources of natural theology in any effort to formulate a viable theodicy. The erosion of the plausibility of Hick's theodicy is an invitation to all philosophers in the Judeo–Christian tradition to explore anew the possibility of natural theology, even if they are not persuaded of the specific account given here. It is to the particular features of Hick's theodicy proper that we turn next.

PART III
THEODICY PROPER

9
John Hick's View of Divine Purpose

Inquiry into the main lines of John Hick's theodicy proper must begin with his notion of teleology, for he envisions this as the "starting-point" for his formulation of "a theodicy for today."[1] This starting point "is a conception of the divine purpose for man, from which follows understanding of both moral and natural evil."[2] This chapter first examines the general principle upon which Hick's teleological theodicy is based and then evaluates his application of this principle to the problems of moral and natural evil. In Chapter 10 I develop the contrasting Augustinian view of divine purpose in relation to the reality of evil.

"SOUL-MAKING" AS DIVINE PURPOSE

Hick uses the term "soul-making" to identify the divine purpose for humanity in terms of which all evils in the world may be understood. He attributes the term to the poet John Keats, who spoke of "the vale of Soul-making" in some correspondence where he "sketches a teleological theodicy."[3] But Hick credits others, particularly Irenaeus (c. A.D. 130–202), with giving this type of theodicy its "first tentative beginnings." Other tentative hints come from Tatian (in his *Oration Against the Greeks,* c. A.D. 175) and Theophilus (in *To Autolycus,* c. A.D. 175). After a long period of dormancy, due chiefly to Augustine's great influence on Christian theodicy, soul-making themes emerge once again in the work of Friedrich Schleiermacher (1768–1834).[4] Since Irenaeus is the great precursor of this "tradition," Hick frequently names his theodicy the "Irenaean type of theodicy," which serves as the title of part III in *Evil and the God of Love.*

The Basic Postulate

It is important to grasp how Hick conceives of this divine purpose for humanity, the starting point for his theodicy: "The basic postulate is that of a divine purpose to make finite persons who have a genuine autonomy and freedom in relation to their creator and who are therefore capable of entering into personal relationship with him. To this end man has not been brought into existence as a perfect being, but as an imperfect and immature creature who is only at the beginning of a long process of development."[5] In Chapters 11 and 12 I explore some of the fundamental implications of Hick's application of the notion of soul-making to the problem of evil. His views about human nature (particularly about human free will) and about human destiny have large roles to play in his formulation of a theodicy. But these are subordinated to the more general consideration of God's purpose in creating finite creatures who have the sort of present nature and future destiny that humans do. The present chapter focuses directly on the concept of soul-making as the divine purpose for humanity. We shall be considering the status of the soul-making purpose as *the* "basic postulate" in Hick's theodicy.

In light of conclusions reached in Chapters 4 and 5 concerning Hick's religious epistemology, it might be expected that Hick's basic postulate would be that God exists, for there could be no "divine purpose" if there was no divine Being. I have described his view as a version of "postulational theism." By this I mean that for him, as for many others, the proposition "God exists" is not to be accepted on the basis of evidence. Hick does not mean that belief in God is therefore irrational. It is just that warrant for theistic belief must be construed differently. Hick does not countenance the project of a natural theology that seeks to positively demonstrate that God exists, yet he affirms the proposition that God exists. Given his approach to justified belief in the existence of God, what could be more basic than his postulate that God exists?

To raise this question is not quite the exercise in trivial pursuit that it may appear to be. The task of framing a theodicy is essentially continuous with the endeavor to recommend acceptance of the proposition that God exists. Whatever the precise nature of one's theodicy, it will always be relevant to a conception of the task and the likely outcome of a theodicy to determine how rational belief in God is to be properly characterized, as an answer to the question, What positively justifies belief in God? Since Hick's theism is postulational at the root, the positing of a divine purpose for human persons can hardly be a starting point, strictly speaking, for theodicy. He means, of course, that as a first principle for formulating a theodicy, *given* the "rational belief" that God exists, identifying some suitably plausible divine purpose for evil is properly fundamental to understanding the presence of evil in the world.

We might ask why theodicy should be addressed in terms of a divine purpose at all, even if God does exist. Nowhere does Hick explain why this is so. Perhaps he thinks it is self-evident that a theodicy must begin with a conception of the divine purpose for human creatures. And perhaps it *is* self-evident, for no one, as far as I know, has yet challenged Hick for making such an assumption. Nevertheless, some justification for positing a divine purpose does seem to be in order. Is it something about the nature of theism itself that suggests to our minds that a divine purpose for humanity is to be expected? If so, does theism contain resources conceptually rich enough to reveal what the divine purpose is? Or is our expectation of a purpose for humanity merely a projection of our own private misgivings about the ultimate meaning of personal existence? This certainly is a logical possibility.

Kurt Vonnegut, Jr., tells a parable that illustrates this possibility:

> In the beginning God created the earth, and he looked upon it in His cosmic loneliness.
>
> And God said, "Let Us make living creatures out of mud, so the mud can see what We have done."
>
> And God created every living creature that now moveth, and one was man. Mud as man alone could speak. God leaned close as mud as man sat up, looked around, and spoke. Man blinked. "What is the *purpose* of all this?" he asked politely.
>
> "Everything must have a purpose?" asked God.
>
> "Certainly," said man.
>
> "Then I leave it to you to think of one for all this," said God.
>
> And He went away.[6]

In his poem "New Year's Eve," Thomas Hardy expresses a similar sentiment, again with God answering the person who demands to know the reason for the world God has created: "Then he: 'My labours—logicless— / You may explain; not I.' "

Why suppose, as theists, that the reality of evil must serve some divine purpose? This is an interesting question to pose for Hick's basic postulate. He says, "The Irenaean way of thinking . . . is inclined to stress that we can know God's purposes and evaluations only in so far as He has revealed them to us in their relation to mankind."[7] He proceeds to argue that it is discoverable that God has certain purposes in relation to humanity and that what these purposes are can be discerned from divine revelation. But what does Hick mean by revelation? What is the locus of revelation regarding God's purposes?

There can be no mistaking what Hick believes to be the proper locus of divine revelation, at least within Christian experience. He states unequivocally that "our positive knowledge of God's nature and purpose still derives from His incarnation in Jesus Christ."[8] He therefore professes to deduce the soul-making purpose for humanity from Christological categories of the divine self-disclosure. Note, however, that he rejects any kind of propositional revelation in favor of a conception of revelation as God's incursion into human experience via revelatory events in history.[9]

The notion of propositional revelation does not accord well with Hick's belief that the universe is religiously ambiguous. In the context of his developed religious pluralism, Hick now refers to Jesus "as the one through whom my own consciousness of God has been largely formed."[10] Others will have formed their concepts of the Ultimate in other ways, presumably with the result that different purposes, or even no purpose at all, will be envisioned to account for the presence of evil in human experience.

On a propositional account of revelation the content of revelation is determined externally and carried to the recipient by language that the recipient can understand. The revelational content is not first received in some other form and then reduced to propositions for subsequent deliberation. Rather, the revelational content comes to the recipient in propositional form, perhaps through speech or writing. The possibility for rich and conceptually clear communication from God to humans is therefore much greater than it would be without propositional revelation. By means of propositional revelation God may break through the phenomenal barrier in making himself known. There is thus a greater chance of correspondence between the Real as it is in itself and the Real as it is experienced by humans when the latter is informed by God's propositional self-disclosure to them. In the use of propositional revelation, God acts to minimize the ambiguity of the religious situation.

With Hick's nonpropositional view of revelation we are once again face to face with his religious epistemology of rational belief founded upon the putatively cognitive nature of religious experience: "The religious mind experiences events both as occurring within human history and as mediating the presence and activity of God."[11] It is in this respect that the Incarnation of Jesus Christ functions as a revelatory event for believers. And what this event reveals, among other things, is a divine purpose for humanity in terms of which evil may be explained.[12]

The upshot of this explication of God's revealed purpose for humanity is that, as M. B. Ahern has observed, there is no way of knowing whether Hick's basic postulate for framing a theodicy (namely, soul-making) is true.[13] This is another weakness in Hick's system. Since the task of theodicy is continuous with the project of positively justifying belief in God, then any difficulty facing the latter will be a difficulty attending the former.

The basic postulate of soul-making, derived from God's self-disclosure in the Incarnation, must reflect the essential message of the Incarnation, which is "the active agape of God at work in human life"; therefore, "a Christian theodicy must be centred upon moral personality rather than upon nature as a whole, and its governing principle must be ethical."[14] Hick points out that God may well have many different purposes for the created order over which he is sovereign, but these must remain unknown to us. "We can glimpse only that aspect of God's purpose for His world that directly concerns ourselves."[15] This purpose can, accordingly, be construed only in terms of "bringing about the high good of man's fellowship with God."[16] But what guarantee does the theist have of this hopeful prospect that does not beg the fundamental question at issue in theodicy? It is in the nature of a teleological theodicy to seek to discover that good that is so high and final that all evil is justified as concomitant to its achievement or realization.[17]

The alleged purpose, which provides the starting point in Hick's theodicy, is God's intention "to lead [Homo sapiens] from human Bios, or the biological life of man, to that quality of Zoe, or the personal life of eternal worth, which we see in Christ."[18] That is, "man is in process of becoming the perfected being whom God is seeking to create."[19] This soul-making purpose for God's human creatures is the fulcrum of Hick's entire theodicy.

Hick's Foremost Criticism of the Augustinian Tradition

Hick states forthrightly that "the Augustinian–Thomist approach to the problem of evil is the main target of the critical part of the book" Evil and the God of Love.[20] His basic postulate of a divine purpose for humanity in terms of personal relationship with God is the precise point of contention for his "most fundamental criticism" of the Augustinian tradition in theodicy. He remarks that a "pervasive presupposition" within the classical tradition of theodicy "is the impersonal or subpersonal way in which God's relationship to His creation is prevailingly conceived."[21] In contrast to this classical approach, Hick takes the notion of a soul-making purpose for humanity to be the definitive feature in his own theodicy, the feature that distinguishes it from and improves upon the Augustinian approach.

For Hick, the real *bête noire* in the Augustinian tradition is its adoption of Plotinian "emanationist philosophy" in its use of such notions as the "principle of plenitude" and "aesthetic perfection,"[22] and, more implicitly than explicitly, the "identity of being and goodness."[23] Even the privative view of evil in the Augustinian tradition is of Neoplatonist origin.[24] All of these ideas are discussed at length in part II of *Evil and the God of Love*. Hick begins this significant section by saying that "St. Augustine . . . has probably done more than any other writer after St. Paul to shape the structure of orthodox Christian belief. . . . It is therefore with Augustine that we begin this study, though with glances back to Plotinus, through whom he absorbed so much from the surrounding thought-world of Neo-Platonism."[25]

Throughout this section of his book Hick refers to Augustine as the true "fountainhead" of the "majority report" in Christian theodicy. But in light of his constant association of Augustine with Plotinus, one might naturally expect Hick to identify Plotinus as the real fountainhead of this tradition. He does not do this, however, for he recognizes that Augustine "alters what he received from Plotinus," making the notions he adopted "more intelligible."[26]

The unifying feature of Hick's criticisms is his rejection of the Augustinian stress on the aesthetic principle in favor of an ethical principle premised on the human person's moral relationship with God. He makes seven comparative observations to clarify the differences between his own view of the divine purpose for humanity and the view embedded in the Augustinian theodicy. These observations are supposed to illustrate transparent shortcomings in the Augustinian system:[27]

1. *Emanation and creation.* God's love extends to his creatures in virtue of his bestowal of being on them, thus filling up the hierarchy of existence.

2. *The self-diffusing divine One.* The relationship between God and his human creatures is characterized by the diffusion of goodness from the One (the Good) to the other (lower-order goods) respectively.

3. *Humanity's niche in creation.* God's purpose for creating humanity is conceived in terms of humanity's fitness for filling a gap in the hierarchy of being, without which the universe would be imperfect because not fully expressive of the divine nature.

4. *Contingency of human nature.* A metaphysical conception of human personality diminishes the dignity of the person and reduces

sin to an impersonal act because human frailty leads one to expect eventual failure.

5. *Evil as nonbeing.* On a privative view of evil, sin is no longer viewed as a failure in humanity's relationship with God. It is, rather, an impersonal malfunction of being requiring a metaphysical "fix" through the application of so-called grace.

6. *Aesthetic harmony.* The premium placed on the aesthetic harmony of the whole order of being diminishes the intrinsic value of individual persons.

7. *Principle of moral balance.* Punishment is meted out by God to his creatures on the basis of merit according to the quantity of their sin, thus impersonalizing the nature of sin, which is really a "breach of personal relationship."

There are at least two reasons why it is difficult to take these misgivings about the tenets (criticisms) of the Augustinian tradition seriously: first, because the Neoplatonist principles behind them are notoriously difficult to formulate, and second, because they seem rather contrived in their unqualified application by Hick to proponents in the "central stream of the Augustinian-theodicy tradition."[28] Illtyd Trethowan rightly protests that "it would be a strange mistake to suppose that the Catholic tradition considers the 'aesthetic perfection' of the universe more important than 'the high good of man's fellowship with God.' "[29] Nevertheless, these are the points that ostensibly militate against a properly personal conception of the divine–human relationship in the Augustinian vanguard. Says Hick, "Indeed, throughout medieval theology the love of God tends to be thought of in metaphysical rather than personal terms."[30] He insists that "the category that inevitably dominates a theology based upon God's self-disclosure in Christ is the category of the personal."[31] Yet the Augustinian tradition, according to him, is misguided from the very outset because it fails to take note of the personal element informing humanity's needful understanding of God's purposes.

HICK ON MORAL AND NATURAL EVIL

Let us now consider how John Hick applies his conception of the teleological principle to both moral and natural evil. Here we are interested in how the fact of evil relates to God's purpose of soul-making for human persons as conceived by Hick. Hick himself classifies evil into these two kinds and defines each as follows: "Moral evil is evil that we human beings originate: cruel, unjust, vicious, and perverse thoughts and deeds. Natural evil is the evil that originates independently of human actions: in disease bacilli, earthquakes, storms, droughts, tornadoes, etc."[32]

Moral Evil

We begin with his account of moral evil. Recall that "the basic postulate is that of a divine purpose to make finite persons who have a genuine autonomy and freedom in relation to their creator and who are therefore capable of entering into personal relationship with him."[33] Accordingly, as in the Augustinian tradition, the notion of freedom has a prominent place in Hick's theodicy. But, as we shall see, the role freedom plays in his system differs significantly from its function in the traditional free-will approach.

Hick identifies moral evil with "the religious concept of sin," meaning that the "basic ethical ideas . . . of wrong action and bad moral character" are interpreted "as expressions of a wrong relationship with God."[34] He assumes a theological context at the outset, and it seems that his justification for doing so would be in terms of cognitively valid religious belief, as discussed in Chapter 4. On his assumption, all moral evil is an expression of "a disorientation at the very center of man's being where he stands in relationship with the Source and Lord of his life and the Determiner of his destiny."[35] Moral evil, considered as sin, constitutes "the heart of the problem of evil" because sin, as such, "belongs to our innermost nature."[36] Hence, the fundamental problem of evil can be expressed with this question: "Why has an omnipotent, omniscient, and infinitely good and loving Creator permitted sin in His universe?"[37] (Note that this question has a distinctly explanation-seeking character. It does not imply skepticism about there being both God and evil.) Hick proceeds to answer this question in terms of God's soul-making purpose for humanity.

It is interesting to note that his reply finds expression in his own version of the traditional free-will defense, which implies that it is significantly continuous with the Augustinian tradition.[38] He commits himself to two fundamental tenets of the free-will defense and owes this much at least to the classical tradition. The first concerns divine omnipotence. He writes, "The self-contradictory, or logically absurd, does not fall within the scope of God's omnipotence."[39] That is, divine omnipotence is not mitigated by what is logically impossible (such as squaring a circle).

A second tenet in the free-will approach embraced by Hick as well is the correlative relationship between moral freedom and human personality: "In order to be a person man must be free to choose right or wrong."[40] In other words, even divine omnipotence, affirmed in the first proposition, cannot make a person without bestowing freedom. To do so would be contradictory. This is especially relevant to Hick's theodicy, which is essentially teleological. Recall that, according to him, "the category that inevitably dominates a theology based upon God's self-disclosure in Christ is the category of the personal."[41] Although God might not have determined to create persons, he did. Therefore, "we can only accept this decision as basic to our existence and treat it as a premise of our thinking."[42] Since it was evidently God's purpose to create persons, it was necessary that they be created with moral freedom.

Hick's analysis of human freedom is the linchpin in his account of moral evil. His own conception of freedom also signals his point of departure from the free-will defense in the Augustinian tradition. It appears that his views about the nature of human freedom crystallize in dialogue with contemporary atheistic thinkers, like Antony Flew and J. L. Mackie, who argue that God might have so constituted persons that they would always freely choose to act uprightly.[43] Since this is a logical possibility, it would seem, Hick grants them their conclusion. However, he demurs somewhat, noting that these atheists overlook one thing:

> According to Christianity, the divine purpose for men is not only that they shall freely act rightly towards one another but that they shall also freely enter into a filial personal relationship with God Himself. There is, in other words, a religious as well as an ethical dimension to this purpose. And therefore, having granted that it would be logically possible for God so to make men that they will always freely act rightly towards each other, we must go on to ask the further question: Is it logically possible for God so to make men that they will freely respond to Himself in love and trust and faith?[44]

Hick's reply to this latter question is negative, "for it is of the essential nature of 'fiduciary' personal attitudes such as trust, respect, and affection to arise in a free being as an uncompelled response to the personal qualities of others."[45] In effect, then, he allows that persons might be constituted so as to always act uprightly toward one another without overruling their freedom with respect to one another. He thinks this is a logical possibility. But it would not be logically possible for persons to relate to God with an authentic positive fiduciary attitude if they did so as a function of their constitution. Therefore, freedom with respect to the latter opens up the possibility of inhumane actions between persons, for interpersonal human relations provide the context for individuals to register their fiduciary attachment to God.

With this creative maneuver Hick thinks he can concede the logical possibility of thwarting the intrusion of moral evil without curtailing human freedom and yet indicate why this logical possibility cannot be fully realized if God also seeks to be worshipped with authentic faith and love by human persons. But in such a scenario it is only a contingent state of affairs that God measures human fiduciary attitudes to himself in terms of their horizontal relationships with one another. Why could God not have so constituted human beings that they would always freely act uprightly toward one another and yet also guarantee their freedom to respond to God with the desirable fiduciary attitude? Could not God have ensured our freedom in our vertical relationship with him without attaching it to the character of our relationships with one another? This would seem to be no less of a logical possibility than the one recommended by Mackie and Flew. If it is, then God would presumably have foreknown it as such and could have prevented the intrusion of moral evil into human society by making the relevant adjustments.

Hick offers no principled reason for assuming that human freedom on the horizontal level must be correlative to human freedom vis-à-vis God. He asserts only that "there would be no point in the creation of finite persons unless they could be endowed with a degree of genuine freedom and independence over against their Maker. For only then could they be capable of authentic personal relationship with Him."[46] He believes that there is a strong analogy between interpersonal human relations and divine–human relations. But this point, even if correct, does not bridge the gap in question. The hidden and problematic premise in this part of his argument is that free fiduciary commitment to God necessitates the kind of freedom in human relationships that risks the eruption of moral evil between persons. But he overlooks the important difference between entailment and analogy. Accordingly, he concludes simply that the contention that "God can without contradiction be conceived to have so constituted men that they could be guaranteed always to freely act rightly in relation to one another" demonstrates "the need for a stronger conception of man's freedom *vis-à-vis* God than that used by Mackie and Flew."[47]

How, then, is human freedom to be conceived? The Flew–Mackie objection does effectively show that human nature must be somewhat determinate and not absolutely amorphous. Otherwise, freedom would be nothing more or less than random behavior.[48] In light of exigencies of this kind, brought to light by the atheist challenge, Hick proposes that human freedom should be conceived as "limited creativity." Here, the notions of a determinate human nature giving rise to certain decisions and of the possibility of unpredictable twists in the moment of decision are compressed to form a richer conception of freedom. "Thus, whilst a free action arises out of the agent's character it does not arise in a fully determined and predictable way."[49] This view allows for persons to act with creative spontaneity in relationship to God, which is a logical requirement for soul-making.

To finally account for moral evil, Hick must explain how interpersonal human relationships are affected in virtue of the freedom that is logically necessary for a fiduciary attitude toward God. I will save a fuller treatment of his anthropology for a later chapter, but I must say something here about his notion of epistemic distance. He maintains that, for genuine human freedom to obtain, whereby the individual is able to come to God voluntarily, "God must set man at a distance from Himself. . . . The kind of distance between God and man that would make room for a degree of human autonomy is epistemic distance."[50] Having been created at an epistemic distance from God, human beings find themselves in a condition that is most conducive to the purpose of responding to God freely in faith. And the manner in which such an epistemic distance is secured makes moral evil possible; indeed, this makes it "virtually inevitable."[51] The mechanism utilized by God to create human beings at the requisite epistemic distance is that of evolution. "And in causing man to evolve in this way out of lower forms of life God has placed His human creature away from the immediate divine presence, in a world with its own structure and laws in which he has a certain relative but real autonomy and freedom over against his Creator."[52] One consequence of employing this effective instrument for securing the epistemic distance of humanity from God is that *Homo sapiens* evolved as a self-centered creature. Thus, "man's spiritual location at an epistemic distance from God makes it virtually inevitable that man will organize his life apart from God and in self-centred competitiveness with his fellows."[53] This self-centeredness, arising naturally in the human person's developmental nature, accounts for the moral evil that one discovers within oneself.

In review of the main features of Hick's account of moral evil, the starting point is a conception of the divine purpose for humanity in terms of soul-making. Soul-making consists in the process whereby human persons voluntarily approach God in trust and love and worship. Hence, humans are regarded as moral personalities in relationship with God. Freedom is required for them to act as personal beings with respect to God. But freedom is guaranteed only if they are created at an epistemic distance from God. Natural evolution is the mechanism used by God to bring humanity into existence such that these conditions will be met. A consequence of this process is *Homo sapiens'* inevitable emergence as a self-centered being in a hostile world. Moral evil arises in this context of human struggle for personal survival, and the way is paved for persons to become the morally mature creatures that God intends.

The logical relationship between the essential elements in Hick's account of moral evil may be illustrated by the following sequence of propositions:

1. God's purpose for humanity is soul-making.
2. The goal of soul-making is predicated on the category of the personal.
3. A human personality must have moral freedom.
4. Moral freedom (vis-à-vis God) necessitates standing at an epistemic distance from God.
5. One's epistemic distance from God makes moral evil inevitable.

The logical sequel in this train of thought consists in the following propositions:

6. What is inevitable in God's created world is God's responsibility.
7. Therefore, God is responsible for moral evil.

There is really nothing radical about the suggestion that Hick's account of moral evil entails ultimate divine responsibility for such evil. First, recall the preliminary account of Hick's overall theodicy in Chapter 3, where I noted his conviction that both the Augustinian tradition and his own theodicy hypothesis "acknowledge God's ultimate responsibility for evil." Hick chastens the Augustinian traditionalist for an unwillingness "to state explicitly what his doctrine covertly implies," namely, that God is ultimately responsible for the existence of evil. He then proclaims that "the Irenaean, in a more rationalist vein, is willing to follow the argument to its conclusion [that is, to God's ultimate responsibility for evil]."[54]

Should there be any lingering doubt that Hick would himself be willing to draw this conclusion explicitly, consider the following remark: "This concept [the idea of divine responsibility for evil] is generated by the belief that God has determined in His absolute freedom all the conditions of creaturely existence, including those out of which sin and suffering have arisen. Given this circumstance, how can God fail to have the final responsibility for the existence of His creation in its concrete actuality, including, as it does, evil as an element within it?"[55] Hick unequivocally calls God "an ultimately responsible moral being" in this regard.[56]

Divine responsibility for evil follows from Hick's belief that evil is "a necessary element in a soul-making universe."[57] The logical formulation with which I have outlined Hick's account shows the step-by-step rationale for this belief. This belief in the omniresponsibility of God is a fundamental motivation behind Hick's universalist soteriology, which I discuss in Chapter 12.

Natural Evil

Hick's account of natural evil is also given in the context of his soul-making teleology: "If, then, God's aim in making the world is 'the bringing of many sons to glory', that aim will naturally determine the kind of world that He has created."[58] The concept of soul-making as God's purpose for humans is the starting point of his account of natural evil no less than his account of moral evil. It is reasonable to expect that the world God created is conducive to his purposes for it. Accordingly, "those who use the problem of evil as an argument against belief in God almost invariably" misconceive God's purpose in making the world. "They assume that the purpose of a loving God must be to create a hedonistic paradise; and therefore to the extent that the world is other than this, it proves to them that God is either not loving enough or not powerful enough to create such a world."[59] The basic postulate in Hick's theodicy is teleological: God's purpose for humans is soul-making, and "we can only accept this decision as basic to our existence and treat it as a premise of our thinking."[60] Consequently, we must ask: "Is this the kind of world that God might make as an environment in which moral beings may be fashioned, through their own free insights and responses, into 'children of God'?"[61] We obviously do not live in a hedonistic paradise and are not pampered by God like cosmic personal pets. But "if our general conception of God's purpose is correct the world is not intended to be a paradise, but rather the scene of a history in which human personality may be formed towards the pattern of Christ." God's purpose of soul-making includes "the realizing of the most valuable potentialities of human personality."[62]

Note that this is the first time that Hick introduces this aspect of his notion of divine teleology. Generally he describes God's purpose as one of bringing individuals to a proper awareness of himself through a freely expressed fiduciary attitude. Now he incorporates the additional element of character development and the adoption of values. This is important to his account of natural evil for reasons he does not seem to make explicit but that are apparent to the careful observer. If God's soul-making purpose is simply to allow humans the freedom to respond to his presence in personal trust, natural evil may be accounted for, but only as a mere concomitant to or consequence of setting up the conditions for this free response. By affirming that the divine purpose includes a character development program, however, Hick can give an account of natural evil as a positive expedient for the realization of God's total purpose for humanity.

As I have already indicated, Hick adapts the evolutionary account of human origins to his purposes in framing a theodicy. His account of moral evil appeals to evolution as the mechanism used by God to create human beings at the epistemic distance necessary if they are to have genuine autonomy vis-à-vis God. Such autonomy is essential to God's purpose for them in their relation to himself. By means of the emergence of *Homo sapiens* through natural evolutionary processes, this unique creature is "placed" in an environment that guarantees personal freedom in virtue of epistemic distance from God. By virtue of humanity's "solidarity" with the natural order, human awareness of God is sufficiently moderate to ensure genuine freedom.

By the same token, human creatures are so embedded in the natural order, which is a "hostile environment," that they come forth as beings in "self-centered alienation from God."[63] The hostilities of the environment from which *Homo sapiens* emerges are presumably the very order of natural evils that a comprehensive theodicy must account for. At least a limited account of natural evil is implicit (subsequently and independently made explicit) in Hick's account of moral evil in terms of postulating the notion of epistemic distance. These evils engage humans in the self-absorbing task of managing the environment just so they will not be immediately aware of the divine presence. Yet this account of natural evil is only partial. In Hick's total theodicy, natural evil serves an additional positive purpose in the divine economy.

The natural order, with its many evils, has positive value as an environment designed for the production of human moral character. God places human beings in a world that not only secures epistemic distance but that is also especially adapted to the production of such virtues of personality as self-sacrifice, care for others, devotion to the public good, courage, perseverance, skill, honesty, unselfishness, truthfulness, good faith, the capacity to love, and compassion.[64] In a different environment, where human beings never encountered hardship, "the race would consist of feckless Adams and Eves, harmless and innocent, but devoid of positive character and without the dignity of real responsibilities, tasks, and achievements." In short, while human creatures would be spoiled without becoming impish, they would not really be human either, for "any such radical alteration in the character of man's environment would involve an equally radical alteration in the nature of man himself."[65] Hick maintains that the goodness of moral human character "could not in fact be created except through a long process of creaturely experience in response to challenges and disciplines of various kinds."[66]

Thus, we find that the world that God made is most fitting in light of his soul-making purposes for humanity. The moral qualities and virtues that characterize a human being as a human being would be altogether missing were it not for the emergence of *Homo sapiens* from the kind of world ours is known to be. Humanity's solidarity with a natural order containing pain and suffering is ultimately constitutive of its very nature. Our world as it is, therefore, fulfills God's purpose as "an environment for personal life."[67] This world is a "vale" of soul-making. And this positive justification of natural evil yields the same conclusion about the locus of responsibility here previously derived concerning moral evil. That is, God is ultimately responsible for both moral and natural evils.

The following propositions illustrate the basic logic of the key notions in Hick's account of natural evil:

1. God's purpose for humanity is soul-making.
2. The goal of soul-making is predicated on the category of the personal.
3. The creation of moral personality requires the production of certain virtues.
4. Virtues of this kind can be produced only in the context of a hostile environment.
5. Such an environment makes natural evils necessary.
6. God is responsible for what is necessary for the realization of his purposes.
7. Therefore, God is ultimately responsible for natural evil.

Let us now turn to an evaluation of Hick's account of the divine purpose for humanity, which is the starting point of his theodicy proper.

DIFFICULTIES WITH HICK'S TELEOLOGY

A number of difficulties attend Hick's teleological account of evil. The first set of difficulties concerns his analysis of the locus of responsibility for evil. The second set has to do with his conception of the precise nature of the divine purpose for humanity.

The Locus of Responsibility for Evil

Trethowan has boldly announced that "the most objectionable conclusion to which Hick leads us is that God *wants* sin—he requires it if
his purposes are to be fulfilled. It is a necessary means to an end."[68]
This difficulty in Hick's theodicy is felt in several respects.

Hick admits that evil is a "necessary element in a soul-making
universe," at least as he conceives of soul-making.[69] He wishes "both
to recognize the essentially demonic nature of evil, and to maintain
the sole ultimate sovereignty and omni-responsibility of God."[70] To do
this, without begging the ultimate question in theodicy, he must give
an account of "the idea of divine responsibility for evil," and this
"depends upon our definition of responsibility."[71]

It is instructive to note how it is that he proceeds to define
responsibility with respect to God and evil. He elects to define divine
responsibility by differentiating it from human responsibility.

> Whether or not we speak of God as being ultimately responsible for
> the existence of evil depends upon our definition of responsibility.
> For there are both differences and similarities between the sense in
> which men are responsible and any sense in which God could be said
> to be responsible. Human responsibility occurs within the context of
> an existing moral law and an existing society of moral beings. But
> God is Himself the source of the moral law and the Creator of all
> beings other than Himself. In His original decision to create He was
> accordingly not responsible *under* any moral law or *to* any existing
> person.[72]

In other words, God is not *culpably* responsible for the existence of
evil. He is, rather, *ontologically* responsible for evil in that "His
decision to create the existing universe was the primary and necessary precondition for the occurrence of evil, all other conditions being
contingent upon this, and He took His decision in awareness of all that
would flow from it."[73] But as we have seen, not only was the existing
universe the primary and necessary precondition for the occurrence
of evil, but the evil itself that arose in virtue of these conditions was
necessary for the realization of God's purposes. So God is ontologically
responsible for evil in the absolute sense of being the ultimate cause
of evil in virtue of the divine will.

The Augustinian tradition, to be examined more closely in the next
chapter, may admit of divine ontological responsibility for evil in some
very qualified sense. For example, it may be that evil "results in every
case from a contingency that is necessarily involved in those determinate conditions which are themselves essential to the creation of a
universe whose ultimate end is the production and progressive devel-

opment of rational, moral selves."[74] However, it is not the case that evil *must* arise if God's ultimate purpose for humanity is to be achieved, for evil runs contrary to the will of God.[75] Evil is not a necessary means to an end but a consequence of human freedom, which is a necessary means to an end. Furthermore, evil is not a necessary consequence of human freedom but only a realized possibility. Hence, in Hick's account, God's ontological responsibility for evil is much more far-reaching. God is the first efficient cause of evil in the world, of moral evil no less than of natural evil since moral evil is the inevitable consequence of humanity's unchosen condition in the natural world. Hick must show how this stronger sense of ontological responsibility for evil does not also entail divine *moral* responsibility.

Hick can escape the conclusion that God is morally responsible for evil, given God's absolute ontological responsibility for evil, only by adopting a voluntarist account of divine goodness. It is, after all, God's moral character that is at stake in the whole theodicy issue, and if absolute goodness is integral to God's character, then moral responsibility for evil would indeed pose an insuperable problem for the existence of the theistic God. But according to Hick God is not morally responsible because there is no meaningful sense in which he could be at the time of his original decision to create.

Hick defines God's ultimacy in terms of his not being responsible "*under* any moral law or *to* any existing person."[76] What, then, can absolute divine goodness mean except "whatever God wills"? If divine goodness is defined as "whatever God wills," then God's goodness is ultimately arbitrary. God could will anything, literally, and never be impugned morally for anything, including the creation of a world with evil that served no purpose whatsoever, whether soul-making or some other. This kind of voluntarist account of God's goodness effectively short-circuits the whole theodicy question, for it removes the possibility of ever knowing what it would mean for God not to be good.

Only an essentialist (or objectivist) account of God's goodness, according to which the absolute goodness of the moral law is a direct consequence of God's nature, can meaningfully address the central concern of the problem of evil: Is God morally blameworthy for creating a world where evil can occur? The voluntarist defines out of existence the possible evil of God's decision to create such a world. But on an essentialist understanding of God's goodness it is possible to know that God cannot be responsible for evil in Hick's strong ontological sense without becoming agnostic about what it is for God to be good. Evil must not be necessary for God's purposes, and its cause must not be attributed to God. Thus, the Augustinian account of divine goodness, which absolutely precludes divine responsibility for evil, is more consistent with the overall task of theodicy.

According to Hick, responsibility for evil is shared by God and human beings. This is because the sinful acts that human individuals perform are no less theirs for being inevitable to God's purposes. Furthermore, any account of moral human freedom would fail to be meaningful apart from moral responsibility. In fact, there would be no such thing as moral evil at the human level if human beings were not somehow responsible for their acts of inhumanity to their fellow humans. But how is this an argument for human culpability? Trethowan trenchantly objects: "We are still waiting to hear how a sin which is inevitable can be anyone's responsibility except God's."[77] While sins may indeed be "our actions," if they are truly inevitable to God's purposes, and if they flow so naturally from our determinate nature since creation, in what sense are they to be regarded as morally reprehensible? It is one thing to attribute some kind of instrumental agency to beings of this sort; it is another matter to hold them accountable if they are merely instrumental agents.

The Divine Purpose for Humanity

A second set of difficulties arises in connection with Hick's conception of the divine purpose for humanity. In the Augustinian tradition, the essential goodness of God requires that we seek some other cause than God for evil. Furthermore, any theodicy that reckons evil as necessary to the realization of God's purpose for humanity cannot do justice to God's essential goodness. It must either be shown that the soul-making purpose that Hick attributes to the divine will does not entail that evil must exist or that this purpose is itself ill conceived and that God's real purpose is different.

According to Hick, God's purpose is to create persons, whereas in the Augustinian tradition, God's purpose is to allow created persons to freely choose God. With the freedom to choose God comes naturally the real possibility that one will not choose God. To direct the will away from God would be an evil; the freedom that makes such an evil possible, however, is itself a good, and a good that is greater than could be achieved if human beings had not been given freedom, for then they could not freely choose God.[78]

Now it is manifestly true that, according to the Augustinian tradition, evil would not be necessary to God's purposes for humanity, although evil would, because of God's purposes in creating humans, be made possible. Some such account of the divine purpose is required once a commitment is made to the existence of a good God who cannot be the cause of evil. As Trethowan remarks, "The alternative is to locate this mystery of iniquity not in ourselves but in the purposes of God. That I regard as fatal to theism."[79]

The only corrective, therefore, is to refine our understanding of God's purposes in light of his total character as revealed in natural theology. We cannot rely on Hick's anthropocentric category of the personal for a full determination of the divine purposes for humans, for in so doing the best that we could hope to construct is an anthropodicy (a defense of human autonomy with respect to God) rather than a theodicy (a defense of the existence and character of God in view of the reality of evil). Only natural theology can rescue our efforts from the subjectivity of discerning the thread of divine *telos* in the fabric of our ostensible nature. This the Augustinian tradition plainly recognizes.

10
The Augustinian View of Divine Purpose

The Augustinian tradition in theodicy does not resist a teleological orientation. Indeed, early proponents of this tradition specified a divine *telos* in terms of which the evil of this world may be appraised. Their conclusions on this matter certainly are the fruit of much sophisticated reasoning. They did not hesitate to borrow philosophical principles from the vault of Greek metaphysical speculation whenever they believed it would aid them in their construction of an effectual Christian natural theology. As St. Thomas Aquinas wrote of St. Augustine: "Consequently whenever Augustine, who was imbued with the doctrines of the Platonists, found in their teaching anything consistent with faith, he adopted it; and those things which he found contrary to faith he amended."[1]

The philosophical reflections of Augustine and Aquinas often receive more theological and devotional expression in their writings. They cannot be accused of neglecting the personal dimension in their formulation of a theodicy. It will not do to point out the obvious parallels, say, between Augustine and Plotinus, or between Aquinas and Aristotle, without also making reference to the vast body of practical writings in which Augustine and Aquinas meditate in a distinctly Christian manner on the personal dimensions of God's relationship with his creatures. Augustine's classic autobiography, *Confessions*, readily comes to mind, and the whole spirit in which he conducted all of his theoretical explorations reflects dependence upon and devotion to God in his search for divine enlightenment.

Jacques Maritain defends Aquinas similarly, informing us that "to understand his ideas on evil it is necessary not only to consult what he says in that particular question of the *Summa* where he considers things from the viewpoint alone of the metaphysics of nature, but also to examine the whole treatise on grace and the one on the redeeming Incarnation, and all the theological context of thomist doctrine."[2]

Leibniz too makes some notably devotional remarks in the third and fourth sections of his *Discourse on Metaphysics:*

> It seems to me that the consequences of such an opinion are wholly inconsistent with the glory of God. . . . For to think that God acts in anything without having any reason for his willing . . . is an opinion which conforms little to God's glory. . . . My opinion is that God does nothing for which he does not deserve to be glorified. . . . The general knowledge of this great truth that God acts always in the most perfect and most desirable manner possible, is in my opinion the basis of the love which we owe to God in all things. . . . I believe that it is difficult to love God truly when one, having the power to change his disposition, is not disposed to wish for that which God desires. In fact those who are not satisfied with what God does seem to me like dissatisfied subjects whose attitude is not very different from that of rebels. I hold, therefore, that on these principles, to act conformably to the love of God it is not sufficient to force oneself to be patient, we must be really satisfied with all that comes to us according to his will.[3]

Why should modern advocates of the Augustinian tradition feel obliged to apologize for staking a claim in metaphysical reasoning on behalf of Christian theology, in which "natural theology" consists?

AUGUSTINE ON BEATITUDE

It is interesting and worthwhile to investigate the manner in which prominent figures in the Augustinian tradition have incorporated a teleological notion, though limitations of space forbid an in-depth treatment of each one. Aquinas's concept of final causality in the so-called fifth way and Leibniz's conception of "the best possible world" both employ teleology in a manner that is instructive for formulating a theodicy. This in addition to the ways in which their theodicies specifically overlap Augustine's. Let us now consider how Augustine himself, the true fountainhead of classical theodicy, whom Hick censures for taking over Plotinian themes, employs a teleological principle in his own formulation of a theodicy.

Augustinian theodicy and Augustinian moral theory go hand in hand; they are to be treated together. To be more exact, the Augustinian theodicy arises out of the context of a general moral theory that the tradition embraces. And Augustine's ethic, like "the typical Greek ethic, . . . proposes an end for human conduct, namely happiness," or beatitude.[4] Such an ethic, in the very nature of the case, attests a teleological principle. Furthermore, Augustine's moral theory "centres round the dynamism of the will,"[5] a distinctively personal relation.

According to Augustine, evil arises through the exercise of human free will. Since God, who is good, cannot be the cause of evil, and since God acts justly in punishing evil deeds, it must be that the human being who sins does so willfully.[6] It is clear that this result depends upon a prior belief in the existence and absolute goodness of God. When we seek a cause for evil, what we are "really asking [is] why we do evil."[7] And Augustine's reply is that it is by our free choice that we do evil. His chief concern, therefore, is with the locus of responsibility for evil. God certainly cannot be blamed for the eventuality of evil, for God is "Creator of all good things which He Himself transcends in excellence, and the most just Ruler, as well, of all that He has created."[8]

It may seem that if free will is the means by which human individuals perform evil acts, then free will must not be a good. But Augustine argues that free choice of the will is a good, for it is given to us by God. But how could God give to us a faculty by which we could sin? The question is whether God *should* have given free will since it could be abused.[9] This is all the more significant since an omniscient God would foreknow the abuse of free will that would come about in time.

The choices are plain: either free will is a good and it must therefore have been given by God, or free choice is not a good and it could not have been given by God. If God did give free will, then the question whether he should have is moot, since God is just in all that he does. The first possibility can be expressed as follows:

1. All goods are created by God.
2. Free will is a good.
3. Therefore, God created free will.

The second possibility takes the following form:

1. God creates only goods.
2. Free will is not a good.
3. Therefore, God did not create free will.[10]

These arguments illustrate that the status of free will depends upon establishing two things: first, whether *all* good things, and *only* good things, come from God; and second, whether free will is a good. These questions, in turn, depend upon whether God even exists. So Augustine makes the following proposal: "Let us take up our search in the following order, if you will. First, how is it proved [*manifestum*] that God exists?, Second, are all things whatsoever, insofar as they are good, from God? Finally, is free will to be counted as a good? When we have answered these three questions, it will be quite clear, I think, whether free will was rightly given."[11]

Augustine proceeds, then, with the first question—whether God exists. The form of his argument for the existence of God will not be repeated here. We have simply to recall from Chapter 2 how Augustine concludes that the existence of God is indubitable. He proceeds to the next question—whether all good things come from God. Here it is the character of Augustine's God that is at issue. And, of course, he concludes that "all good things come from God," by which he means, as well, *only* good things come from God.[12] With the existence and absolute goodness of God thus established, which verities together entail that all good things come from God, only one question remains: "Whether we can establish that free will is to be numbered among the goods."[13] At this crucial point in his cumulative argument Augustine invokes a distinctly teleological principle. An analysis of free will reveals it to be that faculty in the human soul by which, in choosing to live rightly, this soul achieves its proper end, namely, happiness.

Free will is known to be good because of the purpose it serves. That purpose is construed in terms of the judgment that "no righteous act could be performed except by free choice of the will, and . . . that God gave it for this reason."[14] That is, human free will is a necessary condition of genuine human moral responsibility. Augustine reasons that "the happy life—that disposition of the spirit which clings to immutable goods—is man's proper and primary good."[15] And this is what it means "to live rightly": choosing by an act of the will to "cling to immutable goods." It is this clinging to immutable goods that results in beatitude.

What is meant by "immutable goods" is evident from Augustine's argument for the existence of God, an argument based on eternal and immutable truths. These immutable goods converge in God himself. Thus, as Frederick Copleston points out, "Just as the human mind perceives eternal theoretic truths in the light of God, so it perceives, in the same light, practical truths or principles which should direct the free will."[16] There is a divine law implanted within human nature to seek happiness. This is the human person's proper end; it is constitutive of human nature to pursue this divinely ordained objective. But one's end is not merely that one should pursue happiness by living rightly, but that one should discover happiness when, in living rightly, one sees God. Not only was the human person made to seek happiness, it is God's plan that humans find happiness fully and finally only in God. The means for achieving this end are not imposed upon individuals. Persons have free wills that, when properly directed, deliver that happiness that human persons naturally seek.

While it comes naturally for all to seek happiness, it does not necessarily come naturally for persons to seek it by directing their wills to the adoration of God and his will. It is in the proper direction of free will that a "greater good" may be realized than could be if persons were not free.[17] Freedom is a necessary condition for human individuals to live rightly, for they could not live rightly in any meaningful sense if they did so involuntarily. But freedom includes the possibility that they might direct their wills away from immutable goods in their desire for happiness. Such turning of the will away from (*aversio*) immutable goods and turning it toward (*conversio*) its own private good, or toward lower goods, results in unhappiness as its own just punishment.[18] That is, happiness, the proper end of human persons, can be achieved only through right living, which consists in turning the will toward God, and this happiness is forfeited whenever one sins by turning the will toward something else in its pursuit of happiness.

It is quite evident that Augustine employs a teleological principle in his account of the origin of evil, and that this end is conceived in terms of humanity's relationship with God. The Augustinian theodicy incorporates the very element of personal relationship that Hick demands in his own analysis. Evil arises when the will is not directed to its proper end. But how does Augustine ascertain the proper end of humanity? His argument for the existence of God supplies the necessary link. The standard by which persons judge what true happiness is must be grounded in immutable truth. And, according to Augustine's theistic argument, immutable truths require the existence of God as the ground of truth. One's search for the immutable, which is natural enough, leads one to God, and upon discovering God the soul reposes. "For Thou hast made us for Thyself and our hearts are restless till they rest in Thee."[19]

As a result, Augustine's teleological principle has a dual status. On the one hand, it follows logically on the heels of his argument for the existence of God. It is not simply postulated arbitrarily out of some kind of practical necessity. Nevertheless, on the other hand, it gives expression to that which is discoverable in human experience, that sense of being impelled to seek a relationship with God. "St. Augustine, then, in no way denies what we call a 'natural' or 'rational' knowledge of God; but this rational knowledge of God is viewed in close connection with the soul's searching for beatifying Truth and is seen as itself a kind of self-revelation of God."[20] Copleston notes that this self-revelation "is completed in the full revelation through Christ and confirmed in the Christian life of prayer."[21]

Augustine's view of the organic unity of faith and reason in human experience is further manifested in his treatise *De libero arbitrio voluntatis,* where he says:

> Whatever reasoning we performed, within our limited means, concerning such a great question was directed toward *what was obvious,* with *God Himself assisting us* in so perilous a course. These two *facts,* nevertheless, that God exists and that all goods come from Him, were thus discussed—even though we *previously believed them in firm faith*—in such a way that this third question, that free will is to be numbered among the goods, might also appear in *the clearest light.*[22]

That beatitude that all persons seek is known to have *objective* ontological status by means of "a sure though somewhat tenuous form of reasoning."[23]

THE DOCTRINE OF PRIVATION

Aquinas wrote, "Though evil is neither good nor of God, nevertheless to understand it is both good and from God."[24] Part of understanding evil consists in answering the question, What is the nature of evil? As I showed in Chapter 2, the Augustinian tradition answers by saying that evil is a privation. Since the doctrine of privation is often met with incredulity (or something worse) by contemporary philosophers, something needs to be said about the plausibility of this account of evil.

Aquinas concluded that "divine causality reaches to all *beings,* not only in their specific but also in their individual principles, not only in immortal but also in mortal beings. In whatsoever sense they can be said to exist, all things are divinely directed to their ends."[25] This becomes the principal motivation for regarding evil as privation. G. Stanley Kane, who does not accept the doctrine of privation, summarizes the argument admirably:

> Christian doctrine holds that God is the creator of all things. If evil is something that has a positive substance or nature of its own, it would follow that God created evil. If, on the other hand, evil does not have a positive nature but is merely a privation, then the inference from the premise that God created everything to the conclusion that God created evil can be avoided, for the proposition that God created everything is interpreted to mean only that he created everything that has a positive nature. The significance of the privation theory for the question of the origin or cause of evil is thus primarily negative. It enables the theist to avoid the doctrine that God directly created evil.[26]

Kane is not convinced, however, that Augustine and his followers really needed to conceive of evil as privation to absolve God of any moral responsibility for evil. He reasons: "The crucial issue in considering the question of God and evil . . . is whether there is morally sufficient reason for him to create a world in which these evils occur." It is not necessary to argue that God could not have created evil if it is possible instead to argue that "God did indeed create evils when he made the world but that he was morally justified in doing so since these evils are logically necessary to the fulfillment of a divine purpose that is surpassingly good."[27] But then, what evil did God create? According to the deposit of Christian revelation, which informs the Augustinian view, all that God created was declared by God himself to be good.[28]

Kane also complains that "to ground a denial that God directly created evil on a theory of the nature of evil as privation looks very much like a tour de force of definition. Things are so logically defined that it is logically impossible for God directly to create evil."[29] But he fails to notice that the Augustinian denial that God directly created evil is not grounded in any definition of evil. The ground for the denial that God directly created evil is this: God alone creates, and anything that God creates directly is good and therefore cannot be evil. From this it follows that evil must not be created by God and, by extension, that evil is not a created substance. So the definition of evil as privation is grounded in the supposition that God cannot create evil. Thus, the primary reasons for defining evil in this way are "intratheistic."[30]

Even if evil is defined as a privation simply to save the hypothesis of theism (that is, to get God off the hook), the doctrine is not for that reason false. We cannot infer that evil must not be a privation on the grounds that we do not know that it is a privation. Of course, the Augustinian theist does not adopt this definition of evil as a kind of sufficient reason for thinking that God is not responsible for the existence of evil. It is just that, since evil is a reality and not an illusion, and yet it cannot be a substance because all substances are created by God and are therefore inherently good, evil must be a privation of some kind. The notion of privation is not a tour de force of definition, nor is it a veil for the theist to hide behind to say that God cannot cause evil. It is more like a product of transcendental reasoning.

If the creation of evil in the world was logically necessary to the fulfillment of the divine purposes in creating the world, then of course God not only might have but must have created evil. Kane has not, however, demonstrated that evil is logically necessary to the fulfillment of God's purposes. The Augustinian agrees that the possibility of moral evil is logically necessary to the fulfillment of God's purposes.

God directly causes there to be free persons who in turn may cause moral evil. But even they are not efficient causes of evil, since they can will only what is presented to them as some good. When they do not will the good that they ought to, evil is the result. A defect in their willing accounts for the moral evil they bring about. Free persons are thus the accidental causes of evil.

Kane thinks that God might be morally justified in creating evils if "these evils are logically necessary to the fulfillment of a divine purpose that is surpassingly good."[31] It might turn out, however, as Bill Anglin and Stewart Goetz have suggested, that "any function which something inherently evil might serve in the fulfillment of a surpassingly good divine purpose could equally well be served by a privative evil."[32] In that case, no evil that is logically necessary to some divine purpose would necessarily be created by God.

Anglin and Goetz, interpreting Augustine, have stated very briefly what might be construed as a paradigm case argument for accepting the doctrine of privation:

> A typical evil involves no more or less than the loss of some transitory good or the failure to get some object of desire.
> Whatever always accompanies a typical example of something is essential to it.
> Thus privation and nothing but privation is essential to evil.[33]

If it is true of any clear case of evil that the only difference between that instance of evil and its contrary good is the loss of some good or the failure to obtain some desired object, then probably this difference is constitutive of the evil in that case. And since this is true of clear cases of evil, we have reason to think it is true of other cases as well. If Anglin and Goetz are right, then ordinary experience and an analysis of what we mean when we say that something is evil may add plausibility to the doctrine of privation.

There might be cases of evil that are less clearly privative, that may even appear to be counterexamples to the definition, but that are not genuine counterexamples. The possible truth of the generalization that all evil is privative is preserved as long as any alleged counterexample can be answered with a coherent description of how privation might yet be constitutive of the evil in question.

What is interesting about this proposal is that Anglin and Goetz have attempted to confirm the Augustinian definition of evil by an appeal to experience. It is arguable, however, whether either Augustine or Aquinas derived the privation theory inductively as the best way to explain typical cases of evil.[34] Nevertheless, Aquinas did have this to say: "Hence the meaning of evil depends on the meaning of good. Now everything desirable is good, and since every nature loves its own being and perfection, it must be said that the being and perfection of any nature has the force of good. Consequently it cannot be that evil signifies a being, or form, or nature. We are left, therefore, to draw the conclusion that evil signifies some absence of good."[35] In other words, what we mean by calling something evil depends upon what we take to be good. Ordinarily, we determine that something is evil only in reference to some good that is relevantly affected (that is, diminished).

THE PROBLEM OF GRATUITOUS EVIL

Antitheists who acknowledge that evil is not inconsistent with the existence of God often instead argue that the presence of evil makes it highly likely that God does not exist.[36] In connection with this thesis is a developing literature on the significance of so-called gratuitous evil for questions about the existence and fairness of God. Gratuitous evil is evil that serves either no purpose at all or no purpose in God's plan that could not be served without that particular instance or degree of evil. William Rowe, for one, has argued both that gratuitous evil would, if it existed, present a serious challenge to traditional theism and that there probably is gratuitous evil in the world. His argument for atheism "based on the profusion of one sort of evil" is as follows:

1. There exist instances of intense suffering which an omnipotent, omniscient being could have prevented without thereby preventing the occurrence of any greater good.
2. An omniscient, wholly good being would prevent the occurrence of any intense suffering it could, unless it could not do so without thereby preventing the occurrence of some greater good.

Therefore,

3. There does not exist an omnipotent, omniscient, wholly good being.[37]

A few theists, who also think it either likely or possible that there is gratuitous evil in the world, have tried to show that the presence of gratuitous evil in no way undermines the traditional view of God. Michael Peterson has suggested that God does not act with "meticulous providence" such that we can expect him to prevent all gratuitous evils in the world.[38] Ronald Nash, without committing himself to the reality of gratuitous evil, argues that, even if there really were gratuitous evils, they would not count against the existence of God.[39] Peter van Inwagen thinks that "much of what goes on in the world, even much of what seems significant and important to us, is no part of God's plan—and certainly not a part of anyone *else's* plan—and is therefore due simply to chance."[40] When defining a chance event he says: "The event or state of affairs is without purpose or significance; it is not a part of anyone's plan; it serves no one's end; and it might very well have not been."[41] What can be said about the theist who reasons in this fashion?

For one thing, those in theistic quarters who do allow that gratuitous evil exists often are not very impressed with the possibility of natural theology. For example, Peterson states that "a believer may argue that he has convincing proof of God's existence on other grounds, and hence that he knows that the problem of evil must have some answer. Presently, there do not appear to be any such arguments which can be comfortably accepted."[42] He apparently would not appeal to the resources of natural theology in responding to the challenge from so-called gratuitous evil.

Peterson does not say what sort of thing a proof would have to be before it can be "comfortably accepted." Nor does he say why it should matter whether a theistic argument appears acceptable to some proper subset of philosophers. In fact, his claim is stated so generally that it appears that he does not even know of the confidence many contemporary philosophers have in the possibility of natural theology. Furthermore, what Peterson says about theistic arguments holds as well for defenses against the problem of evil. A respectable number of philosophers would say, "There do not appear to be any theodicies which can be comfortably accepted." What is sauce for the goose is sauce for the gander. (Of course, it could also be argued with some plausibility that while many atheologians appeal to the reality of evil as evidence that God does not exist, there is no overwhelming consensus among them about how the argument from evil for the nonexistence of God ought properly to be formulated. Can the general problem of evil therefore be safely ignored?)

If Peterson does not think that natural theology justifies belief in God, he must think that belief in God is to be justified in some other way. He is, after all, a theist with a justificatory task, namely, the articulation of a defense against the problem of evil. If he rests the justification of belief in God upon the quality of religious experience, then he must face the difficulty of justifying belief in God in the face of "gratuitous evil," which he thinks is a feature of human experience. However, the natural theologian can allow that

1. If there is gratuitous evil in the world then there is not an all-powerful, perfectly good God.

Statement (1) is logically equivalent to,

2. If there is an all-powerful, perfectly good God, then there is no gratuitous evil in the world.

If, on the basis of natural theology, the theist is justified in believing that,

3. There is an all-powerful, perfectly good God;

then the theist is justified in thinking that,

4. There is no gratuitous evil in the world.

So the natural theologian does not need to argue for

5. If there is gratuitous evil it does not falsify theism.

Second, there is a reason why it might be imprudent to accept the assumption that there is gratuitous evil in the world (evil that is not justified in terms of God's having a purpose for it). By doing so, Peterson and van Inwagen countenance a state of affairs that it is plausible to think would rule out the existence of God. It is desirable, however, that theists be able to describe in a consistent fashion states of affairs that would, if they obtained, falsify the proposition that God exists. I submit that the existence of genuinely gratuitous evil is just the sort of state of affairs that could exclude the existence of God.

It does not worry me in the least that admitting this will ever lead to the actual falsification of theism, for two reasons: first, because no one who denies that God exists knows what it would be gratuitous for God to permit (and, of course, if God does not exist, then all evil is gratuitous— but then so is everything else); and second, because God does exist, so there must not be any gratuitous evil. We are in a much better position noetically to judge that there must not be any gratuitous evil because God exists than to judge that since there is gratuitous evil in the world there must not be a God who is all-powerful and perfectly good (or that, since there is gratuitous evil God must not practice meticulous providence). That is, it is far easier to be sure that God exists than it is to be sure that there really are gratuitous evils in the world.[43]

The theistic commitment must seem perfectly empty to those who suspect that we have attempted to seal off by definition all possible avenues of criticism of theism. This symptom of current trends in philosophical theology does not bode well for theism. It is an unfortunate consequence of forbidding that gratuitous evil could preclude the existence of God since the claim itself depends upon revising the classical theistic conception of divine providence.

Third, the argument from gratuitous evil rests upon a mistake, and that is the mistake of thinking that we *know* there are gratuitous evils in the world. Arguably, only an omniscient being could know such a thing. Thus, while an atheist may want to argue that the reality of gratuitous evils cannot be ruled out a priori, I would stress that they cannot be ruled in a posteriori. And this is what really matters. This fact places an impossible burden of proof upon the nonbeliever who would cite gratuitous evil as evidence for the nonexistence of God. This being the case, trying to show that gratuious evil does not count against the existence of God does not seem necessary.

Incidentally, those who are confident that there is gratuitous evil, for the reasons they say they are, ought to be even more confident that God exists. Notice the incommensurability between the sort of evidence that is relevant to their claim that there is gratuitous evil and the evidence relevant to the natural theologian's claim that God exists. It is only relatively weakly apparent that gratuitous evil exists. The existence of God is much more apparent. We can give an alternative explanation for any evil that seems to be gratuitous. But we can provide no alternative to explaining the origin of the universe in terms of the existence of God.[44] Therefore, it is simply false to say that "accepting the existence of some gratuitous evil is more consonant with our common experience than is the position which denies gratuitous evil *a priori.*"[45] (Actually, to have natural-theology reasons for thinking that God exists and that therefore there is no gratuitous evil in the world is not, strictly speaking, to deny gratuitous evil a priori.)

Moreover, it is dangerous to think that accepting gratuitous evil is "more consonant with our common experience," and then to extricate the principle of meticulous providence from "the interpretation of theistic commitment" to evade accountability.[46] How far are we willing to go in allowing appearances to determine what can and cannot be included in an interpretation of theistic commitment? How shall we judge the relative weight of appearances that occur together in experience? On the one hand, it appears both to theists and to nontheists that there is gratuitous evil in the world. On the other hand, it appears that if there is gratuitous evil then God does not exist.

In reality, this distinction, which is crucial to Peterson's thesis, is somewhat contrived, for these appearances go hand in hand. That is, they occur together in human experience. For most persons the appearance that God must not exist if there is gratuitous evil in the world is integral to their feeling that there is gratuitous evil. As a phenomenological reading of the experience of seemingly gratuitous evil, if there is gratuitous evil then God does not exist. These are formally distinguishable features of a unitary pattern of the way things seem to those bothered by this problem. If we make the formal distinction, however, it will be difficult to assign a greater value to one appearance than to another. In any case, the further one goes in the direction of abstraction here, the further from the existential feel of the original appearance one gets. Since the negative implication for the existence of God is carried in the appearance that there is gratuitous evil, any account that allows that there is gratuitous evil but forbids the implication fails to take the appearance as such seriously. And any account that takes the appearance of gratuitous evil seriously must take with equal seriousness the appearance that this reflects negatively on the existence of God.

It might seem rather innocuous to allow that, since God does exist, either there is no gratuitous evil or, if there is gratuitous evil, it does not falsify the proposition that God exists. That is, there may seem to be no harm in accepting the full disjunction rather than committing to one or the other disjuncts in defense of theism. But the reasons for accepting one or the other disjunct have to do with our reasons for thinking in each case that gratuitous evil does not falsify theism. And there is an important difference here. In my account we have reasons for thinking this because we have good antecedent and logically independent reasons for thinking that God exists. In contrast, Peterson believes this because he denies a doctrine of meticulous providence (or the sovereignty of God as traditionally conceived). It might be said that if we can be sure both that God exists and that there is gratuitous evil in the world, then we can be sure that gratuitous evil does not falsify the existence of God. But it is not clear how, from a reading of those theists who allow the existence of gratuitous evil, we can be sure that God exists. They are reasonably sure that gratuitous evil exists, however. And they apparently do not think that their positive reasons for believing in God are good enough to overcome the challenge from apparently gratuitous evil.

I myself think it best to circumvent the argument from evil of *any* kind (including alleged gratuitous evil) by showing first how we can be confident that God does exist. It seems much more intuitively plausible to me that if God exists then there is no gratuitous evil, than that gratuitous evil does not rule out the existence of God because God does not engage in meticulous providence. For one thing, to be sure that God does not practice meticulous providence presupposes that God exists. Moreover, I think I can agree with nontheists that God must be less than perfectly good if he is all-powerful but permits gratuitous evil. The admissibility of gratuitous evil largely depends upon what one takes theism to entail. Classical Christian theism is inclusive of some conception of divine providence. On the strength of their reading of Christian Scripture, Christian theists have traditionally believed that divine providence is "meticulous," that God is "ubiquitously meddlesome" even.[47] Many contemporary Christian theists who hold this belief will probably be reluctant to relinquish it in favor of thinking that there is gratuitous evil in the world. What is more likely is that they will chasten the impression that there is gratuitous evil in the world rather than suffer a change in their conception of the divine nature. This, I think, is reasonable for them to do.

The chief reason (if not the only reason) for allowing that there is gratuitous evil is that it seems this way to us. Granted, it does even for me at times seem that certain evils must be pointless. But some have gone on to say:

> Theism isn't worth much if it doesn't help people make sense of the world in which they live. This world is obviously a place in which large amounts of evil that often appears senseless and irrational exists. For many, the arguments [presented here] (which assume the reality of gratuitous evils) help make sense of all this. . . . A universe created by God can contain particular instances of evil that are just as senseless and irrational as they appear.[48]

I find it difficult to accept this for what it means for there to be gratuitous evil is that there is evil that does not make sense. There does not seem to me to be any pragmatic comfort in knowing that there are evils that just happen, that God could have prevented and that serve no purpose in his plan, but that he is somehow justified in permitting. I do not see what reasons there could be at all apart from any reference to the divine purpose, particularly if God could exercise meticulous providence if he wanted to. I even wonder, were it in God's power to do so, whether God could fail to exercise meticulous providence.

The same difficulty lies back of Peterson's claim that "not only are real and potential gratuitous evils not a devastating problem for a theistic perspective, but, properly understood, they are a part of a world order which seems to be precisely the kind God *would* create to provide for certain goods."[49] If we are to expect that God would permit gratuitous evil in the interests of producing certain goods, then gratuitous evil is not finally gratuitous. It has at least a metapurpose, which is what traditional theists have been saying all along. Peterson seems to think that God, being the sort of being that he is, makes it predictable that there would be gratuitous evil in the created world. But I am not sure that we could predict even "significant evil" (that is, nongratuitous evil); certainly we could not predict that there would be gratuitous evil, since that is just the sort of evil that could not be predicted since its predictability would depend upon antecedent conditions that would make it likely. But since the evil in question is supposed to be gratuitous, there could be no such conditions, for these would reflect divine purposes for allowing evil.

As employed in the existing literature, labels like "gratuitous evil" and "meticulous providence" are probably too vague to be very helpful in discussions of the problem of evil. If the doctrine of meticulous providence were to be defined in a way that makes all evil necessary to the plan of God, then I would be reluctant to accept that version of the doctrine. On the other hand, if the denial of meticulous providence means that some evil is not redeemable, then I am not prepared to repudiate the doctrine of meticulous providence. In my view, if God exists, then all evil is in some sense redeemable, though not necessary to the realization of God's purposes. And I assume that some version of the doctrine of meticulous providence is needed to guarantee that all evil is finally redeemable. I take it that this view is in conflict with the supposition that there is gratuitous evil in the world.

Hick has also addressed the question of the admissibility of gratuitous evil: "Let the hypothesis of a divine purpose of soul-making be adopted, and let it be further granted that an environment which is to serve this purpose cannot be a permanent hedonistic paradise but must offer to man real tasks, challenges, and problems. Still the question must be asked: Need the world contain the more extreme and crushing evils which it in fact contains?"[50] Hick recognizes that the particular problem in view here "does not consist in the occurrence of pain and suffering as such. . . . The problem consists rather in the fact that instead of serving a constructive purpose pain and misery seem to be distributed in random and meaningless ways."[51] But Hick does not seek to escape this difficulty by denying the principle of meticulous providence. If anything, Hick has radicalized the principle of providence so that the play of divine providence is meticulous in a way that makes God ultimately responsible for all evil.

In answer to the challenge from "dysteleological evil" (Hick's phrase for gratuitous evil), Hick candidly admits, "I do not now have an alternative theory to offer that would explain in any rational or ethical way why men suffer as they do. *The only appeal left is to mystery.* . . . It may be that the very mysteriousness of this life is an important aspect of its character as a sphere of soul-making."[52] This "frank appeal to the positive value of mystery" depends upon the possibility that seemingly gratuitous evils "contribute to the character of the world as a place in which true human goodness can occur and in which loving sympathy and compassionate self-sacrifice can take place."[53] In other words, they serve the ultimate purposes of soul-making.

Hick denies the serviceability of natural theology but not the principle of meticulous providence. He resists the tendency to think there is gratuitous evil in the world. At least his soul-making theodicy can be interpreted in this way. To the extent that he denies the existence of dysteleological evil he is in company with traditional Augustinians. Since the Augustinian tradition relies upon natural theology to justify belief in God, however, there is no need to respond to the challenge from alleged gratuitous evil by appealing to mystery in the way Hick does. True, many evils that occur seem excessive, even to the natural theologian. But the natural theologian has faith that the positive value of such apparently fruitless evil lies hidden in the unfathomable purposes of God. Such faith, however, is grounded in the positively justified conviction that God exists. While the particular value served by apparently gratuitous evil remains a mystery, that such evil does serve some good purpose is no mystery.

NATURAL EVIL

It is clear that the notion of free will is prominent in the Augustinian account of the problem of evil. The tradition has been aptly called a "Free Will Theodicy."[54] And it is no coincidence that Augustine named his treatise on evil *De libero arbitrio voluntatis* (*On Free Choice of the Will*). In it he is concerned with the origin of evil and with the allegation that God must be the cause of evil. His thesis is that human free will is the cause of evil, and his theodicy, so conceived, is chiefly an account of the origin of moral evil. One must note, however, that in the Augustinian tradition, this free-will theodicy is extended to explain the origin of natural evil as well. It has been common for critics of this tradition to overlook the relevance of the free-will account for natural evils in the world. Nevertheless, Augustinian thinkers have maintained that natural evils are either themselves occasions of moral evil, or a form of divine discipline for moral failure, or the going wrong of natural laws in a universe in which significant human freedom is to be a real possibility, or some combination of the above.

Augustine himself attributes most natural evil to Satan, who is a free moral agent, and some natural evil to divine retribution. Thus, even natural evils are "broadly moral," as Alvin Plantinga says.[55]

Plantinga too has appealed to the logical possibility that what we call natural evil is due to the free action of Satan and his cronies. In contrast to Augustine, however, Plantinga does not make this observation a feature of any sort of theodicy. Rather, it is merely a part of his defense of the claim that the reality of natural evil is compatible with the existence of God in the same way that the moral evil perpetrated by humans is compatible with the existence of God. Of the possibility that much natural evil can be attributed to nonhuman free agents of superhuman power, Plantinga concludes that "the Free Will Defender, of course, does not assert that this is *true;* he says only that it is *possible.*"[56] Richard Swinburne concurs: "This assumption [that fallen angels with free wills have subjected our world to certain 'natural' evils], it seems to me, will do the job [that is, will show that the existence of such evils is compatible with the existence of God], and is not *clearly* false."[57]

Bruce Reichenbach takes a different approach that is also compatible with the general contours of Augustinian theodicy. He offers an explanation of natural evil in terms of the operation of natural law:

> In general what I want to argue is that the natural evils which human persons (and animals) experience (by and large) are not willed by God, but are the consequences of the outworking upon sentient creatures of the natural laws according to which God's creation operates. This creation, in order to make possible the existence of moral agents (in this case, human persons), had to be ordered according to some set of natural laws. Consequently, the possibility arises that sentient creatures like ourselves can be negatively affected by the outworkings of these laws in nature, such that we experience pain, suffering, disability, disutility, and at times the frustration of our good desires.[58]

Here the ordering of creation according to natural laws is for the sake of the freedom of moral creatures. As Stuart Hackett, a defender of this view, contends, "Ethical freedom would not exist apart from its determination from the law of God's being and the existence of a law-abiding universe which makes free acts possible."[59] Both Hackett and Reichenbach admit other considerations into their overall account of natural evil. In any case, they deny that God is responsible for evil and assert that evil arises either as a direct result of morally free acts or "through misappropriate adjustment to the order of natural law."[60]

At any rate, natural evils are connected with the value God places upon protecting human freedom for the sake of human beatitude. As long as the view expressed here does not entail the necessity of evil for the realization of divine purposes, which ultimately makes God the responsible cause of evil, such an account of natural evil is compatible with the Augustinian tradition in general.

In the next chapter we shall investigate Hick's conception of free will, note the problematic role this conception plays in his own theodicy, and compare Hick's account of these matters with that of the Augustinian tradition.

11
Free Will and Evil

It has been necessary to address certain aspects of John Hick's anthropology at various intervals in the discussion of other features of his theodicy. Both his epistemology and his teleology reveal that human personal development is the focal point of his reflections on theodicy. Religious knowledge proceeds from personal human experience, and experience, interpreted religiously, reveals a divine purpose for humanity. Furthermore, Hick assumes a modified free-will defense in his account of both moral and natural evil. Anthropological principles are certainly relevant to any theodicy that accounts for evil in terms of the concept of human freedom.

In this chapter I compare Hick's conception of human freedom more closely with the notion of free will found in the Augustinian tradition of theodicy. I argue that, due to an unsubstantiated assumption about its conception of the goodness of original creation, Hick prematurely jettisons the Augustinian view of human freedom, and that the view of freedom he prefers is inconsistent. Since his concept of human freedom is central to his account of evil, his theodicy may initially be mistaken for the traditional free-will defense. This is obviously a very unlikely parallel, since he makes it quite plain that the Augustinian tradition appears bankrupt to him. As it turns out, the principal difference between the two views (apart from their respective stakes in natural theology) comes precisely at this point: how each conceives of the nature of human freedom and of its relevance in forging a theodicy.

Some philosophers have detected the subtle shift in Hick's conception of the relevance of human freedom for the construction of a theodicy, and one critic has called his view a "hybrid free-will defense."[1] In my own estimation it is more apposite to describe Hick's position as a "quasi-free-will defense." I begin with a background description of the context in which his notion of human freedom is constructed. I then examine two anthropological concepts in his system in terms of which human freedom is conceived and a theodicy is formulated.

CHARACTER DETERMINISM AND HUMAN FREEDOM

Hick's account of human freedom is developed in response to a challenge posed by some atheist philosophers, most notably Antony Flew and J. L. Mackie. This challenge, already discussed briefly in Chapter 10, consists in the claim that "God might have made His human creatures so that they would always in fact freely choose the right."[2] The logic of this argument may be stated as follows:

1. An omnipotent God can achieve anything that is logically possible.
2. It is logically possible for a free moral creature to be constituted in such a way as to always freely choose the good.
3. Therefore, an omnipotent God could create a being who would always freely choose the good.

This argument rests on a definition of freedom according to which a free action is one "that is not externally compelled but flows from the nature of the agent."[3] The idea conveyed here is that a created being as such has a determinate nature. Such a being is therefore free only within the divinely ordained parameters of its particular constitution. Human nature, it is thought, may be so constituted that human beings would always will to act rightly, and that they therefore always would act rightly. The traditional free-will approach resists this challenge by contesting the truth of the claim that God could guarantee that humans *would* always freely choose to act rightly, although no difficulty follows from the logical possibility that humans always *could* choose to act rightly in virtue of their original creaturely freedom. But Hick does not proceed in this fashion. Rather, he believes that the Flew–Mackie objection to the free-will defense, based on the logical possibilities open to an omnipotent Creator, is successful.[4]

Hick's deference to Flew and Mackie on this point paves the way for his account of human freedom. This is reflected in the account Hick gives of the creation of *Homo sapiens,* at which time human nature was determinately constituted. Two anthropological notions, bearing an important mutual relationship, are formulated in his attempt to characterize the true nature of human freedom and its relevance for theodicy. The first is his fundamentally biological conception of the two-stage creation of human beings, and the second is his basically theological idea of epistemic distance.

Biological Aspect: The Two-Stage Creation of Humankind

Modern scientific data lead Hick to posit a two-stage creation of humankind, with certain implications for humanity's moral and spiritual status that are relevant for framing a theodicy.

God's soul-making purpose for humanity requires "a milieu in which the most valuable kind of moral nature can be developed."[5] Hick reasons that, while "we cannot expect to be able to deduce our actual world in its concrete character, and our actual human nature as part of it, from the general concept of spiritually and morally immature creatures developing in an appropriate environment,"[6] the demand that a theodicy hypothesis "be consistent with the data . . . of the world, in respect both of the latter's general character as revealed by scientific enquiry and of the specific facts of moral and natural evil,"[7] leads the modern theodicist to "follow out the implications of the acknowledgment that human beings were created, through the evolutionary process, as morally and spiritually imperfect creatures."[8] In other words, modern biological anthropology places certain constraints upon any Christian thinker who sets out to formulate a rationally credible theodicy. "In the light of modern anthropological knowledge some form of two-stage conception of the creation of man has become an almost unavoidable Christian tenet."[9] In the first stage, by evolutionary means human beings emerge as *Homo sapiens*. In the second stage they mature as free moral creatures.

The implications of modern biological anthropology for humanity's moral and spiritual constitution flow from humanity's "continuity" with the natural order in virtue of its evolutionary emergence from that order. "As animal organisms, integral to the whole ecology of life, we are programmed for survival." Humanity's "survival instinct" derives from its organic unity with "the evolving life of this planet," and "in his basic animal self-regardingness humankind was, and is, morally imperfect." This moral imperfection of human beings inheres in their nature from the very beginning. Their determinate character finds expression in the perpetration of all manner of moral evil, both individual and corporate. In this respect we are not free, for we did not select the conditions of our origin. "The ultimate responsibility for humankind's existence, as a morally imperfect creature, can only rest with the Creator."[10] Nevertheless, this initial stage of creation is preparatory for the next. That is, humanity's solidarity with the natural order is the divine means for securing that measure of epistemic distance between God and humans that will ensure genuine human freedom in relation to God.

Theological Aspect:
Humanity's Epistemic Distance from God

Homo sapiens' appearance on the scene in a morally imperfect state is not superfluous, for it serves an important theological purpose in the divine economy. This is only "the beginning of a long process of further growth and development."[11]

The creation of human beings through the process of biological evolution was expedient for establishing the conditions necessary for the realization of God's soul-making purpose for humanity. This purpose, as we have already seen, requires that human creatures be able to enjoy a degree of autonomy in relationship to God so that they can freely respond to God with the proper fiduciary attitude. "In order to be a person, exercising some measure of genuine freedom, the creature must be brought into existence, not in the immediate divine presence, but at a 'distance' from God." This epistemic distance is thus the intermediate goal of humanity's emergence from the natural order as morally imperfect *Homo sapiens*. This morally imperfect constitution forges "the possibility of the human being coming freely to know and love one's Maker."[12]

The inevitability of human moral imperfection is conceived in terms of the biological aspect of anthropology. Hick attempts to justify this feature of the human creaturely state at the theological level. He maintains that "if the end-state which God is seeking to bring about is one in which finite persons have come in their own freedom to know and love him, this requires creating them initially in a state which is not that of their already knowing and loving him."[13] He does not mean that human beings must emerge as morally innocent or neutral creatures but that they must be created as "imperfect creatures."[14] That is, freedom can be secured only if humans are created with a morally evil propensity. He rejects the hypothesis that humans might not have been morally imperfect at creation, for if this were true, he says, then the whole soul-making process would have been short-circuited: "One who has attained to goodness by meeting and eventually mastering temptations, and thus by rightly making responsible choices in concrete situations, is good in a richer and more valuable sense than would be one created *ab initio* in a state either of innocence or of virtue."[15] The reason why humans cannot, according to Hick, be created at an epistemic distance from God, and also as morally perfect beings, is that "a perfectly good being, although formally free to sin, would in fact never do so."[16]

DIFFICULTIES WITH HICK'S CONCEPTION
OF HUMAN FREEDOM

In the following evaluation of Hick's conception of human freedom I conclude that his position is inconsistent because he posits moral imperfection, according to which humans sin inevitably, as a byproduct of epistemic distance, which in turn is posited to show that humans are free.

Equivocation on the Meaning of "Freedom"

Hick's concession to the atheist challenge forces him into an awkward ambiguity regarding the meaning of human freedom. On the one hand, for purposes of ensuring eventual proper fiduciary commitment to God, human beings are not free. On the other hand, fiduciary commitment is ultimately a function of human free will. Let us look at these polarizations concerning the possession of freedom by human creatures.

Hick's two-stage conception of creation, in terms of which human beings are continuous with the natural order and are therefore morally imperfect, leads to the conclusion that humans are not morally free. Indeed, they are in no way responsible for emerging from the evolutionary process in this condition. They are morally self-regarding creatures, yet this is due to their survival instinct as animal organisms embedded in the processes of the natural world. This line of argument can be standardized as follows:

1. Human beings emerged from the process of creation with a "survival instinct."
2. Their survival instinct "demands" that human beings behave selfishly (that is, in a self-regarding manner).
3. Selfishness is "the essence of moral evil," known theologically as sin (which consists, as Kant observed, in "treating others, not as ends in themselves, but as means to one's own ends").
4. Therefore, human beings were created by God in a morally evil state.[17]

However, Hick's concept of creaturely epistemic distance is invoked to show that humans are religiously free to come to God. In their morally imperfect state, achieved via the primordial stage of creation, the stage is set, so to speak, for human beings to grow toward moral perfection by responding to God in the context of a religiously ambiguous life setting. They are, then, morally free creatures.

I propose the following formulation of Hick's overall account of human freedom to illustrate the fundamental difficulty inherent in his view:

5. Human beings are [religiously] free (to be able to respond to God in personal trust).
6. True [religious] freedom requires that human beings be created at an epistemic distance from God.
7. For human beings to emerge at an epistemic distance from God they must come forth in a morally imperfect state (since the evolutionary mechanism that guarantees their freedom also entails their being sinfully self-regarding creatures).
8. The emergence of humans as morally imperfect creatures means that they must sin.
9. If human beings must sin they are not [morally] free.
10. Therefore, human beings are not [morally] free.

The terms "religiously," "religious," and "morally" are bracketed in propositions (5), (6), (9), and (10) to show the only means at Hick's disposal for avoiding the inconsistency of overtly denying in the conclusion what is affirmed in the initial premise. That is, the freedom affirmed in (5) must differ importantly from the freedom denied in (10). Although Hick does distinguish two aspects or senses of freedom, it is not obvious that this bifurcation succeeds even as a purely formal distinction, much less as an actual distinction in kinds of freedom— one kind capable of being inhibited and the other capable of full expression, both instantiated simultaneously. Something like a difference in kind is apparently in view, however, for Hick thinks it is logically possible for God to create beings with perfect moral freedom and that it is not logically possible for God to create beings with perfect religious freedom.[18]

Any difference which can make that sort of difference I assume must constitute a difference in kind. First, humans are sometimes said to be morally imperfect in relation to one another; at other times it is clear that human moral imperfection includes a definite bias against God. Indeed, it is human failure in personal relationship with God at the outset that accounts for one's morally degrading self-regarding propensity toward other human beings.[19] Second, it is difficult to conceive how religious freedom and moral freedom in relationship to God are different. It seems, rather, that religious freedom is nothing other than moral freedom applied to a human being's relationship to God in contradistinction to this human being's relationship to human fellows. If humans are religiously free to respond to God through faith but they fail to do so, are they not morally culpable? Finally, the supposed logical difficulty that moves Hick to distinguish between religious and moral freedom in the first place (in terms of the Flew–Mackie challenge) is not finally resolved by means of this distinction. This last point deserves further elaboration.

Is There a Logical Difficulty in the Traditional Free-Will Defense?

On Hick's account, humans must be created either with a morally perfect nature or with a morally imperfect nature.[20] Since it would be better if one's attachment to God in personal trust were the result of a free choice rather than a function of internal constitution, one must be created in a morally imperfect condition. In this condition, Hick maintains, humans are free in the sense that they might turn from moral imperfection to moral perfection in virtue of choosing God. They are never absolutely free in an unrestricted sense, for they must be created with some determinate nature.

Hick claims that the free-will defense in the Augustinian tradition is particularly vulnerable in its attempt "to shift the blame for the occurrence of evil from the creator to the creatures" when it begins with the assertion that "the creation was originally perfect."[21] He attacks the Augustinian free-will thesis in a number of contexts, but note the following specific criticism of the Augustinian free-will defense:

> The Creator is preserved from any responsibility for the existence of evil by the claim that He made men (or angels) as free and finitely perfect creatures, happy in the knowledge of Himself, and subject to no strains or temptations, but that they themselves inexplicably and inexcusably rebelled against Him. But this suggestion amounts to a sheer self-contradiction. It is impossible to conceive of wholly good beings in a wholly good world becoming sinful.[22]

Part of the difficulty with this is the connected idea that God could have so constituted human creatures that they would always freely choose to act rightly. If humans had been created in the condition that the Augustinian tradition ostensibly says they were—namely, as "morally perfect" or "wholly good" creatures—then they certainly would have always freely chosen to act rightly.

This *reductio* argument merits a careful reply. The following points endeavor to put the Augustinian free-will defense back on more solid footing, not only in light of these objections but also over against Hick's entire account of human freedom. This reply to Hick's criticism has three parts.

1. *Logical equivalence.* Hick's alternative to the traditional free-will defense, even on the assumption that he has properly character-ized the Augustinian view of humanity's original creaturely state, at best shares the same logical status as the view he criticizes. His criticism of the classical view is based on his acceptance of Mackie's principle: "If their being of this sort is logically possible, then God's making them of this sort is logically possible."[23] Let us call this principle, which has been stated with considerable forcefulness by both Flew and Mackie, the Flew–Mackie principle (FMP):

> If it is logically possible for free creatures to always choose to act rightly, then it is logically possible that God could so constitute them at creation that they *would* always choose to act rightly; and, if God is good, then he *should* have so constituted human individuals, rather than allowing for the possibility for evil to accrue.

On the basis of such a logical possibility, Hick is willing to give up the classical free-will defense. He opts for distinguishing religious freedom from moral freedom, fully expecting that religious freedom is immune to this criticism. But really it is not. David Ray Griffin has noticed this in his own critique of Hick's theodicy. He notes that Hick accepts the soundness of FMP against the free-will defense and then "denies that it is 'logically possible for God so to make men that they will freely respond to Himself in love and trust and faith.' "[24] But Hick is inconsistent, for he claims that human beings will some day, all of them, freely respond to God with these fiduciary attitudes. Hence, since beings of this sort are logically possible, God's originally creat-ing them thus is also logically possible, given FMP. In the final analysis, Hick's rejection of the free-will defender's proposition about moral freedom, and his acceptance of his own proposition about religious freedom, is "purely *ad hoc.*"[25]

This argument takes as its point of departure the fact that Hick thinks all humans will freely trust God in the long run. Of course, this is not to say that all humans must freely trust God in the long run. It may appear that my objection to Hick depends upon illicitly conflating the two statements. Two remarks should help to remove this impres-sion, however.

First, my point at this juncture is not about whether humans must in the long run freely trust God. Rather, it is that if Hick thinks all free creatures eventually will freely trust God, it follows that it must be logically possible for there to be such creatures. This does not, of course, entail any necessity about there ever being such creatures. It is just that, given the sheer logical possibility that free creatures at some time t_1 will freely trust God, and on FMP, which Hick does accept, it is logically possible that these same creatures freely trust God at t_{1-n}, where t_{1-n} could be the moment of their creation as free creatures. Hick cannot accept FMP and yet forbid that free creatures might freely trust God from the start of their personal histories. And yet, he explicitly forbids this: "It would not be logically possible for God so to make men that they could be guaranteed freely to respond to Himself in genuine trust and love."[26]

Second, Hick's confidence that all humans will eventually freely trust God follows from his belief that they must. And he is sure that they must given the love of God *and* the fact that God created them at an epistemic distance from himself so that their moral failings are really his responsibility. It is a requirement of divine justice that God attempt to bring all free creatures to full moral and spiritual perfection. It is a function of divine power that they may be brought to full moral and spiritual perfection, analyzed in terms of freely trusting God. Thus, the power of God and the love of God ensure that what must happen will happen. It is therefore a future matter of fact. Although my argument in this section makes no reference to Hick's belief that all humans must eventually freely trust God, it might have done so without committing any logical mistake.

Alvin Plantinga has proposed a different line of defense against FMP. He appeals to the semantics of possible worlds to show why the principle is false. While I have my doubts about the utility of modal logic for such purposes, I take note of his proposal. He says:

> The essential point of the Free Will Defense is that the creation of a world containing moral good is a co-operative venture; it requires the uncoerced concurrence of significantly free creatures. But then the actualization of a world *W* containing moral good is not up to God alone; it also depends upon what the significantly free creatures of *W* would do if God created them and placed them in the situations *W* contains. Of course it is up to God whether to create free creatures at all; but if he aims to produce moral good, then he must create significantly free creatures upon whose co-operation he must depend. Thus is the power of an omnipotent God limited by the freedom he confers upon his creatures.[27]

Plantinga discusses FMP only in reference to Mackie's particular formulation of it. His comments, however, have general application to any version of it. His main point is that the actualization of any world with free creatures is never up to God alone, and on this he rests his case against FMP.

I am not sure that Plantinga's own counterproposal is quite correct. Actualizing one world from a variety of possible worlds seems to me to be God's prerogative alone, *if* a possible-worlds approach correctly characterizes the opportunities at God's disposal when creating some world. Since I have my doubts about the utility of possible worlds semantics for solving metaphysical difficulties generally, I am not inclined to lean on conceptions about logically possible worlds to answer FMP.[28]

The difficulty, I believe, comes in thinking that *actualizing* a possible world is significantly like *causing* the actions that occur in that world.[29] Taking his own example, Plantinga thinks that it is true either that

1. God's strongly actualizing the state of affairs consisting in Curley's being offered a bribe of $20,000 and being free to accept or reject it results in Curley's accepting the bribe,

or that

2. God's strongly actualizing the state of affairs consisting in Curley's being offered a bribe of $20,000 and being free to accept or reject it results in Curley's rejecting the bribe.[30]

Now Plantinga assumes that either (1) or (2) is true, and adds that this assumption is "fairly innocent" but also "dispensable."[31] But it is neither innocent nor dispensable. It is not innocent because possible-worlds semantics allow that (1) and (2) are both true, (1) in W and (2) in W^*. Even if all states of affairs prior to the time of Curley's decision are the same in both W and W^*, as Plantinga stipulates, in one world these states of affairs are followed by Curley's accepting the bribe (i.e., W) and in the other world they are followed by Curley's rejecting the bribe (i.e., W^*).

Plantinga's assumption is not dispensable either. For if God knows which of these two worlds, though they have the same initial states of affairs, is the one where Curley makes the better choice, why should God not be able to actualize that world on the basis of knowing this? We may not be able to say how God can ensure the creation of the one world and not the other, since the same antecedent states of affairs would be actualized in creating either world. We can at least imagine a role for divine omniscience to play in foreseeing the total states of affairs (including those before and after Curley's decision as well as the decision itself) that God could actualize by creating either world. What is there to forbid the logical possibility that God could actualize whichever of these two possible worlds he wanted? Plantinga's reliance upon the resources of possible-worlds semantics leaves him open to this objection. If the objection stands, then he has not answered Mackie.

Anybody who takes the general framework of possible worlds

seriously faces a paradox that can be illustrated in the context of our discussion. On the one hand,

1. It is logically possible that at least one possible world contains significantly free creatures who never go wrong with respect to any moral choice, such that that world contains no moral evil.

This logical possibility is ensured by the fact that creatures in this world are significantly free *ex hypothesi.* The force of FMP derives from this supposition. On the other hand,

2. It is logically possible in all possible worlds with significantly free creatures that at least one free creature will freely go wrong with respect to some moral choice, such that any such world will contain a modicum of moral evil.

This second logical possibility is ensured by the fact that the creature in question is significantly free *ex hypothesi.* This is the point underlying Plantinga's response to FMP. He is therefore committed to denying (1). But the denial of (1) severely undercuts the intuitive appeal of using the semantics of possible worlds to solve metaphysical problems. We grope in vain for a way to decide between the distinct metapossibilities (1) and (2), which cannot both be actualized. There is no uncontroversial rule in modal logic for finding our way between this Scylla and Charybdis of logical possibility.

What I think is right in Plantinga's position, however, is the hint that what is logically possible may not always be actually achievable, especially in view of the purposes God may have in creating some world. There are accounts of possibilia other than those present in various versions of possible-worlds semantics. It may, just to note one example, be better to analyze the ontological status of possibilia in terms of their existence as ideas in the mind of God. There is, of course, a long tradition of thinking along such lines about possibilia. This, indeed, is what Leibniz himself had in mind in his discussions about possible worlds as a way of solving problems of theodicy.

If this Leibnizian approach is right, then included among the possibilia as a regulative factor is the particular set of goals that God has in creating a world. In formulating these goals, God is sensitive to those concepts and qualities that, as it were, cry out for existence. What determines that these particular concepts and qualities be actualized has to do with the inner dynamics of the divine consciousness. And this is something to which we have, as philosophers, precious little access. What access we do have to the inner determinations of the mind of God concerning worlds he might have made depends largely upon our making correct observations about the world he has made. As Leibniz was fond of saying, "If all things were well known to us, it would clearly appear that a better world than that made by God could not even be desired."[32] From our limited perspective we imagine that alternative worlds would be more desirable. Nevertheless, our limited perspective does not prevent us from realizing in our more reflective moments that this world might be the most desirable arrangement. This confidence begs no questions as long as we are antecedently justified in believing in God.

We may even begin to appreciate why the actual world arrangement is to be preferred over the logically possible one preferred by Flew and Mackie. Their objection (FMP) rests upon the possibility of valuing genuine human freedom. They think that this freedom that we rightly value could be preserved even if God had arranged to make us free beings who never would in fact sin. But what is the basis of their assurance of this? The context in which we happen to value freedom includes the experience of moral failings. Do we know that the value we place upon our freedom in such a context is no greater than what we would place upon our freedom if we lived in the sort of world Mackie and Flew recommend? Even if God could have achieved this logical possibility it may not have been more desirable for him to do so. If, as free creatures, we are even now able to choose the better of two alternatives, and we often do not choose the better but take the morally less desirable course, what guarantees that we can now nevertheless judge that our preference for another kind of world is due to its moral superiority? Moments of moral crisis enable us to appreciate what we have as free creatures. Our own awareness of the possibility of willing wrongly contributes to our capacity to value our freedom. And our awareness of this capacity is made more sure by the fact that we do sometimes will the wrong thing.

It is perhaps not uncommon for morally serious persons to experience a certain reluctance when contemplating a moral decision they are about to make. Our choices are seen to be "momentous," to use a Jamesian term, when we are conscious of what is at stake. I wonder if this would be possible in the sort of world Mackie and Flew say they would prefer.

The point of FMP is that the value of freedom can be preserved by God without his creating a world where free persons use their freedom sinfully. But this assumes without argument that the freedom in this case is to be valued in the same way that freedom in the actual world is valued. Even if the freedom is the same in other respects, which also may be questionable, it does not follow that it can be valued in the same way in both kinds of worlds. Speaking abstractly, there are worlds with persons having both freedom and dignity (such as our world is), there are worlds with persons having freedom but little dignity (such as Mackie's hypothetical world may be), and there are worlds with persons having neither freedom nor dignity (such as B. F. Skinner's and Patricia Churchland's worlds would be). We know ourselves to be free when we err and realize that we might not have, and when we do right and realize that we might have done otherwise.

2. *Locus of responsibility.* All else being equal at the purely logical level, the Augustinian free-will defense is clearly still the better choice since it rescues the theodicist from the unacceptable conclusion that God is responsible for evil. If the problem posed by atheists like Flew and Mackie, in terms of logical possibilities, can be answered along the lines I have suggested, then it is also desirable to hold that free moral beings who do sin are responsible for their own moral choices. As Illtyd Trethowan remarks, "God does not 'permit' sin in the sense of making it a part of his plan. He does indeed bring good out of evil, but he does not *arrange* for evil in the interest of doing so."[33] Evil is a contingency that might well erupt in a world created for the realization of certain goods. It is in this sense that God is the *per accidens* cause of certain physical evils. Or, as Germain Grisez puts it, "The creator causes states of affairs which involve evil, but does not cause evil, since evil does not require a creative cause."[34] If evil is a privation, as the Augustinian tradition affirms, then it is true by definition that evil does not need a creative cause. "Evil is the nonobtaining of what might have obtained and ought to have obtained but does not obtain. What does not obtain does not require a cause of its nonobtaining as such."[35]

Recall that Hick is not as concerned with defining the nature of evil as those within the Augustinian tradition are. He writes: "The Augustinian tradition embodies the philosophy of evil as non-being. . . . In contrast, the Irenaean type of theodicy is more purely theological in character and is not committed to the Platonic *or to any other philosophical framework.*"[36] It cannot be said, however, that a certain conception of evil is not presupposed by Hick's theodicy. He may not make the precise nature of evil explicit in his account, but however "purely theological" his conception of evil turns out to be, it does not follow from the theological character of any definition that it will fail to be the least bit philosophical. Nor is it clear what Hick means by a purely theological characterization of evil and how adherence to this ideal is supposed to aid the cause of the theodicist. He suggests only that the Augustinian preoccupation with defining evil involves theodicists of this school in needless difficulty. But why should not the difficulty Hick has in mind here pertain to philosophical definition in general and not merely to the particular definition proposed by Augustinian defenders?

Moreover, Hick's desire to remain strictly theological does not relieve him of the responsibility to give some meaningful characterization of the nature of evil. He seems to think it a virtue of his system that it does not succumb to the temptation to define evil. But it is surely an awkward theodicy that does not provide some account of the nature of the reality that is supposed to be problematic for the existence of God. It seems right to say that "very little progress can be made in any philosophical discussion unless the participants know what they are talking about. Thus it is crucial in considering the question of God and evil to have a correct analysis of the concept of 'evil.' "[37] Any analysis of evil so called needs to be more rigorous than occurs in most discussions of the problem of evil. In the Augustinian tradition a metaphysically scrupulous analysis of the nature of evil is given in terms of privation.

In connection with his misgivings about any philosophical definition of evil, Hick believes that attributing responsibility for evil to human beings as a result of their own volitions to act wrongly "amounts to postulating the self-creation of evil *ex nihilo*."[38] But it is not appropriate to speak of the ex nihilo creation of something that is never regarded as a substance in its own right, something that is a privation in a thing rather than a substantive thing. Ironically, it is Hick's account of the intrusion of evil—despite his silence regarding the nature of evil—that is susceptible to his accusation. In his schema, evil has more of a substantial nature by virtue of its necessity in the divine economy (discoverable there at the outset) and of its integral relation to the whole creative process of evolution by which *Homo sapiens* emerges from the outset as a morally imperfect being.

Hick neglects (even repudiates) the significance of the Augustinian conception of evil as a privation and, on this basis, claims that God's ultimate responsibility for evil is acknowledged even in the Augustinian tradition, albeit only implicitly. If the Augustinian doctrine of privation is taken seriously, however, then this is one effective means by which ultimate divine causative responsibility for evil can be ruled out. The prior conviction that God is absolutely good, justified by means of natural theology, removes the possibility in principle that God might be the cause of evil. The theory of privation facilitates the effort to understand how, God being omnibenevolent, evil could ever arise. And this is the fundamental task of theodicy.

Proponents of the Augustinian tradition can agree with Hick when he writes, "*Ultimately* God alone is sovereign, and evil can exist only by His permission. This means that God has willed to create a universe in which it is better for Him to permit sin and evil than not to permit them."[39] It is absolutely proper, however, for Augustinian theists to demur when Hick goes on to conclude that "this brings us back, however reluctantly, to some kind of instrumental view of evil."[40] By an "instrumental view of evil" Hick means that God did more than allow evil into the world; he had some purpose to fulfill that could not be fulfilled without the presence of evil, and therefore evil is a necessary instrument: "Our theodicy must find the meaning of evil in the part that it is made to play in the eventual outworking of that [soul-making] purpose."[41] Here the need for viewing evil as instrumental depends upon the notion that God, being sovereign, is ultimately responsible for evil.[42]

In the Augustinian tradition, however, evil is instrumental only in the sense that the *possibility* of evil is necessary to God's good purposes and, should that possibility be actualized, that God may bring some higher good out of evil. Evil is redeemable within the scope of God's purposes, but not necessary to the realization of those purposes. Since God's purpose with respect to humans is chiefly to allow them the freedom to choose God as their proper source of beatitude, if they perpetually refused to exercise their freedom to do evil, which is a logical possibility, then God's purpose would not fail thereby. The doctrine of the sovereignty of God requires only that all evil be redeemable, not that any evil be necessary.

3. *Morally perfect versus morally neutral beings.* Hick's charge against the traditional free-will defense is based upon an inaccurate characterization of the Augustinian conception of humanity's original nature at creation. Stephen Davis, a contemporary proponent of the traditional free-will defense, answers the charge that "a fall into sin seems logically impossible for a perfectly morally good being," asserting that the free-will defense "is not committed to the view that humans were created perfectly morally good." Davis suggests, rather, that "God judged his creation to be very good in that it was a harmonious, beautiful, smoothly working cosmos. . . . Since God wanted [human beings] to be free moral agents, he must have created them as spiritually immature, morally neutral creatures, capable of choosing either good or evil."[43]

Notice that humans may have been created in a state that is both morally neutral and spiritually immature, according to the Augustinian account. Spiritual immaturity is not necessarily constitutive of any kind of moral defect. Surely it is logically possible for humans to be so constituted at their creation that they would be able to make their own moral decisions and that in making such decisions they might either grow in moral perfection or sink to moral corruption. There is no reason why they should not be created in a morally *innocent* state, capable of bringing moral guilt upon themselves in the exercise of their wills in an environment replete with moral choices. And God might have some good purpose for so constituting humans at the outset.

According to the Augustinian tradition, this exactly describes the original state of the first humans. God created humans to seek their own beatitude. Furthermore, he formed them in such a way that their beatitude could be maximized only by freely choosing God. Nevertheless, by virtue of their free choice, humans might knowingly repudiate the good, thus forfeiting for themselves the experience of true happiness. Their constitution is indeed "determined" in certain respects. Humans cannot help but desire to be happy. Still, they must elect how they will seek to satisfy their longing for satisfaction. Their God-given, morally sensitive conscience enables them to know what is proper in this regard. Yet their conscience does not choose for them, or absolutely efficaciously compel them to choose, the proper realization of their natural end. Humans are genuinely free; they are created in a state of unexercised freedom and consequently of moral innocence. Their pristine condition is not that of moral perfection, although their moral perfection is intended and desired by God, else he would not have constituted them so as to be able to enjoy the beatitude that they seek.

Hick presumes that the only options with respect to the original human state are either moral perfection or moral imperfection. He objects to the former, the alleged Augustinian viewpoint, with the observation that "to say that an unqualifiedly good (though finite) being gratuitously sins is to say that he was not unqualifiedly good in the first place."[44] This is exactly the point that free-will defenders wish to make, however. Humans were not created as "unqualifiedly good" beings. Failing to appreciate the possibility described above, representative of the Augustinian anthropology, Hick argues for the moral imperfection of humans at creation, thus appearing to account for the existence of evil but failing to account for evil in terms of the exercise of human freedom. Consequently, his conception of human freedom, and of humanity's share in the responsibility for evil, is ultimately incoherent.

I submit that only subsequent to creation, and precisely through the exercise of free-will, did humans become morally imperfect. In our present condition "we are not merely imperfect creatures who must be improved: we are, as Newman said, rebels who must lay down our arms."[45] As Trethowan rightly observes, "From the point of view of experience we must surely say that we are aware of our responsibility as absolute. We know that what we are called upon to do is reasonable, eminently reasonable, yet we know that we have the power to refuse it."[46]

12
Evil and the Afterlife

In John Hick's theodicy proper there are, broadly speaking, major areas of overlap with the Augustinian tradition. Both systems are teleological in their orientation; that is, both appeal to the purpose or purposes of God in accounting for evils of all kinds, whether moral or natural. Furthermore, in the area of anthropology, both Augustinian theodicists and Hick assign a prominent role to human free will, although each conceives of the nature and specific role of freedom differently. What remains is to consider the matter of eschatology in Hick's theodicy, where again it is not surprising to find certain affinities between his theodicy and that of the Augustinian tradition, but also important differences. This appraisal of Hick's theodicy, from a natural-theology perspective, concludes with an examination in this chapter of the emphasis he places upon the eschatological resolution of the problem of evil.

THE ROLE OF ESCHATOLOGY IN HICK'S THEODICY

The importance of the eschatological component in Hick's overall theodicy is unmistakable: "But there is one further all-important aspect of the Irenaean type of theodicy, without which all the forego-ing would lose its plausibility. This is the eschatological aspect."[1] An afterlife for all human individuals is a non-negotiable postulate of the soul-making theodicy. The ultimate justification of evil, according to Hick, is rooted in God's purpose for humans and in the final compre-hensive fulfillment of that purpose. It is not enough that God intend the full moral and spiritual perfection of all human beings; God must also ensure that this objective is brought to full realization. Otherwise, the problem of evil is an everlasting embarrassment to the Judeo–Christian conception of the divine nature.

The Need to Postulate an Afterlife

The integral relationship between Hick's teleological postulate of an overarching divine purpose for humans in terms of their moral perfection (soul-making) and his eschatological postulate of an afterlife is evident by the following standardization of his reasoning:

1. *God's purpose for humans is soul-making.*   Recall that soul-making is the "basic postulate" in Hick's theodicy. Soul-making envisions the end state of the human developmental process. This creative process unfolds in two general stages: first, the evolutionary emergence of *Homo sapiens* from the natural world order in epistemic distance from God and, as a result, in a state of moral imperfection; second, the gradual moral perfection of humans through personal travail in a hostile environment and their ultimate commitment to God displayed in a variety of fiduciary attitudes. It is the infinite good of the end state of human persons, preenvisioned in God's soul-making purpose for them, that ultimately justifies the existence of any and all evil in the world: "For the justification of evil, according to this Irenaean type of theodicy, is that it is a necessary part of a process whose end product is to be an infinite good—namely, the perfection and endless joy of all finite personal life."[2] Here Hick anticipates the inevitable moral outcome for all human persons at the end of a long and arduous process that has been supervised by God. "Men may eventually become the perfected persons whom the New Testament calls 'children of God', but they cannot be created ready-made as this."[3] Since it is this alleged purpose of God that is supposed to justify all evil, this purpose must eventually be realized completely. The ultimate justification of evil is contingent upon the final fulfillment of the soul-making process. This is especially so since evil is *as a necessity* included in the process of soul-making, meaning that the quality of human soul that God seeks could not be achieved apart from evil.

2. *God's soul-making purpose is not fully realized in the present personal life of most human beings.*   The ultimate justification of the existence of evil in a theistic universe, according to Hick, depends upon the fruition of God's soul-making purpose. However, "It is quite evident that the creating of human animals into children of God is not usually completed by the moment of bodily death and that if it is ever to be completed it must continue beyond this life."[4] Simple observation, both of the present conditions in the world of humankind and of "the entire scroll of recorded history," reveals that "we are not entitled to say either that all sin leads to redemption or that all suffering is used for good in its final issue."[5] Individuals remain

unrepentant even at death. For such as never are morally and spiritually perfected in this life, God's purpose of soul-making fails and a relevant measure of evil persists, as yet unjustified.

3. *Therefore, we must postulate an afterlife—or series of afterlives—during which God's soul-making purpose may yet be fully realized for all humans.* "If there is any eventual resolution of the interplay between good and evil, any decisive bringing of good out of evil, it must lie beyond this world and beyond the enigma of death."[6] When humans reach the end state there can be no residual evil, otherwise God will have failed to accomplish his purpose, which is postulated as the only means of justifying his permission of evil. In short, "Human immortality is essential to this type of theodicy."[7] Hick admits that his entire theodicy hypothesis, constrained by his picture of the present world as the context for the making of human souls, "can make sense only if we see this life as part of a much larger existence in which that creative process continues to completion beyond this world."[8] That is, to sustain the ultimate plausibility of his theodicy hypothesis, it is not enough for Hick to formulate his basic postulate in terms of God's soul-making purpose. He must include the postulate of the final and complete eschatological realization of that purpose lest the justification for evil collapse. Without this eschatological component, the rest of his theodicy proper would "lose its plausibility."[9]

The Universalist Imperative

The nature of the end state envisioned by the soul-making purpose leads Hick to "question the validity of belief in hell" and to posit the universal salvation of humankind.[10] His reasoning is related to the nature of the purpose of soul-making and its role in theodicy. Again, Hick's argument can be given formal expression.

1. *Theodicy seeks to justify the existence of evil by appealing to an infinite good.* In Hick's theodicy, the justification of the existence of evil hinges on God's purpose for allowing evil. But Hick also admits that, given the divine purpose of soul-making, the obtrusion of evil into the world is an inevitable necessity. (It is therefore misleading to speak of the divine "permission" of evil, for God himself is ultimately ontologically responsible for evil's existence.) The only thing that can ultimately justify the incursion of evil into the soul-making process is the final realization of some infinite good at the end of the process. In Hick's theodicy, "the justification of evil within the creative process lies in the limitless and eternal good of the end state to which it

leads."[11] If evil is instrumental to some divine purpose, then the only justification for employing evil in the realization of that purpose is the nature of the good that results. If the end product is not an infinite good, then the employment of evil by God is not ultimately justified. Although Hick addresses this matter in terms of an "infinite good," the crux of his identification of an infinite good is his conception of the divine purpose for humans, namely, soul-making—their moral and spiritual perfection.

2. *The infinite good is identified with God's soul-making purpose for humans.* It is not that the process of soul-making is itself an infinite good but that the process finally yields an infinite good. This infinite good is identified with "the perfection and endless joy of all finite personal life."[12] The good that comes at the end of the soul-making process is "infinite" in at least two respects. First, it is infinite because it is eternal. The process "eventually succeeds" so that evil is no longer necessary. Once eradicated, evil will never again supervene upon the human situation. Second, its eventual success entails the fruition of the soul-making purpose for the entire realm of humanity. God's purpose is "the perfection and endless joy of all finite personal life," which is what Hick means by salvation.[13] This is the end state of humanity for which the soul-making process was divinely ordained, a process that necessarily included a modicum of evil. "If the justification of evil within the creative process lies in the limitless and eternal good of the end state to which it leads, then the completeness of the justification must depend upon the completeness, or universality, of the salvation achieved."[14] The fulfillment of soul-made perfection must extend to *all* human beings.

3. *Thus, there can be no eternal hell, or even annihilation, awaiting any human beings.* God's soul-making purpose must be fulfilled if evil is to be justified. But, "if only some arrive at that fulfillment, whilst others are eternally lost, then the depravity and suffering of human history will only have been partially redeemed."[15] Thus, the realization of an "infinite good" constitutes a tremendous presumption against the validity of the Christian doctrine of hell. "If part of humankind is in the end condemned to hell, this will itself constitute an infinite, because unending, aspect of the problem of evil. God's good purpose will have been eternally frustrated, leaving the eternal evils both of sin and punishment."[16] In the end state there can be no such "permanently unredeemed evils"; that, says Hick emphatically, "would constitute the most intractable aspect of the theodicy problem!"[17] He concludes that "the doctrine of hell therefore rules itself out."[18] Annihilationism, according to which the sinful lost eventually

"fade out of existence," cannot be allowed either, for "the evil that has brought them to this end remains eternally unredeemed, not made to serve any eventual good, and thus constitutes a perpetual marring of the universe."[19]

4. *Therefore, all humans will eventually freely choose God.* The conclusion to which Hick is led on the basis of the foregoing reasoning is that

> it can be predicted that sooner or later, in our own time and in our own way, we shall all freely come to God; and universal salvation can be affirmed, not as a logical necessity but as the contingent but predictable outcome of the process of the universe, interpreted theistically.[20]

A certain "antinomy" emerges with this conclusion:

> On one side is the omnipotent divine love intending man's salvation. If that divine intention is never fulfilled, then God is not after all the sovereign lord of his own universe: he is a limited God, defeated by an evil which he has permitted to exist but which he cannot now overcome. And on the other side is our human freedom. If man is saved against his will, or without his will, then he does not after all make a free, personal response to his Maker. In forcing man into his kingdom God would have turned the human thou into an it.[21]

Because of his determination to defend human freedom, Hick admits that "men can damn themselves." Still, he wants to say that, in view of God's sovereignty, although humans can damn themselves, "in the end none will."[22] He argues that although one might perish if one failed to yield to God, it is "a true deduction from God's power and goodness that in the end man *will* somehow be drawn freely to open himself to his Maker."[23]

Hick indicates several means at God's disposal to propel humans toward an awareness of God without obstructing their personal freedom: "Through the work of prophets and saints, through the resulting religious traditions, and through the individual's religious experience."[24] On the one hand, Hick observes that "the affirmation that all will be saved without their freedom being at any point overridden has the status, not of a scientific prediction, but of a hope."[25] Hence, based on his conviction that the divine love and power precludes, in view of God's purpose in creating humans and permitting evil, the final lostness of any person, he "speaks of real people being *drawn towards* their perfection in an existence which extends far beyond this present life."[26] On the other hand, he insists that this hope has the status of "a true deduction."[27]

The Character of the Afterlife

Hick's conviction that all humans must eventually be irreversibly perfected, coupled with the realization that seldom does anyone experience complete moral perfection in this life, leads him not only to conclude that there must be an afterlife but also to speculate about the nature of such an afterlife. Here, as well, he is constrained by the permutations of his soul-making theodicy. In general, the possibilities are twofold: "If, then, God's purpose of the perfecting of human beings is ever to be fulfilled, it must either be brought to an instantaneous completion by divine fiat, perhaps at the moment of death, or else take place through a continued development within some further environment in which God places us."[28] He reasons that divine fiat is improbable and favors, by way of elimination, the conclusion that human sanctification is progressively realized following death.

There seem to be two related reasons for Hick's doubts that imperfect humans would be transmuted in the twinkling of an eye into perfect creatures. First, on the divine fiat theory, there would be no basis for affirming the continuity of a person who died as an imperfect being with someone instantaneously perfected thereafter. In other words, such an account raises the whole question of personal identity in an afterlife, which is hotly disputed in debates about human immortality. It seems impossible to specify identity conditions if the divine fiat theory obtains.

A second reason has to do more directly with the alleged soul-making purpose God has ordained for humans. As Hick puts it, if human moral perfection is brought about instantaneously by divine fiat, then "the whole earthly travail of faith and moral effort is rendered needless."[29] Perfection by divine fiat, even if it occurred after death, would seem to undercut the earlier thesis that an imperfect human being must be brought to moral perfection gradually "through his own responses and assent."[30] That is, the logical impossibility that precludes the pristine constitution of free human persons in proper fiduciary relationship with God also foredooms the plausibility of the eventual perfectibility of humans by divine fiat. With no other alternative close at hand, Hick opts for "the conception of a continued life in an intermediate state."[31]

In a chapter of his book *Death and Eternal Life* entitled "A Possible Pareschatology," Hick asks and answers the provocative question: "What, then, is likely to happen in the next stage of this journey?"[32] He willingly suffers a departure from the classical Christian tradition in his highly speculative account of the nature of an afterlife. He employs the notions of purgatory and of a kind of postmortem progressive sanctification in his descriptive eschatology. Elsewhere he argues that "any continuation of the person-making process beyond death will consist in a series of lives, each with its own beginning and end; for it is the boundaries of life that provide the pressure that constitutes it a person-making history."[33]

He believes that a viable Christian theodicy must envision a peculiar kind of afterlife. First, one must postulate some sort of afterlife to ensure the completion of the soul-making purpose. Furthermore, since the soul-making purpose is realized only gradually through a painstaking process that accounts for the necessary existence of evil, that process itself cannot be foreshortened by any immediate or abrupt perfection of humans following death. Nevertheless, the requirement that God's purpose *eventually* succeed implies "an eternal heavenly life eventually supervening upon an intermediate or purgatorial postmortem existence."[34] That is, an intermediate state during which the soul-making process necessarily continues does not last indefinitely, with the perpetual postponement of the end state said to represent the infinite good of humankind's total moral and spiritual perfection. Still, the intermediate state, intervening between one's earthly sojourn and one's introduction into eternal heavenly life, may include any number of stages, the extent and duration of which are "determined by the degree of *un*sanctification remaining to be overcome at the time of death."[35]

A complicating feature in the determination of the duration of the intermediate state is the fact that humans sometimes regress rather than unfailingly progress upward toward perfection. The probable complexity of the entire situation regarding this intermediate state is certainly one reason why Hick is willing to allow reincarnationist elements to inform his total eschatological outlook: "Reincarnation is not, and has never been, an orthodox Christian belief. But it does not absolutely follow from this that it could never become an orthodox Christian belief. The history of Christianity shows a number of instances of important ideas which at one time formed no part of accepted Christian teaching but which at a later time have been taught in substantial parts, at least, of Christendom."[36]

Hick proceeds to cite four principal reasons "for the widely accepted view that the idea of reincarnation is incompatible with Christian truth," none of which strikes him as particularly decisive for a proper evaluation of the possibility of wedding this Eastern doctrine with Christian belief. As he states it, however, neither is he "able to come to a clear-cut conclusion either that the doctrine [of reincarnation] is true or that it cannot be true."[37] Briefly, these four reasons are as follows: (1) reincarnation is not taught in the New Testament; (2) this present life is regarded in Christian teaching as the time when a person's final destiny is determined; (3) the Christian doctrine of a bodily resurrection seems incompatible with reincarnation; and (4) personal salvation comes through Christ's unique atoning death, which does not recur endlessly as one might expect on a reincarnationist interpretation.[38]

Nevertheless, in articulating his own version of the "many-lives doctrine," Hick is careful to distinguish his view only from those reincarnationist theories that include the belief that humans have experienced past lives *on the earth*. Hick feels sure that human existence does not extend into an infinite past. He only advances the notion that "something like the more 'solid' conception of reincarnation can apply to the idea [Hick's own] . . . of future lives in other worlds."[39]

In his account of the eschaton, Hick indulges a striking interest in seeking further points of convergence between Eastern and Western conceptions of reality. He takes up the Eastern notion of the total absorption (metaphorically expressed in terms of "the raindrop merging into the sea") of individual human personalities into a cosmic unity to express his own view that, with the eventual realization of God's purpose to create a morally perfected human community, all the "personal centers" that make up that community "will have ceased to be mutually exclusive and will have become mutually inclusive and open to one another in a richly complex shared consciousness." This union of "personal centers" will yield the experience of "an intimacy of personal community which we can at present barely imagine."[40] He employs the term "atman" to name "this deeper or higher consciousness or self, of which human individuals are constituent aspects . . . because the idea of the ultimate oneness of mankind, although not confined to the religions of indian origin, has been most explicitly affirmed by them."[41]

Anticipating a possible point of convergence with Christianity, Hick refers to the Christian doctrine of the Trinity to illustrate the interrelationship of wedded human personalities in the eschaton. Says Hick: "Let us now apply this trinitarian conception of the one-in-many and many-in-one to the eschatological community of human persons."[42] One final element that Hick weaves into the tapestry of his overall vision of the eschaton—also an element borrowed from Eastern thought—is the possibility that "the ultimate state, in which human selves have found their unity in the atman, is beyond both matter and time."[43]

AN AUGUSTINIAN APPRAISAL OF HICK'S ESCHATOLOGY

One aspect of Hick's theodicy that defenders of the Augustinian tradition have approved in general is his emphasis on the need for an eschatological realization of God's purposes respecting the permission of evil.[44] Probably anyone who adheres to the Christian tradition will agree that human immortality is not only an essential Christian doctrine but that it is also relevant to the formulation of an adequate Christian theodicy. Still, there are important problems with Hick's eschatology, and these can be traced back to a fundamental difference between himself and Augustinian theodicists in their respective conceptions of the divine purpose for humans.

The Notion of an Infinite Good

The Augustinian tradition accepts the postulate of an afterlife but rejects both universalism and modified reincarnationism. (In the Augustinian tradition it is not necessary to characterize the epistemic status of belief in an afterlife as a postulate. It is a revealed truth.) Now Hick's overall argument appears to move logically from premise to premise, beginning with the basic postulate of the divine soul-making purpose and ending with the completion of this soul-making purpose for all persons beyond this world in an "eternal heavenly life eventually supervening upon an intermediate or purgatorial postmortem existence." To avert the conclusions that Hick draws regarding universalism and the intermediate state (for which Augustinian Christians interested in preserving orthodoxy have plenty of incentive), there must be some premise in the initial stage of his argument, where he defends the postulate of immortality, that his detractors in the Augustinian tradition would be willing to dispute.

Indeed, it is a rather simple matter to lay hold of the problematic proposition: Hick's conception of theodicy as involving the justification of the necessary existence of evil in God's soul-making purpose for humans leads him to posit an "infinite good" that is altogether foreign to the Augustinian tradition (though the classical tradition does speak of comparative goods) and that is attended by certain philosophical difficulties as well. Within the framework of Augustinian theism, Hick's "infinite good" is, forgive the neologism, "impositable."

Whereas Hick concludes that only an infinite good can truly justify the occurrence of necessary evil in the world, in the classical tradition of Christian theodicy it is only necessary that the possibility of evil be the occasion of some higher good. It is crucial to keep in mind that in Hick's theodicy evil is regarded as a necessary feature of the soul-making process, an emphasis that distinguishes his theodicy in an important respect from the Augustinian perspective. Because evil is seen as necessary in Hick's system, God is responsible for the existence of evil. Hick concludes that the only way to justify God's instrumental inclusion of evil in the soul-making process is if, at the end of the process, some "infinite good" results. In his theodicy, such an infinite good is characterized by the eventual success of God's purpose, which includes the salvation of all human persons.

The Augustinian tradition conceives of the divine purpose somewhat differently. God's purpose is for humans to seek their own beatitude by the free exercise of their wills and to discover that beatitude whenever they direct their wills toward God. Richard Swinburne defines beatitude as "worthwhile happiness" that results "when the agent has true beliefs about his condition and gets his happiness from doing what is worthwhile."[45] This is a fundamentally Augustinian conception of beatitude.

Since evil arises only as a consequence of turning the will away from God, evil is never construed as a necessary concomitant to the completion of God's purpose for humans. Free choice of the will in moral contexts entails the possibility that evil will ensue. The Augustinian tradition insists only that the purpose God has for humans regarding the freedom to choose God as the good must represent a greater good than could be achieved apart from risking the actualization of evil through the creation of morally free agents. In the nature of the case, the capacity for moral self-determination is such a good that even the permission of evil is a good in that the freedom of morally significant action is thereby guaranteed. (In this type of perspective, it is not in the slightest degree disingenuous to speak of God "permitting" evil.) This difference has important implications for the eschatological perspective in the Augustinian tradition.

According to the Augustinian tradition, God intends the culmination of human beatitude in what is sometimes called the "Beatific Vision." By virtue of their specialized nature, inclusive of intellect and free will, humans are able to "formally possess God."[46] The Beatific Vision identifies the ultimate possession of God by a human person in heaven "through the splendor of [God's] own countenance."[47] The doctrine of the Beatific Vision is virtually the antithesis of Hick's notion of epistemic distance. It represents a direct knowledge of God by virtue of which humans experience the full complement of joy and happiness (beatitude) for which they were created. This moment is the occasion of an individual's complete moral perfection. It could even be said that this transformation of the human person happens by divine fiat, though this judgment must be attended by certain qualifications to be mentioned in a moment. It is possible to forfeit this singular encounter with God, and consequently to forego personal moral perfection, by turning the will away from God. It is the exercise of free choice with respect to this decision—either by turning the will toward God or by turning it away from God to some lesser good—that determines the ultimate destiny of any human agent. Naturally, one's character and moral disposition are molded in the process, but ultimate moral perfection is contingent upon whether one finally freely chooses God in this earthly life.

By contrast, Hick regards soul-making as the ultimate purpose of God for humans, and evil is supposed to be instrumental in bringing this about. Therefore, God must be dedicated to perfecting all human souls rather than to honoring the freedom of all human souls to personally decide whether they will be perfected by choosing God as the highest good. Hick would have to conceive of a Beatific Vision in very different terms if he wanted to include this feature of the Augustinian tradition in his own theodicy.

For the Augustinian, the prior attachment of the will to God is a condition for experiencing the Beatific Vision. The will of the one who receives the Vision is already properly oriented toward God before receiving the Vision. The Vision itself brings about a correlation of character with this orientation of will. For Hick, something like a Beatific Vision is needed to elicit final fiduciary trust. The epistemic blinders that prevent free beings from trusting God must finally be removed. This is not strictly speaking the created agent's responsibility. God creates persons at an epistemic distance and then gradually moves within view until everyone is irresistibly drawn into moral and spiritual perfection. God moves as a condition for experiencing the Beatific Vision, rather than the person who is thereby brought to moral and spiritual perfection. This subtle but all-important distinction in terms of divine purpose between Hick's theodicy and that of the Augustinian tradition accounts for their respective differences regarding universalism, the nature of an intermediate state, and the character of the end state of humans as individuals.

The Doctrine of Hell

Perhaps Hick realizes that a loving God could justifiably allow an unrepentant person to descend to a hellish state of eternal duration. But he insists that a loving God cannot allow anyone to remain unrepentant. Why not? Because on Hick's view God is responsible for their moral imperfection; human moral unsavoriness is reflected in an original constitutive bias against God effected by God in creating them at an epistemic distance from himself. On such an account it would surely be unjust for God to hold humans finally responsible for a moral orientation they did not choose. This explains Hick's commitment to extreme universalism.

Hick is a "hard universalist" in that he maintains, in light of God's sovereign love, that all humans *must* be saved eventually.[48] Although it is logically possible, in view of their possession of freedom, for individuals to remain unrepentant forever, and therefore to finally perish, it is not logically possible, in view of God's sovereign ability to perform all that he wills, for anyone to actually remain eternally unrepentant. Of course, not all logical possibilities may obtain, for the actualization of some will preclude the actualization of others. This is the case in Hick's account of universalism, when he himself says that "having insisted that it is logically possible that some, or even all, men will in their freedom eternally reject God and eternally exclude themselves from His presence, we may go on to note the actual forces at work and to consider what outcome is to be expected and expected with what degree of confidence."[49]

Since the range of all logical possibilities cannot obtain simultaneously, some logical possibilities are actually unachievable. That they are unachievable is a contingent truth. In other words, which logical possibilities turn out to be actually unachievable depends upon which other logical possibilities are actualized. In the Augustinian view, if God creates free creatures, which is one logical possibility, and at least some of those creatures perpetually refuse to acknowledge God, a second-order logical possibility that supervenes upon the previous one, then the logical possibility of bringing all free creatures to eventual moral and spiritual perfection will be actually unachievable. Either the logical possibility that some free creatures will remain morally and spiritually recalcitrant or the logical possibility that all free creatures will realize full moral and spiritual perfection must be actually unachievable. The contingent state of affairs that will finally determine which of these logical possibilities fails to obtain is tied up with how humans exercise their free wills.

The only feature of God's character that will prove relevant to this outcome is the divine commitment to permit humans to act with genuine freedom. This commitment to preserve freedom will constitute an expression of the love of God. The love of God does not determine the outcome of logical possibilities in favor of universal salvation, as Hick suggests. The "actual forces at work" do not consist solely of acts of divine persuasive appeal, but of human acts of moral defiance as well. Contra Hick, there is no a priori way of deciding in advance which will prove decisive. These conflicting sets of "actual forces at work" delimit the possibilities. Recognizing the nature of this conflict, the Augustinian tradition makes allowance for the real possibility of interminable human resistance to the soul-making process. Hick has yet to explain why this logical possibility must be actually unachievable.

We see, then, how Hick's universalism flows from his basic postulate concerning God's purpose of soul-making. But it is not the case that universalism follows with the same practical necessity from the Augustinian conception of the divine purpose. Anti-universalism is not a liability for the Augustinian tradition, as it would be for Hick's theodicy, once the precise nature of the divine purpose is understood. If God's purpose is to secure the greater good of human freedom, which when properly exercised leads the way to ultimate beatitude but also creates the possibility of the refusal to choose God, then hell, even if it involves eternal torment, may be justly permitted since it reflects God's eternal commitment to this good purpose.

Free-will defenders take no exception with Hick's contention that the heavenly eschaton must be "unqualifiedly good."[50] They do, however, proceed to specify *for whom* heaven will be unqualifiedly good. It will be good only for those who have freely chosen God as the highest good. Rebellious creatures surely could not be happy in the eternal presence of the God they perpetually refuse to honor. As Swinburne writes: "The principal occupation of heaven is the enjoyment of the friendship of God. . . . Friendship with persons involves acknowledgment of their worth. So friendship with God, the supremely good source of being, involves adoration and worship."[51] These are the primary activities of those who will spend eternity in the presence of God. And "a man who has molded his desires so as to seek only the good and its continuation would not, given the Christian doctrine of God, be bored in eternity."[52] The point is, "the only people who will be happy will be people with a certain character," and the present life provides the context for humans to choose the kind of character they wish to manifest by either directing their wills toward God or away from God.[53]

Hell is reserved for the unrepentant as the place where persons can exercise their free wills in turning away from the Creator without the recrimination of additional and unsolicited persuasive influences that would ostensibly coax them to do otherwise. In the Augustinian tradition, according to which hell is crucial to the free-will defense, God's purposes for humans are in no way "eternally frustrated," for his purposes respecting human freedom are eternally fulfilled by virtue of separating those who choose God and those who do not in heaven and hell, respectively. C. S. Lewis called this "the Great Divorce."[54] Hence, it is more apropos to speak of a soul-*deciding* theodicy rather than of a soul-*making* theodicy.[55]

Furthermore, according to the Augustinian tradition, the doctrine of hell does not entail that there will be permanently unredeemed evils, for this accusation is operable only on the assumption that evil is substantial rather than privative. And the ongoing permission of impious diversion of human wills away from God is itself a good, for it ensures that God never forces beatitude upon unwilling persons. From the Augustinian point of view, God's determination of human freedom to achieve universal human perfection would represent a malignancy in the relationship between God and human persons, a malignancy for which God himself would be responsible. To block the exercise of human free will in the name of divine love would not be love at all but an unprecedented and unredeemable evil on God's part.

Moral Voluntarism

In Hick's theodicy, God does not just foreknow that all humans will eventually yield their wills to his. Strangely enough, Hick never even mentions divine foreknowledge in this connection. His defense of universalism depends not upon divine omniscience concerning future contingent sates of affairs but upon a certain necessity contained within the concept of divine love for persons. Again, his voluntarist account of divine goodness, discussed in Chapter 9, proves too much. If Hick is right when he says that God's ultimacy entails that he is not responsible "under any moral law or to any existing person," then Hick could never be sure that the love of God necessitates universalism. It would always be far from plain what it means to assert that God is love and what the love of God must entail for divine–human relationships. Hick risks equivocation when he argues in one context that God's direct responsibility for the reality of evil is morally neutral, and insists in another context that God must perfect all humans because of his love. We have already seen in Chapter 9 that Hick assigns to God responsibility for evil. Now we find that Hick's conception of God as infinitely loving forbids us to think that God might send some persons to hell or even that he might annihilate anyone's soul.[56] But if God so transcends moral principles as to be free from moral evaluation in connection with purposing to use evil as a necessary condition for making persons, then God is also above moral reason in the operation of his love for humans. And God might well have morally sufficient reasons of his own for banishing some persons to hell or altogether annihilating their souls. Indeed, on a voluntarist account of divine goodness, *any* reasons God might have will be morally sufficient just in virtue of being *his* reasons.

Since I have objected to voluntarism here and yet accept that we do not have limitless insight into the nature of divine goodness, perhaps a word of explanation is in order. Orthodox Christians believe that because Jesus Christ was divine, any act he performed during his earthly life was righteous—including certain surprising actions: scourging the money changers, rebuking his mother, and so forth. These actions surprise us because they do not comport well with our initial intuitions about how a righteous person will behave.[57]

That our own prereflective conception of righteousness would leave little room for this sort of activity does not require the kind of voluntarism I have argued against. It does, however, illustrate the difficulty involved when humans attempt to judge whether God is righteous in performing or even allowing certain acts. The rejection of voluntarism does not entail the possibility of full human comprehension of what it means for God to be good or of what God's goodness specifically requires in particular circumstances. What matters is that some analogy exist between the use of the term "goodness" in ordinary moral discourse and its use as a predicate of the divine nature. As long as something of the meaning of divine goodness may be apprehended by us, through the application of our normal concept of "goodness," we may be justified in our belief that even startling acts performed by God are characteristically good. Furthermore, while we may witness certain acts of God behind a veil of ignorance at the present, upon reflection or through access to revelation we may come to apprehend the virtue of these acts in a way compatible with our fundamental beliefs about morally praiseworthy action.

The Mechanism for Sanctification

Augustinians must also take a dim view of the character of the end state Hick describes as "unqualifiedly good" and as an "infinite good." First, he expects the fulfillment of the soul-making purpose to be "decisive," characterized by "endless joy," successful to the point of eradicating all evil and establishing irreversible moral perfection.[58] It is one aspect of the infinite nature of this eschatological good that it is eventually instantiated on a permanent basis. But this is a rather difficult claim to make good, particularly within the constraints of Hick's own theodicy hypothesis. He insists that the soul-making process is necessarily gradual and that it takes longer for those who are most unsanctified to reach moral and spiritual perfection. Yet it is a "true deduction" that this gradual process will have its terminus in the goal it seeks to fulfill.

The divine objective to make souls cannot, according to Hick, be brought about by divine fiat. So what is the mechanism that ensures the permanent fulfillment of this ideal, and what guarantees that the end state of humans, characterized as moral and spiritual perfection, will persist eternally? Most important, what change is effected in human persons such that they retain their identities, reach moral and spiritual perfection, remain free creatures, and never fall into recidivism? The transformation implicit in such a state of affairs must call for something radical within the soul-making process to bring it about, for all empirical data about human behavior indicate that this sort of permanent alteration of character evades the reach of most (if not all) humans.

Even instances of the most remarkable moral progress achieved by persons in this life do not approach the quality of character picked out by the idea of perfection. All of the saints and prophets that come most readily to mind as our best moral and spiritual exemplars (with the notable exception of Jesus) humbly confess how meager is their own progress in comparison with the moral and spiritual distance that remains to be traveled. Indeed, we look upon it as a sign of spiritual attainment when such humble disclaimers are sincerely uttered. Often, the most recognizably saintly figures seem themselves to await a kind of complete sanctification by divine fiat.

Theodicists of the Augustinian persuasion do not fail to acknowledge the soul-making potential of human beings living in this sort of world. But in their view this gradual transformation cannot be brought to realized perfection apart from what amounts to a transfusion of divine grace into the life of the one who freely entrusts oneself to God by faith. On their own humans show no promise of ever reaching their intended moral and spiritual destination, though some (I do not say all) express their desire for moral perfection with utmost sincerity. What progress they do manifest is not even qualitatively the same as what moral perfection entails. Behavior may conform to a divine moral ideal while character remains substantially unchanged. It is character transformation that corresponds to moral and spiritual perfection, and this is brought about by a unique vision of the goodness of God, which most Catholic theologians call the "Beatific Vision" and many Protestant theologians refer to as "glorification."

In the very nature of the case, this kind of reconstitution of the moral dimension of human nature is nothing less than radical and cataclysmic. In the eschaton, God will uphold the intention of those who would but often fail to direct their wills toward him in the present order of human existence. Through his direct enablement, their character will finally and perfectly conform to that pattern which God wills for them. Those whom we recognize as "saints" in this life have already begun to give evidence of an uncommon partnership with God in this respect.

Hick produces nothing of the same order that is equal to the task of decisively achieving the soul-making end for humans. What Hick does describe is a vaguely conceived state of "unity in the atman," a "richly complex shared consciousness."[59] But this serves only to characterize, however obscurely, the nature of the end state, not the manner in which it is, in the quintessential moment of process, finally achieved.

Furthermore, it invites the suspicion that Hick's former worries about identity conditions for humans in the eschaton are now forgotten. He should say what he means by a "richly complex shared consciousness." It may well turn out that there is little difference between the end state Hick envisions here and the annihilationist proposal he finds so repugnant. For it would seem that even on his view there no longer are, in the final analysis, individual souls.

Difficulties about identity conditions for humans throughout the soul-making process are acute at both ends of the process. My remarks here have to do with the existence of this tension in connection with the realization of the end state of perfection, vaguely denoted by "unity in the atman." But it could just as well be observed that this tension exists for Hick's conception of human evolution, where the human condition develops from one of epistemic distance to one of moral responsibility, from the original pre-*Homo sapiens* position to the eventual status of free moral creatures. Hick does not explain how entities that are not yet persons undergo the ontological change of becoming persons without suffering a corresponding change in identity. This is the question of how an entity can sustain a change in ontological status and yet remain the same entity. And it is a very general problem for the theory of evolution.

Hick abjures *any* picture of realized perfection in which humans are depicted as being "transmuted in the twinkling of an eye into perfect creatures."[60] Unfortunately, the same considerations he thinks militate against this possibility in Augustinian theodicy undercut the reasonableness of his own doctrine that ultimate human moral perfection is irreversible. What could guarantee the outcome he envisions? He thinks that God might be able to bring about the sort of qualitative difference denoted by moral and spiritual perfection "through the work of prophets and saints, through the resulting religious traditions, and through the individual's religious experience."[61] However, none of these has yet proved effectual—that is, never yet has a single individual become fully human by these means. What assurance does Hick have that these previously tried methods— and not something radically different—will eventually, after much persistence and patience on God's part, succeed?

The Soul-making Process and the End State

Hick has also suggested that "it is the boundaries of life that provide the pressure that constitutes it a person-making history." A peculiar sort of "psycho-analytic experience" that one undergoes during the "temporary *bardo* phase" of one's life history, intervening between one life and the next, is supposed to be enough to elicit the self-awareness sufficient to prompt upward progress on the ladder of soul-making.[62] Hick acknowledges that the character of this mental state is not sufficient to absolutely prevent moral retrogression. He does not say what evidence supports this thesis, but perhaps the familiar occurrence of deathbed conversions could count as evidence that the human psyche operates in this fashion.

Still, the model is seriously problematic for a number of reasons. It might be questionable whether humans act with complete sincerity in such circumstances. The effectiveness of this scenario would depend upon the deception—or false belief, if one prefers—that this life avails the only opportunity for one to choose God. But anyone who is already convinced of Hick's many-lives hypothesis could understandably be less inclined to leap with faith into the loving arms of God, for one would have many future opportunities to be reconciled with him. Suppose certain individuals, knowing that they will have as many opportunities in the future as they require, decide to wait indefinitely. What could motivate them to change their minds? The means said to be at God's disposal often work only on the presupposition that time is running out. The prophet's plea and the saint's example, strong incentives that they are, are generally interpreted in the context of a sense of urgency and finality.

In the final analysis, Hick must rely entirely on the prospects of private religious experience to awaken human interest in God's program of making souls. But then the question arises: What assurance do we have that experiences of this kind are effectual? If it is the power and love of God that provides the guarantee, then we are back to wondering why God must wait so indefinitely to conjure the required quality of religious experience for the reluctant saint-in-the-making. At this point we run out of explanatory postulates, keeping in mind that Hick's view forbids the possibility of any kind of cataclysmic moment of fully realized moral perfection that smacks of divine fiat.

His conception of the end state is a fugitive vision, not because it is unverifiable but because it is unachievable.[63] Something like the machinery of a Beatific Vision is needed to permanently secure the faithful devotion of persons to the God of love. In Hick's eschatological construct, there is nothing to ensure that some will not eventually slip away from the state of moral and spiritual perfection, for he disallows any kind of action by divine fiat to realize such a moral state on a permanent basis. Human freedom, in his system, must then put the divine purpose at interminable risk of nonfulfillment. If human freedom does not entail this possibility, then the postulation of many lives is the postulation of a needlessly protracted course for human history. Indeed, it would make more sense to postulate an infinite process of soul-making, with no pledges whatsoever about the possible final fulfillment of human perfection. But this cannot justify evil any more than can the scenario that includes either eternal hell or annihilation. Worse yet, an infinite process of soul-making for recalcitrant individuals would mean that the end state must be perpetually postponed, permitting these individuals to "blackmail the universe."[64]

Fairness and the Afterlife

Some free-will defenders wish to acknowledge the emotional appeal of universalism without acquiescing to the logic behind it. The problem of evil can seem "a bit less intractable for the universalist than for the non-universalist."[65] This sentiment is ultimately unwarranted, however. Unqualified sympathy with those who endorse universalism represents a failure to reflect on the implications of universalism. First, human freedom is ultimately denied if humans are universally, because irresistibly, drawn to God despite their initial bias against God. Related to this is the fact that, with the dissolution of genuine human freedom, the possibility of moral activity is withdrawn and the "category of the personal," to which Hick is so committed, is thereby rendered nugatory. Furthermore, universalism exacts a heavy price in terms of a proper appraisal of the divine character. God cannot be truly loving if he compels his creatures, by means of even the most subtle manipulation, to love him in return. Also, he cannot be ultimately just if he makes heaven indiscriminately compulsory for all, so that the most stubborn "converts" share in the same heavenly blessings as those who show less resistance to God's persuasive love.[66]

There remains the matter of "unfinished business" of "incalculable scope"[67]—the grossly depraved actions of human agents living on this earth. It is morally repugnant to imagine that the accounts are not balanced by proper punishment in the afterlife. Frederick Buechner, who with tongue in cheek characterizes the full body of Christian doctrine as essentially wishful thinking, remarks that the Christian doctrine of retribution for the wicked "reflects the wish that somewhere the score is being kept."[68] Even in his discussion of postmortem sanctification, brought about through a series of purgatorial lives, Hick omits all reference to a proper theory of punishment. But this matter begs to be addressed. Justice and God's love for the victims of human cruelty make it a necessity. Does Hick believe that punishment is altogether unwarranted?

Furthermore, it is, arguably, "good that God should not let a man damn himself without much urging and giving him many opportunities to change his mind, but it is bad that someone should not in the all-important matter of the destiny of his soul be allowed finally to destroy it."[69] As John Roth points out, on Hick's view of the matter "it is questionable whether virtue will ever be its own reward."[70] The Augustinian tradition affirms a literal hell in defense of God's justice in treating real moral evil as reprehensible and culpable—God's love and justice demand that humans be held accountable for the manner in which they exercise their moral freedom.

Finally, as Stephen Davis observes, in positing universalism Hick fails to meet his own "requirement that in order to be acceptable a theodicy must be 'consistent with the data . . . of the religious tradition on which it is based.' "[71] Universalism does not accord well with the Christian tradition to which Hick nominally subscribes. If Hick's universalism is based on the moral repugnance of the notion of hell, then perhaps these considerations provide the necessary corrective to this logically deficient and evidently emotive response.

The free-will defense naturally seeks to explain the justification of hell in terms of human freedom to turn the will away from God. Free-will defenders charge universalists with revoking human freedom by making the eventual choice for God inevitable. "Free will is a good thing, and for God to override it is to all appearances a bad thing," explains Swinburne.[72]

Hick answers the charge about divine manipulation by suggesting that humankind is "endowed with a certain nature" that exhibits "a basic Godward bias," and he cites Augustine's famous line of the *Confessions* in support of this contention: " 'Our hearts are restless until they find their rest in Thee.' "[73] This appeal to Augustine is rather odd since Augustine thought that human restlessness evinced a tendency to recoil from God, not that restlessness is a function of any kind of bias or propensity to choose God.

At any rate, Hick's account of human freedom in terms of determinate human nature results in a "denatured" free-will defense. Certainly humans must have a determinate nature as existents. This is part of what it means for humans to be members of a class. But if their nature includes moral freedom, then there must be something indeterminate about their moral character as well. This is what it means for them to be free. In effect, human freedom comes to nothing, on Hick's view, since it is defined in terms of the inevitable determinateness of human nature, which again is why I have called Hick's account a quasi-free-will defense. This is the focus of M. B. Ahern's criticism of Hick:

> Furthermore, although he believes that all men, no matter how evil in this world, will share the blessedness of an afterlife, Hick gives no clear ground for certainty of this. If unforced moral response to God and to good is a supreme value, it is difficult to see how it could be certain, either before creation or after it, that all men will actually make this response in this life or in the next. For his belief Hick claims not absolute certainty but practical certainty because of God's power to win people to Himself. However, he does not explain how this power of God's is to be reconciled with unforced moral responses in every instance.[74]

Hick's Modified Reincarnationism

If Hick's universalism represents a departure from Christian orthodoxy, his willingness to embrace reincarnationist themes only accentuates this departure. Although a full evaluation of his westernized reincarnationism would require a thorough examination of his book *Death and Eternal Life,* any extensive appraisal of his theodicy cannot fail to make a few critical observations about this aspect of his system.

Hick's notion of the progressive sanctification of humans *after* death is based on an analogy with the present life and the nature of God's soul-making purpose for humans. Both progression and retrogression characterize the moral development of humans in this life. According to Hick, God's purpose of soul-making is by nature a long process that includes personal travail. Seldom if ever does the process reach completion in the life of any human individual before death. Therefore, this process must continue after death in some way analogous to its perdurability in this life.

What is true about the soul-making process in this life "is presumably true of the intermediate state in which the sanctifying process, begun on earth, continues towards its completion, its extent and duration being determined by the degree of *un*sanctification remaining to be overcome at the time of death."[75] But the very affinity that the intermediate state must have with this earthly life is also the basis for questioning the credibility of Hick's thesis. Davis makes this point when he objects that "if people are as morally and spiritually free after death as they are now—as Hick claims—then the evidence of how people behave here and now does not give me much hope that the human race will gradually improve till all are the God-conscious 'persons' God intended."[76] If the process of soul-making must go on as it has in this life, the similarity that holds between this life and the afterlife proves too much.

Just as Davis inveighs against Hick's universalism by appealing to his own criterion of adhering to the Christian tradition, so might one challenge Hick's "Christian reincarnationism" on similar grounds. This aspect of his thinking is radically avant-garde vis-à-vis the Christian tradition. His association of the Hindu notion of "atman" with the Christian doctrine of the Trinity is particularly unsettling. If for no other reason, this propensity alone renders his overall theodicy suspect as a candidate for being a bona fide "Christian alternative." It is not just that his sympathy for reincarnationist doctrine militates against the traditional Christian doctrine of resurrection. To suggest that a doctrine as far removed from the historical consensus of Christianity as reincarnation might eventually become orthodox is to play havoc with the notion of orthodoxy.

It is ironic that Hick has felt compelled to buttress the creditability of his theodicy by linking it with the historic figure of Irenaeus when he is so willing to give up universally acknowledged conditions of orthodoxy within the Christian tradition. There are moments when he refers to Irenaeus as "the first great representative" of the sort of theodicy he embraces and develops, and he emphasizes the point that this theodicy "originated in the earliest and most ecumenical phase of Christian thought."[77] The reader is left with the distinct impression that something important is to be gained by tethering the soul-making theodicy of its contemporary proponents to the reputation of a stalwart of the patristic period of the Christian church. Indeed, Hick considers it a desirable feature of a Christian theodicy that it be recognizably continuous with the Christian religious tradition historically.[78] He maintains, therefore, that, in the spirit of perennial variety that has characterized theological development in the history of the church, two distinctive theodicies have their inception in very early proponents, namely, Augustine and Irenaeus.

The point is that Hick expresses great respect for maintaining solidarity with the chief lines of Christian theology shared by its earliest champions. However, belief in reincarnation has always been a mark of heterodoxy for the Christian community of faith, though the current century has witnessed unprecedented experimentation with the possibility of a Christian doctrine of reincarnation.[79]

Quite apart from misgivings about Hick's conception of an emergent orthodoxy, there is reason to wonder about the prudence of embracing reincarnation for the sake of theodicy. Once again, if the Augustinian conception of the divine purpose is accepted then there is no compelling reason to postulate the kind of intermediate afterlife that is virtually unavoidable in Hick's account. In the Augustinian tradition, this earthly life provides every individual ample opportunity to make an ultimate commitment to God. If one resists until death, then God honors the choice that is freely made, for only freely made choices are compatible with God's purpose in creating humans as free moral agents. In creating free creatures divine omnipotence submitted, as it were, to this possibility. The Sovereign of the universe created the possibility of having his own will resisted. "The one principle of hell is—'I am my own.' "[80] That is, the reality of a hell underwrites the Augustinian conviction that God has not stacked the deck against human freedom.

As Lewis wrote, "I willingly believe that the damned are, in one sense, successful, rebels to the end; that the doors of hell are locked on the *inside*."[81] Humans who turn their wills away from God do, indeed, forfeit the Beatific Vision; but in the hell they choose instead they eternally reveal the justice and love of God.

Afterword
by John Hick

It is not often that a book includes a critical review of itself! This is however, in effect, what Professor Geivett has invited me to provide; and I am grateful for the invitation.

The difference in point of view between the main part of the book and this Afterword is that between "conservative" and "progressive" (or "liberal") forms of Christianity. This is today a major tension, and the long-term danger is that increasing polarization should result, in effect, in two Christianities. If this can be avoided, it will be by dialogue between the two positions; and hopefully this book, although dealing only with one aspect of the conservative/progressive debate, may encourage such dialogue.

Douglas Geivett's book makes two claims. One is that rational argument can establish the existence of God to the satisfaction of a reasonable person. The second is that a theodicy of the traditional Augustinian type is to be preferred to one of the Irenaean kind, such as I have advocated.

Although related, these are logically independent claims. That is to say, one could hold that it is possible to prove, as a valid philosophical conclusion, that God exists (thus producing, in Cardinal Newman's terms, a notional but not a real belief in God) and at the same time to accept an Irenaean-type theodicy; and likewise one could deny that any such proof is possible and at the same time accept an Augustinian-type theodicy. However, Geivett is right in noting that I myself both reject the theistic arguments and accept an Irenaean theodicy, and that I regard this as a coherent and viable combination.

Of course, if one had an absolute proof of the reality of a perfectly good and all-powerful deity, the need for a theodicy would be much less pressing than it is on the contrary assumption. For we should know both that God exists and that God must have a good reason for permitting evil, whether or not we can discern that reason. Geivett does not claim, however, that there is such a proof. He offers something less than logical demonstration. Hence his need, like my own, for a theodicy.

I shall return to theodicy and the relation between theodicy and the grounds for theistic belief. But first let me explain my misgivings about Geivett's own proposed theistic argument. It may initially seem strange that one who believes firmly in the reality of God should criticize an attempt to establish this by sound reasoning. However, the project of natural theology—of trying to prove God's existence or, more modestly, of trying to show it to be more probable than not—has failed in the opinion of most contemporary philosophers, including most theistic philosophers. And if they are right, as I believe that they are, one is only storing up disappointment and disillusion by leading people to rely on arguments that will not withstand critical examination. And when Christian philosophers, including myself, point out the defects of the various kinds of natural theology and recommend a different epistemological approach, this is in the interests of a more enduring basis for belief in God.

For many centuries it was generally assumed within Christendom that we can establish God's existence, either by St. Anselm's ontological proof, St. Thomas's cosmological proofs, or the arguments from (or to) design that flourished in the eighteenth and nineteenth centuries, mainly in Protestant circles. But almost any textbook in the philosophy of religion today recounts the demolition of these arguments by Hume, Kant, and others. There was, it is true, a valiant attempt in the 1960s and 1970s to reestablish the ontological argument in its recently (re)discovered second form, but after a flurry of discussion this has not proved convincing to more than a few.

As a result of this history most of those who continue to advocate a natural theology have lowered their aim from proof to probability. The most considerable recent attempt to show, to the satisfaction of any rational person, that the existence of God is more probable than not, is that of Richard Swinburne in *The Existence of God* (1979). He sees that if this argument is to be more than the expression of a personal hunch, it must be numerically quantified, and he accordingly tries to prove, by a carefully constructed process of reasoning, that the probability of divine existence is more than 0.5. But it turns out, as others have argued (and as I have also argued in *An Interpretation of Religion*, chap. 6), that his assignment of numerical values to the various elements of the equation is, and in the nature of the case can only be, arbitrary, so that his impressive panoply of logical formulae covers only a personal estimate of likelihood.

Operating in what has thus become hostile territory for the natural theologian, Geivett is properly cautious in what he claims to have achieved. He says, "Finally, I have not pretended to demonstrate the existence of God. Rather, I have argued that the rational person should conclude that there is a God." Since his argument is not an attempted demonstration, it presumably falls within the more modest category of probability arguments. The probability remains, however, unquantified. But Geivett seeks to balance the vagueness of an unquantified judgment of probability by his claim that theism is the *only* explanation of the puzzling phenomenon of the existence and nature of the universe, so that whatever its degree of probability it is still the best explanation available.

We should remember, however, that a best-available explanation may or may not be the true explanation. The only available (and therefore the best) explanation of the movement of the sun across the sky was once that the sun revolves around the earth, but this was not in fact the true explanation. And there is always the possibility that our information is insufficient to reveal to us the true explanation of the universe as we find it. There is also the more radical possibility that the universe had no beginning and no explanation in terms of a prior reality that brought it into being.

Geivett's argument hinges, indeed, upon the claim that the universe had an absolute beginning in the big bang of some fifteen or more billion years ago. I can agree with him on two important points: (1) if the big bang was indeed an absolute beginning, its occurrence is an absolute mystery from the point of view of the natural sciences, and (2) the natural scientist would then have either to accept this absolute mystery as final or postulate a creative force of some kind external to our universe.

Suppose, for the moment, that the big bang was an absolute beginning and that an external force is accordingly postulated to account for it. Could we justifiably assume that this unknown cause of the big bang has the specific features of the God of Christian faith? I do not think so. Geivett's own argument that the postulated creative force must be a non-natural, morally good, personal agent relies at each point on question-begging assumptions. If the total universe is such as to produce our universe by the big bang, why must that totality be personal? Or good? Geivett's reasons are, to my mind, ones that appeal to the already convinced rather than to those who need convincing. All that we should be logically entitled to infer is that the total universe (in the sense of all that is) is more comprehensive than our own universe and is such as to have produced our own universe within it. But whether this happened by deliberate intent, by the operation of natural law, or otherwise remains open.

Returning, however, to the big bang: the fifteen or so billion year expansion has produced an immense universe of galaxies spread out over increasing distances of millions of light years, within which our earth is one of the planets of a very minor star on the edge of a very minor galaxy somewhere in the vastness of space; and this speck in the immensity of the cosmos will have produced conscious life for an infinitesimal flash of time within the total history of the universe. To assume that the entire universe is designed for the sake of we human creatures during this brief microsecond of cosmic history is rightly called the "anthropic principle." For it sets humanity at the center of the cosmos in essentially the same spirit as the old Ptolemaic astronomy. So far from such anthropic thinking establishing the truth of religion, it presupposes an already-existing religious faith. From within the circle of faith the heavens do indeed declare the glory of God; but from outside that circle, although the anthropic prejudice undoubtedly appeals to our human self-esteem, the view can be very different. As the physicist Steven Weinberg (quoted by Geivett) says, "It is very hard to realize that [the earth] is just a tiny part of an overwhelmingly hostile universe. It is even harder to realize that this present universe has evolved from an unspeakably unfamiliar early condition, and faces a future extinction of endless cold or intolerable heat. The more the universe seems comprehensible, the more it also seems pointless."

But we need to consider directly Geivett's conviction that the big bang was an absolute beginning. He argues this on both scientific and philosophical grounds. I cannot find either argument convincing. The two main options at present in scientific cosmology are that the expansion that began some fifteen billion years ago will continue indefinitely or that it will in due course be reversed by the gravitational pull of the matter in the universe, collapsing back into a single intensely dense point. The most recently reported research (April 1992) suggests that there is a vast amount of hidden matter, and that the present expansion will eventually be reversed. This likelihood (as it seems at present) fits one of the currently available cosmological models, that of a beginningless and endless series of expansions and contractions. According to this model the present phase of the universe had a beginning and will have an end; but the universe in its totality may have neither beginning nor end.

However, we cannot today responsibly claim it as more than a possibility either that the big bang was an absolute beginning or that it was the latest in a series. At present (1992) the latter possibility seems more likely. But nothing has been definitively established; and it is even possible that there will never be final certainty. In this situation any claim that scientific cosmology has either established or ruled out the existence of God is, in my view, an expression of wishful thinking. An endlessly expanding universe would not guarantee that the big bang constituted an absolute beginning, and a series of expansions and contractions would be compatible with the entire series being a divine creation.

The religious objection, then, to this type of natural theology is that, although initially attractive, it is liable in the end to disappoint the candid inquirer, turning him or her away from religious commitment.

In contrast to this line of apologetic my own view has long been, and still is, that the universe is religiously ambiguous—meaning by this, not that it has no definite character, but that it is capable from our present point of view within it of being consistently thought and experienced in both religious and naturalistic ways. Each aspect of the universe that prima facie supports a religious understanding of it (for example, the fact of moral goodness) can also be incorporated into a naturalistic worldview, and each aspect that prima facie supports a naturalistic understanding (such as the reality of evil) can also be incorporated into a religious worldview. And there is no objective sense of probability in which it can be shown that one of these interpretations is more probable than the other.

What leads a person to adopt and live in terms of either a religious or a naturalistic understanding of the universe is participation or nonparticipation in one of the historical streams of religious experience. Considered as evidence from which (along with other evidences) one might infer the existence of God, religious experience is open to contrary naturalistic interpretations. But considered, not as an item of evidence authorizing an inference, but as a putative experience of God, it takes us into a different epistemic situation. The question now is whether it is rational to trust this mode of experience so as to base both our beliefs and our lives upon it. I believe that it is. I have argued this at length elsewhere (e.g., in *An Interpretation of Religion,* chap. 13) and will not repeat the discussion here.

I thus hold that the correct philosophical defense of the rationality of religious belief consists in the empiricist argument for the rationality of basing beliefs on our experience, plus the extension of this to include religious experience. The general empiricist principle is of course subject to possible defeaters (or overriders), for there are circumstances in which it may not be rational to trust one's experience (e.g., if one has recently consumed a large amount of alcohol). And the extension of the empiricist principle to religious experience opens up a further range of possible defeaters, arising principally from the differences between sensory and religious experience. The former is universal, is compelling in that to trust it is biologically necessary, and is formed throughout the world by much the same system of concepts; whereas the latter is not universal, is not such that we distrust it at peril to our lives, and is formed by partially different sets of concepts within the different religious traditions. The proposed defeater to these defeaters consists in showing how these differences are correlated with differences in the supposed objects of the two modes of experience. Whereas the physical environment compels us to know it aright, God leaves us free to become or fail to become aware of God's presence, for the limitlessly valuable divine reality must be responded to freely. And because we exercise our cognitive freedom in terms of culturally varying conceptual systems, awareness of the divine is formed in different ways within the different religious traditions of the world. But the full discussion of the experiential ground of religious belief is considerably more complex; see, for example, the recent extensive treatment by William Alston in *Perceiving God* (1991).

The fact of evil—wickedness and suffering—stands in a different relationship to religious belief than these potential epistemological defeaters. The theodicy issue is a part—a very important part—of the debate about the religious ambiguity of the universe. Evil is not a defeater to the veridicality of religious experience as such, as is the claim that it lacks some feature of sense experience in virtue of which we habitually trust the latter. But insofar as the universe could be shown not to be ambiguous, but to point away from a religious understanding of it, to that extent the case for basing belief upon religious experience would be indirectly weakened. And so the theodicy debate figures as a major part of the larger debate about the religious ambiguity or otherwise of the universe.

For me, then, belief in God is not the outcome of a balancing of pro and contra items of evidence, with the fact of evil figuring in the contra column, but from participation in one of the historical streams of religious experience within a religiously ambiguous universe. As a ground of religious belief this can, in principle, be defeated either by attacks upon its epistemic parity with sense experience, or by considerations, such as the problem of evil, that would show—independently of religious experience—that the universe has a nontheous character. It is at this point that theodicies come on the scene to attempt to counteract this threat. They cannot establish the reality of God, but they may restore the religious ambiguity of the universe, which the fact of evil had seemed to upset.

Geivett has well outlined the Irenaean type of theodicy. It comes from an earlier phase of Christian thinking than that in which St. Augustine formed the orthodoxy that was to dominate the church for some fourteen centuries. For Augustine, the doctrine of the fall of humanity from an initial ideal state was crucial. (Stephen Davis's move away from this, cited by Geivett, represents his modification of an otherwise largely Augustinian theodicy to include an Irenaean element.) For St. Irenaeus and several of the other Hellenistic Fathers, Adam and Eve were created as immature creatures, sometimes even pictured as children, who were to grow in grace through the experience of living in (to use Keats's phrase) a "soul-making" world. The greatest modern Christian thinker to develop this profound early insight was Friedrich Schleiermacher, and many others have since followed him.

Created at an epistemic distance from God, as part of the larger phenomenon of animal life, we share a basic instinct for self-preservation that, at a higher level of consciousness, is our human self-centeredness. We are thus imperfect (or in Augustinian language "fallen") creatures. But we also have a capacity for self-transcendence, or love, and are in our heart of hearts oriented toward God as our highest good. Within this complex dual nature we exercise moral freedom. (Thus we are not, as Geivett suggests, deprived of moral freedom by our animal nature.)

The kind of environment that is appropriate for the growth of morally free beings is not a static paradise but a world process that contains challenges and problems and that calls forth self-sacrifice on behalf of others. Thus we find ourselves as imperfect beings in an imperfect world and immersed in the problem of evil—of why God permits both human acts of cruelty and malevolence, and the harsh and dangerous aspects of the natural world. From an Irenaean point of view, human wrongdoing is part of the price of freedom, and a world functioning in accordance with its own laws, in which there are real perils and in which real disasters can occur, is part of the cost of person-making.

As Geivett rightly points out, such a theodicy requires an eschatological dimension. To come to completion, the person-making process must continue beyond this life to its fulfillment in a state of human perfection in which our epistemic distance from God has been overcome and we exist at last in God's presence in the divine "kingdom." This completion is an infinite, because eternal, good that justifies the pain and heartache of our long temporal journey toward it. (Geivett rejects the idea of an infinite good as foreign to an Augustinian theodicy. But I do not see why a traditionally Augustinian theologian need deny that eternal life is good and is therefore an infinite good.)

There is of course much more to this kind of theodicy than can be indicated in a few sentences. Some of the further aspects are described by Geivett, and yet other aspects in my *Evil and the God of*

Love. An informed judgment concerning my own version of this theodicy must presuppose a reading of that book.

There is, however, one further topic that should be mentioned here. Geivett accepts the traditional Augustinian doctrine of hell. He says, "If God's purpose is to secure the greater good of human freedom, which when properly exercised leads the way to ultimate beatitude but also creates the possibility of the refusal to choose God, then hell, even if it involves eternal torment, may be justly permitted since it reflects God's eternal commitment to this good purpose." Again, "In the Augustinian tradition, according to which hell is crucial to the free-will defense, God's purposes for humans are in no way 'eternally frustrated,' for his purposes respecting human freedom are eternally fulfilled by virtue of separating those who choose God and those who do not in heaven and hell, respectively."

This traditional doctrine of hell is one of the aspects of conservative Christianity that repels the typical modern mind. It seems morally incredible that a perfectly loving Creator should devise a situation in which millions of men and women suffer eternally. The alternative to this, however, is not that God should (in Geivett's phrase) "force beatitude upon unwilling persons." For our freedom is always freedom within a given nature. And it may be that God has initially formed us as "religious animals," our hearts set, in Augustine's famous phrase, *ad te domine,* "towards you, lord." (This may or may not be consistent with other aspects of Augustine's thought, but few, if any, large bodies of writings, produced over a long span of years, are totally consistent!) Thus whilst it remains logically possible that any (or indeed all) humans will eternally reject God, the actual constitution of our nature is such that sooner or later the infinite resourcefulness of infinite love, working without temporal limit, will enable all to find their ultimate fulfillment. (For a fuller and more adequate discussion, see my *Death and Eternal Life,* chap. 13.)

May there not, however, be a logical problem in this combination of free will and universal salvation? For on the one hand it is said to follow from the fact of God's omnipotence and love that all *will* in fact be saved, so that (1) it is necessary that all will be saved. But on the other hand it is said that this saving is contingent, occurring through our own free will, so that (2) it is not *necessary* that all will be saved. Is there not here a logical contradiction? The answer, I think, is no. For we have to remember the distinction between *de dicto* and *de re* necessity. Proposition (1) is a case of *de dicto* necessity: what it affirms to be necessary is the truth of the proposition "all will be saved," that is, contingently saved. Proposition (2) on the other hand is a case of *de re* necessity: it affirms that it is not of the essential nature of the "all" that they will be saved, that is, they are not saved of logical necessity, but contingently. Thus "It is necessary that all will be saved" is not affirmed and denied in the same sense. It is affirmed *de dicto* and denied *de re,* and there is accordingly no logical contradiction.

The suggestion I have made that further person-making beyond this life may well occur in a series of finite lives, because of the creative pressure exerted by the boundaries of birth and death, is offered as a reasonable speculation, not as theological dogma. It is a suggestion to be considered on its merits in comparison with alternative possibilities. It is not, however, properly identified with the idea of reincarnation, as the term is normally used, since this refers to repeated lives in our present world.

It would be possible to prolong these comments indefinitely. But the purpose is only to remind the reader that there are many sides to all these questions, and that continued discussion is in order. Douglas Geivett has written a stimulating series of reflections on natural theology and on theodicy that will, I hope, assist the ongoing conservative/progressive dialogue.

NOTES

CHAPTER 1

1. Bertrand Russell, *The Autobiography of Bertrand Russell: 1872–1914* (Boston: Little, Brown, 1967), pp. 3–4.

2. Gabriel Marcel, *The Philosophy of Existentialism* (Secaucus, N.J.: Citadel, 1956), p. 19.

3. Langdon Gilkey, *Message and Existence: An Introduction to Christian Theology* (San Francisco: Harper & Row, 1979), p. 14.

4. See Jeffrey Burton Russell's four-volume history of the personification of evil. These works reference allusions to evil in art, literature, and the popular culture, as well as in philosophy and theology (*The Devil: Perceptions of Evil from Antiquity to Primitive Christianity* [Ithaca, N.Y.: Cornell University Press, 1977]; *Satan: The Early Christian Tradition* [Ithaca, N.Y.: Cornell University Press, 1981]; *Lucifer: The Devil in the Middle Ages* [Ithaca, N.Y.: Cornell University Press, 1984]; and *Mephistopheles: The Devil in the Modern World* [Ithaca, N.Y.: Cornell University Press, 1986]). See also his summary volume *The Prince of Darkness: Radical Evil and the Power of Good in History* (Ithaca, N.Y.: Cornell University Press, 1988).

5. Harold S. Kushner, *When Bad Things Happen to Good People* (New York: Avon, 1981), p. 1.

6. Ibid., p. 5.

7. Philip Yancey, *Where Is God When It Hurts?* (Grand Rapids, Mich.: Zondervan, 1977), p. 16.

8. Thomas Malthus, *An Essay on the Principle of Population* (London: Penguin, 1970), pp. 211–12.

9. Boethius *De consolatione philosophiae* (*The Consolation of Philosophy*) 1. pr 4. The quotation is from the Loeb Classical Library edition (Cambridge, Mass.: Harvard University Press, 1946), p. 151. Scholars conjecture that Boethius is here quoting Epicurus, in dependence upon Lactantius *De ira Dei* 13. 21.

10. David Hume, *Dialogues Concerning Natural Religion*, pt. 10. The quotation is from the Norman Kemp Smith edition (Indianapolis, Ind.: Bobbs-Merrill, 1947), p. 198.

11. Martin Gardner, *The Whys of a Philosophical Scrivener* (New York: Morrow, 1983), p. 243.

12. John Bowker, *Problems of Suffering in Religions of the World* (New York: Cambridge University Press, 1970), p. 2.

13. For two distinct ways in which evil is problematic or otherwise of

interest to atheists, see Germain Grisez, *Beyond the New Theism: A Philosophy of Religion* (Notre Dame, Ind.: University of Notre Dame Press, 1975), p. 301; and F. C. Copleston, *Aquinas* (Baltimore, Md.: Penguin, 1955), p. 148.

14. Nicolas Berdyaev, *The Destiny of Man* (New York: Harper & Brothers, 1960), p. 23.

15. See Kai Nielsen, *Ethics Without God* (Buffalo, N.Y.: Prometheus, 1973).

16. John Hick, "Evil, The Problem of," in *The Encyclopedia of Philosophy*, ed. Paul Edwards (New York: Macmillan, 1967), 3:136.

17. J. L. Mackie, "Evil and Omnipotence," in *God and Evil: Readings on the Theological Problem of Evil*, ed. Nelson Pike (Englewood Cliffs, N.J.: Prentice Hall, 1964), p. 47.

18. Antony Flew, *God and Philosophy* (London: Hutchinson, 1966), p. 48.

19. Brian Davies, *An Introduction to the Philosophy of Religion* (Oxford: Oxford University Press, 1982), p. 16.

20. See George Mavrodes, *Belief in God: A Study in the Epistemology of Religion* (New York: Random House, 1970), p. 99.

CHAPTER 2

1. John Hick, *Evil and the God of Love*, rev. ed. (San Francisco: Harper & Row, 1978), p. 12.

2. Augustine *On Free Choice of the Will*, trans. Anna S. Benjamin and L. H. Hackstaff (Indianapolis, Ind.: Bobbs-Merrill, 1964), p. xv. All quotations from Augustine's *De libero arbitrio voluntatis* are from this edition.

3. Ibid., p. xx.

4. Augustine *De libero arbitrio* 1.1.

5. Others have interpreted Augustine as much less natural-theology-oriented than I do. Alan Richardson is a clear example (see his manual on *Christian Apologetics* [London: SCM, 1947]). Ronald H. Nash, who acknowledges the complexity of Augustine's views about the relation of faith and reason, is a *possible* example (see his study *The Light of the Mind: St. Augustine's Theory of Knowledge* [Lexington: University Press of Kentucky, 1969]). Much of what Nash says in his monograph on Augustine is compatible with regarding him as a natural theologian. For an account that clearly regards Augustine as a natural theologian, see Ralph M. McInerny, *A History of Western Philosophy: From St. Augustine to Ockham* (Notre Dame, Ind.: University of Notre Dame Press, 1970), pp. 32–36. Etienne Gilson cites a number of European figures who have offered conflicting interpretations of Augustine's views on theistic proof (*History of Christian Philosophy in the Middle Ages* [New York: Random House, 1955], p. 594 n. 33).

6. Gilson, *Christian Philosophy*, p. 77.

7. Augustine *De libero arbitrio* 2.15.

8. Augustine *De libero arbitrio* 1.2.

9. Augustine *De libero arbitrio* 2.16.

10. Augustine *De libero arbitrio* 2.17.

11. Augustine *De libero arbitrio* 2.17.

12. Augustine *De libero arbitrio* 2.17.

13. Augustine *De libero arbitrio* 2.17.

14. For an extension of this line of thinking, see the next section, which discusses Thomas Aquinas and the notion of God as *per accidens* cause of certain evil states of affairs.

15. Augustine *De libero arbitrio* 3.17.

16. Augustine *De libero arbitrio* 2.18.

17. Augustine *De libero arbitrio* 2.18.

18. Augustine *De libero arbitrio* 2.20.

19. Augustine *De libero arbitrio* 2.19.

20. Augustine *De libero arbitrio* 3.1.

21. Augustine *De libero arbitrio* 3.3.

22. Augustine *De libero arbitrio* 3.3.

23. Augustine *De libero arbitrio* 3.3.

24. Several contemporary philosophers have suggested that God is "the direct cause of freedom," or that divine causality is "a condition of" human freedom, or that divine creation is a "necessary condition of" the occurrence of all free actions. See, respectively, Herbert McCabe, "God. II. Freedom," *New Blackfriars* 61 (1980): 460; James Ross, "Creation II," in *The Existence and Nature of God*, ed. Alfred J. Freddoso (Notre Dame, Ind.: University of Notre Dame Press, 1983), p. 131; and Brian Davies, *Thinking About God* (London: Geoffrey Chapman, 1985), pp. 208–9, 221–22. Davies quotes Aquinas: "Every operation, therefore, of anything is traced back to him [God] as its cause" (p. 209). This *may* approximate what Augustine had in mind. Davies thinks this view requires rejecting the free-will defense. Augustine certainly did not have *this* in mind, and neither did Aquinas. As Alvin Plantinga states, "Although of course God may cause it to be the case that I *am* free with respect to [an action] *A*, he cannot cause it to be the case either that I freely take or that I freely refrain from this action—and this though he is omnipotent" (*The Nature of Necessity* [Oxford: Clarendon Press, 1974], p. 171). See the discussion in Chapter 11.

25. This is the thrust of Augustine's discussion in *De libero arbitrio* 3.4.

26. See Augustine *De libero arbitrio* 3.5.

27. Norman L. Geisler and Winfried Corduan, *Philosophy of Religion*, 2d ed. (Grand Rapids, Mich.: Baker, 1988), p. 325.

28. Hick, *Evil and the God of Love*, p. 93.

29. Thomas Gilby, trans., *St. Thomas Aquinas: Philosophical Texts* (Durham, N.C.: Labyrinth, 1982), p. xiii.

30. Thomas Aquinas *Summa theologiae* 1a.2.3. This quotation is from Anton C. Pegis, ed., *Introduction to St. Thomas Aquinas* (New York: Modern Library, 1948). Unless otherwise noted, all quotations of the *Summa theologiae* are from this source.

31. Thomas Aquinas *Summa theologiae* 1a.2.3.

32. Thomas Aquinas *Summa theologiae* 1a.2.2.

33. See Thomas Aquinas *Summa theologiae* 1a.2.3.

34. Thomas Aquinas *Summa theologiae* 1a.2.3. Thomas is quoting Augustine's *Enchiridion* 11 (italics in Pegis edition).

35. Thomas Aquinas *Summa theologiae* 1a.3.
36. Thomas Aquinas *Compendium theologiae* chap. 21. The quotation is from Cyril Vollert, trans., *Compendium of Theology* (St. Louis, Mo.: Herder, 1947), p. 23.
37. Thomas Aquinas *In libros Posteriorum Analyticorum expositio* (Commentary on Aristotle's *Posterior Analytics*) lect. 6 (as cited in Gilby, *Philosophical Texts*, p. 69).
38. Thomas Aquinas *Summa theologiae* 1a.4.2 (as cited in Gilby, *Philosophical Texts*, p. 73).
39. Thomas Aquinas *Summa theologiae* 1a.4.2 (as cited in Gilby, *Philosophical Texts*, p. 74).
40. Thomas Aquinas *Summa contra gentiles* 37.2. All quotations of the *Summa contra gentiles* are from idem, *Summa Contra Gentiles, Book One: God*, trans. Anton C. Pegis (Garden City, N.Y.: Image Books, Doubleday, 1955).
41. Thomas Aquinas *Summa contra gentiles* 37.1.
42. Thomas Aquinas *Summa contra gentiles* 37.3.
43. See Thomas Aquinas *Summa contra gentiles* 38.
44. See Thomas Aquinas *Summa contra gentiles* 39.
45. Thomas Aquinas *Summa theologiae* 1a.48.3. Aquinas says, "Hence the meaning of evil depends on the meaning of good" (1a.48.1 [as cited in Gilby, *Philosophical Texts*, p. 164]).
46. Thomas Aquinas *Summa theologiae* 1a.48.4.
47. F. C. Copleston, *Aquinas* (Baltimore, Md.: Penguin, 1955), p. 151.
48. Thomas Aquinas *Summa theologiae* 1a.49.1.
49. Thomas Aquinas *Summa theologiae* 1a.49.1.
50. Thomas Aquinas *Summa theologiae* 1a.49.1.
51. Paul J. Glenn, *A Tour of the Summa* (Rockford, Ill.: Tan, 1978), p. 44.
52. Ibid., p. 43, in exposition of *Summa theologiae* 1a.49.1 (see especially Thomas's "Reply to Objection 3").
53. Copleston, *Aquinas*, pp. 154–55.
54. Thomas Aquinas *Expositio in Job ad litteram* (Commentary on Job) Prologue (as cited in Gilby, *Philosophical Texts*, p. 163).
55. Ninian Smart, *Philosophers and Religious Truth* (New York: Macmillan, 1964), p. 75.
56. Hick, *Evil and the God of Love*, p. 154.
57. Cited in Benson Mates, *The Philosophy of Leibniz: Metaphysics and Language* (New York: Oxford University Press, 1986), p. 33.
58. Richard H. Popkin, "Bayle, Pierre," in *The Encyclopedia of Philosophy*, ed. Paul Edwards (New York: Macmillan, 1967), 1:257.
59. James Collins, *God in Modern Philosophy* (Chicago: Henry Regnery, 1959), p. 131. Still, "in his writings Bayle rarely discussed religion without making Manichaeanism or Judaism seem either more plausible or more significant than Christianity" (Popkin, "Bayle, Pierre," p. 261).
60. Antony Flew, *A Dictionary of Philosophy*, rev. 2d ed. (New York: St. Martin's Press, 1984), p. 39.
61. Pierre Bayle, *Historical and Critical Dictionary: Selections*, trans. Richard H. Popkin (Indianapolis, Ind.: Bobbs-Merrill, 1965), p. 298.

62. Ibid., p. 429.

63. James Collins, *A History of Modern European Philosophy* (Milwaukee, Wis.: Bruce, 1954), p. 254.

64. Collins, *God in Modern Philosophy*, p. 128.

65. See Gottfried Wilhelm von Leibniz *Monadology* 45, and his discussion of this proof in his *New Essays on Human Understanding* 4.10.7.

66. Leibniz *Monadology* 38. All quotations are from idem, *Monadology and Other Philosophical Essays*, trans. Paul Schrecker and Anne Martin Schrecker (Indianapolis, Ind.: Bobbs-Merrill, 1965). Leibniz states the principle of sufficient reason in the *Monadology* 32 and uses it in his a posteriori argument for the existence of God in sections 36 to 38.

67. H. J. McCloskey, *God and Evil* (The Hague, Netherlands: Martinus Nijhoff, 1974), p. 78.

68. M. B. Ahern, *The Problem of Evil* (New York: Schocken, 1971), p. 59.

69. Flew, *Dictionary of Philosophy*, p. 201.

70. McCloskey, *God and Evil*, p. 79.

71. John S. Feinberg, *Theologies and Evil* (Washington, D.C.: University Press of America, 1979), p. 26.

72. McCloskey, *God and Evil*, p. 79.

73. Gottfried Wilhelm von Leibniz, "The Problem of Evil," in *Historical Selections in the Philosophy of Religion*, ed. Ninian Smart (New York: Harper & Row, 1962), p. 146.

74. Ibid.

75. Ibid.

76. Ibid., p. 147.

77. Ibid.

78. Ibid., p. 151.

79. See ibid., pp. 147–48.

80. Ibid., pp. 151–52.

81. Ibid., p. 152.

82. Martin Gardner, citing John Stuart Mill in agreement, in *The Whys of a Philosophical Scrivener* (New York: Morrow, 1983), pp. 416–17 n. 3.

83. Ibid., p. 417. Gardner says that "as a Christian, Leibniz believed in the rewards and punishments of an afterlife, and the reality of hell, though his hell was considerably less populous than Augustine's" (p. 259).

84. Wolfhart Pannenberg, "Theological Questions to Scientists," in *The Sciences and Theology in the Twentieth Century*, ed. A. R. Peacocke (Notre Dame, Ind.: University of Notre Dame Press, 1981), p. 14.

85. Leibniz, "Problem of Evil," p. 147.

CHAPTER 3

1. Jerry H. Gill, "John Hick and Religious Knowledge," *International Journal for Philosophy of Religion* 2 (Fall 1971): 129.

2. Ibid.

3. John B. Cobb, Jr., and David Ray Griffin, *Process Theology: An Introductory Exposition* (Philadelphia: Westminster, 1976), p. 56.

4. William L. Rowe, "Ruminations About Evil," in *Philosophical Perspectives, 5: Philosophy of Religion, 1991*, ed. James E. Tomberlin (Atascadero, Calif.: Ridgeview, 1991), p. 88 n. 22.

5. Illtyd Trethowan, "Dr. Hick and the Problem of Evil," *Journal of Theological Studies* 18 (October 1967): 407.

6. David Ray Griffin, *God, Power, and Evil: A Process Theodicy* (Philadelphia: Westminster, 1976), pp. 174–78.

7. See Roland Puccetti, "The Loving God—Some Observations on John Hick's *Evil and the God of Love*," *Religious Studies* 2 (April 1967): 255–68; Trethowan, "Dr. Hick," 407–16; Keith Ward, "Freedom and the Irenaean Theodicy," *Journal of Theological Studies* 20 (1969): 249–54; and John M. Rist, "Coherence and the God of Love," *Journal of Theological Studies* 22 (1972): 95–105.

8. John Hick, *Evil and the God of Love* (London: Fontana Library, Collins, 1968); rev. ed. (San Francisco: Harper & Row, 1978). All references to *Evil and the God of Love*, cited in all chapters hereafter as *EAGOL*, are from the revised edition, unless otherwise noted.

9. Hick, *EAGOL*, p. 3.

10. John Hick, "The Problem of Evil in the First and Last Things," *Journal of Theological Studies* 19 (October 1968): 591.

11. Paul Edwards, "Difficulties in the Idea of God," in *The Idea of God: Philosophical Perspectives*, ed. Edward H. Madden, Rollo Handy, and Marvin Farber (Springfield, Ill.: Charles C. Thomas, 1968), p. 55.

12. John Hick, *God Has Many Names* (Philadelphia: Westminster, 1980), pp. 16–17.

13. John Hick, *Evil and the God of Love* (London: Fontana Library, Collins, 1968), p. 250.

14. John Hick, *Philosophy of Religion*, 3d ed. (Englewood Cliffs, N.J.: Prentice Hall, 1983), p. 57.

15. John Hick, *Arguments for the Existence of God* (New York: Herder & Herder, 1971), p. 107.

16. Ibid., p. 101.

17. Hick, *EAGOL*, p. 244.

18. Hick, *Arguments*, p. 109; see also idem, *An Interpretation of Religion: Human Responses to the Transcendent* (London: Macmillan, 1989), pp. 73–95, 210–11, 219, 221.

19. Hick, *Arguments*, p. 109.

20. John Hick, "God, Evil and Mystery," *Religious Studies* 3 (April 1968): 539.

21. John Hick, "Religious Faith as Experiencing-as," in his *God and the Universe of Faiths: Essays in the Philosophy of Religion* (New York: St. Martin's Press, 1973), pp. 51–52.

22. Hick, *EAGOL*, p. 244.

23. Ibid., pp. 244–45.

24. Ibid., p. 3.

25. Ibid.

26. Ibid., p. 4.

27. Ibid.

28. Ibid., p. 5.

29. John Hick, "Remarks" (on "The Problem of Evil"), in *Reason and Religion*, ed. Stuart C. Brown (Ithaca, N.Y.: Cornell University Press, 1977), p. 124.

30. Hick, "Remarks," p. 124.

31. Hick, "God, Evil and Mystery," 540.

32. Hick relinquishes all claim to originality by citing the second-century Bishop of Lyon, Irenaeus, as the one in whom we find "the outline of an approach to the problem of evil which stands in important respects in contrast to the Augustinian type of theodicy" (*EAGOL*, p. 214); hence, Hick's "soul-making theodicy" is often also called the "Irenaean theodicy." Hick maintains that the themes developed by Irenaeus on theodicy had even earlier "tentative hints" in Tatian, in his *Oration Against the Greeks* (c. 175), and in Theophilus, in his treatise *To Autolycus* (c. 175) (see Hick, *EAGOL*, pp. 210–11).

33. Hick, *EAGOL*, p. 256.

34. Hick, "God, Evil and Mystery," 540.

35. Hick, *EAGOL*, p. 255.

36. Ibid., pp. 254, 256.

37. Ibid., p. 256.

38. Ibid., p. 255.

39. Ibid., p. 256.

40. John H. Hick, "An Irenaean Theodicy," in *Encountering Evil: Live Options in Theodicy*, ed. Stephen T. Davis (Atlanta, Ga.: John Knox Press, 1981), p. 46.

41. Hick, *EAGOL*, p. 257.

42. Hick, "Irenaean Theodicy," p. 47.

43. Ibid., p. 39.

44. Hick, *EAGOL*, p. 255.

45. Ibid.

46. Ibid., p. 256.

47. Hick, "Remarks," p. 125.

48. Ibid.

49. Hick, *EAGOL*, p. 261.

50. Hick, "Irenaean Theodicy," p. 51.

51. Ibid., p. 52.

52. See Hick's discussion in the section entitled "Theodicy Versus Hell," in *EAGOL*, pp. 341–45.

53. Ibid., pp. 374–75.

54. John H. Hick, *Death and Eternal Life* (San Francisco: Harper & Row, 1976).

55. Hick, *God Has Many Names*, p. 22.

56. Hick, *Death and Eternal Life*, p. 456.

57. Ibid.

58. Ibid.

59. Hick, *Interpretation of Religion*, p. 236.

60. Ibid., p. 279.

61. See ibid., pp. 118–21.
62. Ibid., pp. 359–60.
63. I have responded elsewhere to Hick's religious pluralism (see R. Douglas Geivett, "John Hick's Approach to Religious Pluralism," *Proceedings of the Wheaton College Theology Conference* 1 [Spring 1992]:39–55). Hick's pluralistic hypothesis has greatly influenced him to see Christian theodicy as myth.
64. Hick, *EAGOL*, p. 385.
65. Ibid.
66. See ibid., pp. 236–37.
67. Ibid., pp. 238–40.
68. Thomas Aquinas *Summa theologiae* 1a.25.3 (cited in Thomas Gilby, trans., *St. Thomas Aquinas: Philosophical Texts* [Durham, N.C.: Labyrinth, 1982], pp. 120–21).
69. Hick, *EAGOL*, p. 250.
70. Ibid.; see also pp. 62–64.
71. Ibid., p. 55.
72. Ibid., p. 56.
73. Ibid., p. 57.
74. Ibid., p. 77.
75. Ibid., pp. 76–82.
76. Ibid., pp. 90–168.

CHAPTER 4

1. This discussion of Hick's religious epistemology is based chiefly on the essays "Rational Theistic Belief Without Proofs," in his *Arguments for the Existence of God* (New York: Herder & Herder, 1971), pp. 101–20; and "The Nature of Faith," in his *Faith and Knowledge,* 2d ed. (Ithaca, N.Y.: Cornell University Press, 1966), pp. 95–119. More recently, Hick has repeated concise statements of his religious epistemology, with a few modifications, in his *Problems of Religious Pluralism* (New York: St. Martin's Press, 1985) and in his Gifford lectures published as *An Interpretation of Religion: Human Responses to the Transcendent* (London: Macmillan, 1989).

2. See R. Douglas Geivett, "John Hick's Approach to Religious Pluralism," *Proceedings of the Wheaton College Theology Conference* 1 (Spring 1992):39–55.

3. John Hick, *God Has Many Names* (Philadelphia: Westminster, 1980), pp. 16–17.

4. Hick, *Arguments,* pp. 101, 102.

5. John Hick, *Evil and the God of Love* (London: Fontana Library, Collins, 1968), p. 250.

6. John Hick, *Philosophy of Religion,* 3d ed. (Englewood Cliffs, N.J.: Prentice Hall, 1983), p. 30.

7. John Hick, "Our Experiences of God," in *Why Believe in God?* ed. Michael Goulder and John Hick (London: SCM, 1983), p. 33.

8. Hick, *Interpretation of Religion,* p. 219.

9. Hick, *Arguments*, p. 102.

10. Ibid., p. 103.

11. Ibid., p. 104.

12. Ibid., p. 107.

13. Ps. 19:1; see also Isa. 45:18.

14. Rom. 1:20.

15. Thomas V. Morris, *The Logic of God Incarnate* (Ithaca, N.Y.: Cornell University Press, 1986), p. 74.

16. Ernest Nagel, *The Structure of Science: Problems in the Logic of Scientific Explanation* (Indianapolis, Ind.: Hackett, 1979), p. 11.

17. Ibid.

18. H. D. Lewis, *Our Experience of God* (London: Allen & Unwin, 1959), p. 51.

19. The important distinction between "belief-that" and "belief-in" is treated extensively by H. H. Price in his article "Belief 'In' and Belief 'That,'" *Religious Studies* 1 (1965): 1–27. Price plausibly suggests that belief-in can be further divided into "factual belief " and "evaluative belief."

20. See Frederick Ferré, *Basic Modern Philosophy of Religion* (New York: Scribner's, 1967), p. 111.

21. Ps. 14:1; Ps. 53:1.

22. Friedrich Nietzsche, *The Antichrist* 47, in *The Portable Nietzsche*, trans. W. A. Kaufmann (New York: Viking, 1954), p. 627.

23. A. C. Ewing, *The Fundamental Questions of Philosophy* (London: Routledge & Kegan Paul, 1951), p. 191.

24. Hick, *Arguments*, p. 101.

25. Ibid., p. viii.

26. Ibid., p. 101.

27. Hick, *Philosophy of Religion*, pp. 21, 23.

28. See ibid., pp. 25–26.

29. Alvin Plantinga, "The Probabilistic Argument from Evil," *Philosophical Studies* 35 (1979): 3 (italics in the original). Plantinga's exposition of the free-will defense is given in his *God, Freedom, and Evil* (Grand Rapids, Mich.: Eerdmans, 1977).

30. For Plantinga's own account of "Reformed epistemology," see his composite essay "Reason and Belief in God," in *Faith and Rationality: Reason and Belief in God*, ed. Alvin Plantinga and Nicholas Wolterstorff (Notre Dame, Ind.: University of Notre Dame Press, 1983). Plantinga has suggested that theists and nontheists do not share the kind of nontrivial standards of rationality needed for natural-theology arguments to persuade nontheists of the rationality of belief in God (see his "Discussion Article II: Existence, Necessity, and God," *New Scholasticism* 50 [Winter 1976]: 71–72). He has in the past and for some time offered a general objection to natural theology by criticizing the foundationalist epistemology upon which it has been based. In a recent attempt to assimilate the value of natural theology to the framework of Reformed epistemology, however, he has put his readers on notice that "there are many good theistic arguments" ("The Prospects for Natural Theology," in *Philosophical Perspectives, 5: Philosophy of Religion, 1991*, ed. James E.

Tomberlin [Atascadero, Calif.: Ridgeview, 1991], pp. 287–315). Indeed, he mentions a surprising variety of arguments he thinks are worthwhile. Good theistic arguments have at least two things going for them: first, they can be viewed as somehow *adding to* the warrant for what is initially a properly basic belief in God (and thus, perhaps, they may even transform mere true belief into knowledge); and second, they pass muster according to less exalted and more realistic standards than have customarily been applied to natural-theology arguments (see "Prospects for Natural Theology," pp. 310–12). Plantinga's proposal is provocative, but it needs to be explored in detail. How is a mere true belief, held in the basic way, converted into knowledge when that belief is already *properly* basic and therefore to some degree already justified? What does it mean for a properly basic belief to be a mere true belief that falls short of bona fide knowledge such that having evidence of the kind referred to in natural theology converts that belief into knowledge? Plantinga's version of the epistemic doctrine of the proper function of our noetic faculties must play a central role in answering these and other questions. It remains to be seen, however, whether a merger between Reformed epistemology and natural theology is possible, and if so, how it is to be achieved.

31. Keith E. Yandell, *Christianity and Philosophy* (Grand Rapids, Mich.: Eerdmans, 1984), p. 227.

32. Brian Davies, *An Introduction to the Philosophy of Religion* (Oxford: Oxford University Press, 1982), p. 25. See also D.J.B. Hawkins, *The Essentials of Theism* (New York: Sheed & Ward, 1950), p. 138; Bruce Reichenbach, "The Inductive Argument from Evil," *American Philosophical Quarterly* 17 (1980): 224; Norman L. Geisler and Winfried Corduan, *Philosophy of Religion*, 2d ed. (Grand Rapids, Mich.: Baker, 1988), p. 344; and F. J. Fitzpatrick, "The Onus of Proof in Arguments About the Problem of Evil," *Religious Studies* 17 (1981): 27–30.

33. M. B. Ahern, *The Problem of Evil* (New York: Schocken, 1971), p. 75 n. 3; see also Clement Dore, "Do Theists Need to Solve the Problem of Evil?" *Religious Studies* 12 (1976): 389. Ahern's claim is an especially strong one. It is not at all clear how proof of the existence of God entails the justification of evil unless such proof also establishes the relevant attributes of omniscience, omnipotence, and omnibenevolence.

34. Nelson Pike, "Hume on Evil," in his *God and Evil: Readings on the Theological Problem of Evil* (Englewood Cliffs, N.J.: Prentice Hall, 1964), p. 102.

35. Michael Scriven, *Primary Philosophy* (New York: McGraw-Hill, 1966), p. 158 (italics in the original).

36. Wallace I. Matson, *The Existence of God* (Ithaca, N.Y.: Cornell University Press, 1965), p. 137. I do not think the proposition that this is the best of all possible worlds is a strict corollary of the outcome of the cosmological argument, for there could well be a future world that is the best and that is brought about in part by the actualization of a world such as ours. If there is a "strict corollary" that is entailed by a valid cosmological argument, it is not that this is the best possible world but that theodicy is possible.

37. See William L. Rowe, "The Problem of Evil and Some Varieties of Atheism," *American Philosophical Quarterly* 16 (1979): 335–41, reprinted in R. Douglas Geivett and Brendan Sweetman, eds., *Contemporary Perspectives on Religious Epistemology* (New York: Oxford University Press, 1992), pp. 33–42.

38. Michael Martin, *Atheism: A Philosophical Justification* (Philadelphia: Temple University Press, 1990), pp. 340–41.

39. H. J. McCloskey, *God and Evil* (The Hague, Netherlands: Martinus Nijhoff, 1974), pp. 9–12.

40. Ibid., p. 12.

41. John H. Gerstner, *Reasons for Faith* (Grand Rapids, Mich.: Baker, 1967), pp. 134–35 (italics added).

42. Yandell defines theodicy as "an attempt by a theist to explain the fact that there is evil" (*Christianity and Philosophy*, p. 237 n. 7).

43. See Aristotle *Rhetoric* 1358b1.

44. Ralph Barton Perry, *Present Philosophical Tendencies* (London: Longmans, 1929), p. 289.

45. Robert Nozick, *Philosophical Explanations* (Cambridge, Mass.: Harvard University Press, 1981), p. 8.

46. Ibid., p. 9.

47. See ibid., p. 10.

48. Ibid., p. 11.

CHAPTER 5

1. John Hick, *An Interpretation of Religion: Human Responses to the Transcendent* (London: Macmillan, 1989), p. 211.

2. See especially John Hick, *Arguments for the Existence of God* (New York: Herder & Herder, 1971), pp. 101–20; and idem, "The Rationality of Religious Belief," in *Interpretation of Religion*, pp. 210–30, reprinted in R. Douglas Geivett and Brendan Sweetman, eds., *Contemporary Perspectives on Religious Epistemology* (New York: Oxford University Press, 1992), pp. 304–19. See also William P. Alston, who has argued in a similar way in his essay "Religious Experience and Religious Belief," *Nous* 16 (1982): 3–12, reprinted in Geivett and Sweetman, *Contemporary Perspectives*, pp. 295–303.

3. Hick, *Arguments*, p. 109.

4. Ibid., pp. 109–10.

5. Hick, *Interpretation of Religion*, p. 221.

6. Ibid.

7. Hick, *Arguments*, p. 110.

8. Hick, *Interpretation of Religion*, p. 221.

9. Hick, *Arguments*, p. 110.

10. See Hick, *Interpretation of Religion*, pp. 359–60.

11. Hick, *Arguments*, p. 111.

12. Hick, *Interpretation of Religion*, p. 221 (italics added).

13. Ibid., p. 215 (italics added).

14. Ibid. (italics added).

15. Hick, *Arguments*, p. 111.

16. See John Hick, *Faith and Knowledge,* 2d ed. (Ithaca, N.Y.: Cornell University Press, 1966), pp. 97–98.

17. Hick, *Arguments,* p. 112.

18. Ibid.

19. Hick, *Interpretation of Religion,* p. 221.

20. See ibid. (italics added).

21. Hick, *Arguments,* p. 113.

22. Hick describes three realms or levels of "situational significance": the natural, the ethical, and the divine spheres. Each level bears a certain relationship to the other two, but the category of natural experience is basic to the others: "As ethical significance interpenetrates natural significance, so religious significance interpenetrates both ethical and natural. The divine is the highest and ultimate order of significance, mediating neither of the others and yet being mediated through both of them. . . . The primary locus of religious experience is the believer's experience as a whole" (*Faith and Knowledge,* pp. 107–114). See also Brian Davies's discussion of Hick in his *Introduction to the Philosophy of Religion* (Oxford: Oxford University Press, 1982), pp. 74–76.

23. Acts 17:27–28.

24. Rom. 1:20: "Ever since the creation of the world his invisible nature, namely, his eternal power and deity, has been clearly perceived in the things that have been made. *So they are without excuse*" (italics added).

25. See Jacques Maritain, *Existence and the Existent: An Essay on Christian Existentialism,* trans. Lewis Galantiere and Gerald B. Phelan (Garden City, N.Y.: Image Books, Doubleday, 1956).

26. Frederick Copleston, *A History of Philosophy, 2: Medieval Philosophy, Augustine to Scotus* (Westminster, Md.: Newman Press, 1950), p. 325.

27. Ibid.

28. See ibid., p. 340.

29. Ibid., p. 325.

30. Hick, *Arguments,* p. 101.

31. In his book *Religious Experience* (Berkeley: University of California Press, 1985), William Proudfoot has put forward a convincing statement of this sort of objection to the direct religious experience approach to justified belief in God. The chapter in which he develops this objection is reprinted under the title "Explaining Religious Experience" in Geivett and Sweetman, *Contemporary Perspectives,* pp. 336–52.

32. Hick, *Arguments,* p. 112.

33. Hick, *EAGOL,* p. 3.

34. Philip Yancey, *Where Is God When It Hurts?* (Grand Rapids, Mich.: Zondervan, 1977), pp. 15–16.

35. Hick, *Interpretation of Religion,* p. 221.

36. Ibid., p. 215 (italics added).

37. See ibid., pp. 123–24.

38. See ibid., p. 123.

39. Hick, *EAGOL,* p. 244.

40. See Jerome I. Gellman, "A New Look at the Problem of Evil," *Faith and Philosophy* 9 (April 1992): 210–16. Gellman agrees that the experience of evil is a potentially very strong defeater of belief in God when that belief is grounded in religious experience. Unfortunately, Gellman misconstrues the relation between theistic arguments and religious experience so that, in his view, natural theology cannot overcome this defeater.

41. Larry Laudan, *Progress and Its Problems: Toward a Theory of Scientific Growth* (Berkeley: University of California Press, 1977), p. 13.

42. For explicit treatments of the relation between justified belief in God and patterns of explanation encountered in scientific practice, see Robert Prevost, *Probability and Theistic Explanation* (Oxford: Clarendon Press, 1990); and Edward Schoen, *Religious Explanations* (Durham, N.C.: Duke University Press, 1985).

43. Laudan, *Progress and Its Problems,* p. 14.

44. Ibid.

45. Ibid., p. 15.

46. Ibid.

47. See my discussion of this in Chapter 6.

48. Laudan, *Progress and Its Problems,* p. 18.

49. Ibid., p. 20.

50. The basis for the discussion in this section is chap. 5 in Hick's *Faith and Knowledge.*

51. See Frederick Ferré, *Basic Modern Philosophy of Religion* (New York: Scribner's, 1967), pp. 237–44.

52. Ibid., p. 247.

53. Recall, however, the discussion of Hick's conception of theism toward the end of Chapter 3.

54. Hick, *EAGOL,* p. 245.

55. Ibid., p. 244.

56. Hick, *Interpretation of Religion,* pp. 213–14.

57. Kenneth Surin, *Theology and the Problem of Evil* (Oxford: Basil Blackwell, 1986), p. 38.

58. M. B. Ahern, *The Problem of Evil* (New York: Schocken, 1971), p. 64.

59. A number of writers distinguish between the logical and the evidential forms of the problem of evil: Michael Peterson, *Evil and the Christian God* (Grand Rapids, Mich.: Baker, 1982), pp. 43–44; Bruce R. Reichenbach, *Evil and a Good God* (New York: Fordham University Press, 1982), p. 1; and C. Stephen Evans, *Philosophy of Religion: Thinking About Faith* (Downers Grove, Ill.: InterVarsity Press, 1985), p. 132.

CHAPTER 6

1. See Richard Swinburne, *The Existence of God* (Oxford: Clarendon Press, 1979), p. 13. See also J. L. Mackie, *The Miracle of Theism: Arguments For and Against the Existence of God* (Oxford: Clarendon Press, 1982), p. 10; and Antony Flew, *God and Philosophy* (London: Hutchinson, 1966), p. 141.

2. Flew, *God and Philosophy,* p. 141 (italics added).

3. Ibid., p. 63. See also Alasdair MacIntyre, *Difficulties in Christian Belief* (London: SCM, 1959), p. 63.

4. See Basil Mitchell, *The Justification of Religious Belief* (New York: Oxford University Press, 1981), pp. 39–40; see also idem, "The Justification of Religious Belief," in *New Essays on Religious Language,* ed. Dallas M. High (New York: Oxford University Press, 1969).

5. Mitchell, *Justification of Religious Belief,* p. 40.

6. Ibid.

7. For a helpful discussion of the chief differences between Swinburne and Mitchell, see William J. Abraham, *An Introduction to the Philosophy of Religion* (Englewood Cliffs, N.J.: Prentice Hall, 1985), pp. 98–129.

8. Swinburne, *Existence of God,* pp. 274, 277–91.

9. Ibid., p. 14.

10. Richard L. Purtill, *Reason to Believe* (Grand Rapids, Mich.: Eerdmans, 1974), pp. 108–15.

11. John E. Smith, "The Present Status of Natural Theology," *Journal of Philosophy* 55 (October 1958): 935.

12. Michael Tooley, "The Argument from Evil," in *Philosophical Perspectives, 5: Philosophy of Religion, 1991,* ed. James E. Tomberlin (Atascadero, Calif.: Ridgeview, 1991), p. 129; see also pp. 102–4.

13. Ibid., p. 103.

14. See Thomas V. Morris, *Our Idea of God: An Introduction to Philosophical Theology* (Downers Grove, Ill.: InterVarsity Press, 1991), pp. 35–40, 51–56; and idem, "The Necessity of God's Goodness," in his *Anselmian Explorations: Essays in Philosophical Theology* (Notre Dame, Ind.: University of Notre Dame Press, 1987), pp. 42–69. For more on this approach, both pro and con, see Swinburne, *Existence of God,* pp. 97–102; Keith Ward, *Rational Theology and the Creativity of God* (Oxford: Basil Blackwell, 1982), chaps. 6, 8; Winfried Corduan, *Handmaid to Theology: An Essay in Philosophical Prolegomena* (Grand Rapids, Mich.: Baker, 1981), pp. 122–23; and Stephen T. Davis, *Logic and the Nature of God* (Grand Rapids, Mich.: Eerdmans, 1983), chap. 6.

15. See Mackie, *Miracle of Theism,* p. 95.

16. Abraham, *Philosophy of Religion,* p. 116.

17. See his *Faith and Reason: Searching for a Rational Faith* (Grand Rapids, Mich.: Zondervan, 1988), p. 93.

18. Ibid., pp. 96–97

19. Stephen T. Davis seems to have a very similar account of proof that I here give of demonstration. See his "What Good Are Theistic Proofs?" in *Philosophy of Religion: An Anthology,* ed. Louis P. Pojman (Belmont, Calif.: Wadsworth, 1986), pp. 80–84. See also Terence Penelhum, *Problems of Religious Knowledge* (New York: Herder & Herder, 1972), pp. 36–40.

20. Mackie, *Miracle of Theism,* p. 7.

21. With Richard Purtill I believe this to be the basic pattern of all good arguments for the existence of God. See his article "The Current State of Arguments for the Existence of God," *Review and Expositor* 83 (Fall 1985): 521–33.

22. Alvin Plantinga, "Is Theism Really a Miracle?" *Faith and Philosophy* 3 (April 1986): 127.

23. Ibid., 133.

24. Alvin Plantinga, "The Prospects for Natural Theology," in *Philosophical Perspectives, 5: Philosophy of Religion, 1991,* ed. James E. Tomberlin (Atascadero, Calif.: Ridgeview, 1991), p. 312 (Plantinga's italics).

25. Ibid., pp. 311–12 (italics added).

26. Steven Weinberg, *The First Three Minutes: A Modern View of the Origin of the Universe* (New York: Basic Books, 1977), p. 5. For a survey of the "generally accepted history of the universe," thought to be "in agreement with all the observational evidence that we have today," see also Stephen W. Hawking, *A Brief History of Time: From the Big Bang to Black Holes* (Toronto: Bantam, 1988), pp. 116–21.

27. Robert Jastrow, *Journey to the Stars: Space Exploration—Tomorrow and Beyond* (Toronto: Bantam, 1989), pp. 43, 47. Jastrow is himself agnostic about religious matters.

28. Paul Davies, *God and the New Physics* (New York: Simon & Schuster, 1983), p. 18.

29. Ibid., p. 55–56.

30. Ibid., p. 57.

31. Fred Hoyle and others speak this way: Hoyle, *From Stonehenge to Modern Cosmology* (San Francisco: Freeman, 1972), p. 56; Joseph Silk, *The Big Bang: The Creation and Evolution of the Universe* (San Francisco: Freeman, 1980), pp. 22, 94, 108; Jayant V. Narlikar, *Introduction to Cosmology* (Boston: Jones & Bartlett, 1983), pp. 123–24, 242–45, 253–54; and idem, *The Primeval Universe* (Oxford: Oxford University Press, 1988), pp. 66–67. Narlikar claims that "Hoyle's approach to the steady state theory . . . was designed to attack the problem of *primary creation of matter*" associated with the big bang singularity (*Introduction to Cosmology,* p. 254 [italics added]); see also Hugh Ross, *The Fingerprint of God* (Orange, Calif.: Promise Publishing, 1989), pp. 109–117. Michael Rowan-Robinson gives a brief description of the empirical evidence for "a universe of finite age" (*Cosmology,* 2d ed. [Oxford: Clarendon Press, 1981], pp. 56–57).

32. Stewart C. Goetz, "Craig's *Kalam* Cosmological Argument," *Faith and Philosophy* 6 (January 1989): 99. Goetz is responding to William Lane Craig's effort to demonstrate that the universe was caused to exist *ex nihilo* by a personal Creator. Craig's argument involves an appeal to the impossibility of an actually infinite series and the impossibility of traversing an actual infinite. Goetz does not challenge these principles. He notes, rather, that there being a quiescent universe is consistent with them. Thus, the argument does not establish that the universe was created ex nihilo.

33. William Lane Craig, "The *Kalam* Cosmological Argument and the Hypothesis of a Quiescent Universe," *Faith and Philosophy* 8 (January 1991): 106; see also idem, *The* Kalam *Cosmological Argument* (New York: Barnes & Noble, 1979), pp. 101–2.

34. Craig, "Hypothesis of a Quiescent Universe," 107.

35. See Weinberg, *First Three Minutes;* Ivan R. King, *The Universe Unfold-*

ing (San Francisco: Freeman, 1976); John Gribbin, "Oscillating Universe Bounces Back," *Nature* 259 (1976): 15; Jeno M. Barnothy and Beatrice M. Tinsley, "A Critique of Hoyle and Narlikar's New Cosmology," *Astrophysical Journal* 182 (1973): 343–49; J. Richard Gott III, James E. Gunn, David N. Schramm, and Beatrice M. Tinsley, "An Unbound Universe?" *Astrophysical Journal* 194 (December 1974): 543–53; idem, "Will the Universe Expand Forever?" *Scientific American* (March 1976): 65; and G. J. Whitrow, *The Natural Philosophy of Time*, 2d ed. (Oxford: Clarendon Press, 1980), pp. 23–24.

36. James S. Trefil, *The Moment of Creation: Big Bang Physics from the First Millisecond to the Present Universe* (New York: Scribner's, 1983), p. 215.

37. See John Gribbin, *Spacewarps* (New York: Delacorte, 1983), pp. 165–69.

38. Bertrand Russell, *Human Knowledge: Its Scope and Limits* (New York: Simon & Schuster, 1948), p. 14 (italics added).

39. Arthur S. Eddington, "The End of the World: From the Standpoint of Mathematical Physics," *Nature* 127 (1931): 450 (cited in Ross, *Fingerprint of God*, p. 66).

40. Fred Hoyle, "A New Model for the Expanding Universe," *Monthly Notices of the Royal Astronomical Society* 108 (1948): 372 (cited in Ross, *Fingerprint of God*, p. 76). In one of his textbooks, Hoyle encourages students to reflect upon the significance of the problem of evil for theistic belief in the context of the laws of physics, chemistry, and biology (see Hoyle, *Astronomy and Cosmology: A Modern Course* [San Francisco: Freeman, 1975], p. 522). In this text he also remarks, "I do not believe that an appeal to metaphysics is needed to solve *any problem of which we can conceive* (p. 685 [italics in the original]).

41. There is a growing literature on this point. See especially Craig, *Kalam Cosmological Argument*, (esp. pp. 102–10); idem, "Philosophical and Scientific Pointers to *Creatio ex Nihilo*," *Journal of the American Scientific Affiliation* 32 (March 1980): 5–13, reprinted in R. Douglas Geivett and Brendan Sweetman, eds., *Contemporary Perspectives on Religious Epistemology* (New York: Oxford University Press, 1992), pp. 185–200; and Dallas Willard, "Language, Being, God, and the Three Stages of Theistic Evidence," in J. P. Moreland and Kai Nielsen, *Does God Exist? The Great Debate* (Nashville, Tenn.: Thomas Nelson, 1990), pp. 202–8, reprinted under the title "The Three-Stage Argument for the Existence of God" in Geivett and Sweetman, *Contemporary Perspectives*, pp. 212–24.

42. See Bertrand Russell, *Our Knowledge of the External World*, rev. ed. (London: Allen & Unwin, 1926), pp. 159–88, and esp. pp. 160–61, 187.

43. Anthony Kenny, *The Five Ways: Saint Thomas Aquinas' Proofs of God's Existence* (Notre Dame, Ind.: University of Notre Dame Press, 1969), p. 66.

44. Mackie, *Miracle of Theism*, p. 94. Mackie is discussed here because his views are representative. His book is widely regarded as a powerfully articulated contemporary defense of the atheistic position and a formidable challenge to the "miracle" of theistic belief.

45. Ibid.

46. Ibid.

47. David Hume, letter to John Stewart, February 1754, in *The Letters of David Hume*, ed. J.Y.T. Grieg (Oxford: Clarendon Press, 1932), 1:187.

48. David Lewis, *On the Plurality of Worlds* (Oxford: Basil Blackwell, 1986), pp. 134–35.

49. Mackie, *Miracle of Theism*, p. 85 (italics added).

50. Ibid., pp. 86–87.

51. Ibid., pp. 85–86.

52. See Dallas Willard, "The Three-Stage Argument for the Existence of God," in Geivett and Sweetman, *Contemporary Perspectives*, pp. 215–16.

53. Mackie, *Miracle of Theism*, p. 92.

54. Ibid., p. 94.

55. Ibid., p. 7.

56. Ibid., p. 95.

57. Ibid., p. 6.

58. William Pepperell Montague, *Belief Unbound: A Promethean Religion for the Modern World* (New Haven, Conn.: Yale University Press, 1930), p. 73.

59. For fairly rigorous arguments from consciousness to the existence of God, see two books by Richard Swinburne, *Existence of God*, pp. 152–75, and *The Evolution of the Soul* (Oxford: Clarendon Press, 1986); and one by J. P. Moreland, *Scaling the Secular City: A Defense of Christianity* (Grand Rapids, Mich.: Baker, 1987), pp. 77–103. See also Robert M. Adams, "Flavors, Colors, and God," in his *Virtue of Faith* (New York: Oxford University Press, 1987), pp. 243–62, reprinted in Geivett and Sweetman, *Contemporary Perspectives*, pp. 225–40.

60. As Hume himself put it: "The separation, therefore, of the idea of a cause from that of a beginning of existence, is plainly possible for the imagination; and consequently the actual separation of these objects is so far possible, that it implies no contradiction nor absurdity; and is therefore incapable of being refuted by any reasoning from mere ideas; without which 'tis impossible to demonstrate the necessity of a cause" (*A Treatise of Human Nature* 1.3.3). The quotation is from the 2d L. A. Selby-Bigge edition (Oxford: Clarendon Press, 1978), pp. 81–82.

CHAPTER 7

1. Richard Swinburne, *The Existence of God* (Oxford: Clarendon Press, 1979), pp. 19–20 (italics added).

2. It is beyond the scope of this book to argue for a doctrine of human freedom. The following discussion assumes that some such doctrine at least is neither intuitively nor demonstrably false.

3. See Swinburne, *Existence of God*, pp. 20, 32–42, 57–62. Unlike Swinburne, I see no special difficulty in thinking of "personal explanation" as a type of scientific explanation.

4. Charles Darwin, *On the Origin of Species*, 3d ed. (New York: American Library, 1958), Introduction (cited in Norman L. Geisler, *Knowing the Truth About Creation* [Ann Arbor, Mich.: Servant, 1989], p. 134).

5. C. S. Lewis, "Christianity and Literature," in his *Christian Reflections* (Grand Rapids, Mich.: Eerdmans, 1967), p. 10.

6. Carl Sagan, *Cosmos* (New York: Random House, 1980), p. 199.

7. Stephen W. Hawking, *A Brief History of Time: From the Big Bang to Black Holes* (Toronto: Bantam, 1988), p. 175.

8. Steven Weinberg, *The First Three Minutes: A Modern View of the Origin of the Universe* (New York: Basic Books, 1977), pp. 154–55.

9. Ronald E. Beanblossom and Keith Lehrer, eds., *Thomas Reid's Inquiry and Essays* (Indianapolis, Ind.: Hackett, 1983), p. 333. Reid's view is defended by William L. Rowe, "Two Concepts of Freedom," *Proceedings and Addresses of the American Philosophical Association* 61 (suppl) (September 1987): 43–64.

10. Roderick Chisholm, "Human Freedom and the Self," in *Free Will*, ed. Gary Watson (Oxford: Oxford University Press, 1982), p. 31.

11. John Finnis also endorses the doctrine of agent-causation to account for human freedom and sees an analogy between free-choice instances of first-cause causation and the first cause of the universe (*Natural Law and Natural Rights* [Oxford: Clarendon Press, 1980], pp. 389–90; and idem, *Fundamentals of Ethics* [Washington, D.C.: Georgetown University Press, 1983], pp. 145–46).

12. Chisholm, "Human Freedom," p. 28.

13. Ibid., p. 33.

14. Richard Taylor, *Metaphysics*, 3d ed. (Englewood Cliffs, N.J.: Prentice Hall, 1983), p. 48.

15. Ibid.

16. Daniel C. Dennett, *Elbow Room: The Varieties of Free Will Worth Wanting* (Cambridge: Cambridge University Press, 1984), p. 76.

17. Taylor, *Metaphysics*, p. 48.

18. Chisholm, "Human Freedom," p. 24.

19. Janet Levin, of the University of Southern California, suggested this to me.

20. Dennett, *Elbow Room*, p. 76.

21. Richard Swinburne, "The Argument from Design," *Philosophy* 43 (July 1968): 204, reprinted in R. Douglas Geivett and Brendan Sweetman, eds. *Contemporary Perspectives on Religious Epistemology* (New York: Oxford University Press, 1992), pp. 201–11.

22. Swinburne, "Argument from Design," 204.

23. Ibid., 205–6.

24. David Hume, *Dialogues Concerning Natural Religion*, pt. 12 (italics in the quoted edition). The quotation is from the Norman Kemp Smith edition (Indianapolis, Ind.: Bobbs-Merrill, 1947), p. 227.

25. Antony Flew, *God and Philosophy* (London: Hutchinson, 1966), p. 62.

26. George Gale, "Anthropocentrism Reconsidered," in *Human Nature and Natural Knowledge*, ed. A. Donagan, A. N. Perovich, Jr., and M. V. Wedin (Dordrecht, Netherlands: D. Reidel, 1986), p. 236 (quoted in Michael Martin, *Atheism: A Philosophical Justification* [Philadelphia: Temple University Press, 1990], p. 132).

27. Alan H. Guth, "Inflationary Universe: A Possible Solution to the Horizon and Flatness Problems," *Physical Review* D23 (1981): 348 (cited in Hugh Ross, *The Fingerprint of God* [Orange, Calif.: Promise Publishing, 1989], p. 124).

28. For a discussion of these and other parameters, see John D. Barrow and Frank J. Tipler, *The Anthropic Cosmological Principle* (Oxford: Oxford University Press, 1986); Paul Davies, *The Accidental Universe* (Cambridge: Cambridge University Press, 1982); idem, *God and the New Physics* (New York: Simon & Schuster, 1983), pp. 177–89; Hugh Montefiore, *The Probability of God* (London: SCM Press, 1985), pp. 23–42; Ross, *Fingerprint of God*, pp. 121–28; John Wiester, *The Genesis Connection* (Nashville, Tenn.: Thomas Nelson, 1983), pp. 27–36, 47–50; John Leslie, "Anthropic Principle, World Ensemble, Design," *American Philosophical Quarterly* 19 (April 1982): 141–50; and J. P. Moreland, *Scaling the Secular City: A Defense of Christianity* (Grand Rapids, Mich.: Baker, 1987), pp. 52–54.

29. George Greenstein, *The Symbiotic Universe: Life and Mind in the Cosmos* (New York: Morrow, 1988), p. 27.

30. See Robert T. Rood and James S. Trefil, *Are We Alone? The Possibility of Extraterrestrial Civilizations* (New York: Scribner's, 1983) (cited in Ross, *Fingerprint of God*, p. 132).

31. Swinburne, *Existence of God*, p. 181 (see chap. 10 for a full development of the "argument from providence"); see also Finnis, *Natural Law and Natural Rights*, pp. 30, 388, for brief remarks along the same lines. In chaps. 3 and 4 Finnis discusses in greater detail a number of human goods he takes to be "irreducibly basic." For similar treatments and lists of this kind, see Germain Grisez and Russell Shaw, *Beyond the New Morality: The Responsibilities of Freedom* (Notre Dame, Ind.: University of Notre Dame Press, 1974), chap. 7; and William K. Frankena, *Ethics*, 2d ed. (Englewood Cliffs, N.J.: Prentice Hall, 1973), pp. 87–88. See also Abraham H. Maslow's psychological account in his *Motivation and Personality* (New York: Harper, 1954), pp. 80–106. For the related views of Thomas Aquinas, see the *Summa theologiae* 1a2ae.94.2.

32. Swinburne, *Existence of God*, p. 181.

33. Swinburne's argument from providence has theodicy elements in it. See the discussion by Michael Martin, *Atheism*, pp. 221–22.

34. Swinburne, *Existence of God*, p. 187.

35. Moreland, *Scaling the Secular City*, p. 231.

36. William P. Alston, "The Fulfillment of Promises as Evidence for Religious Belief," *Logos* 12 (1991): 1–26.

37. As the author of the New Testament book of Hebrews puts it in Heb. 11:6.

38. For good discussions of Pascal's Wager, see William G. Lycan and George N. Schlesinger, "You Bet Your Life: Pascal's Wager Defended," in *Reason and Responsibility: Readings in Some Basic Problems of Philosophy*, 7th ed., ed. Joel Feinberg, (Belmont, Calif.: Wadsworth, 1989); and Thomas V. Morris, "Pascalian Wagering," *Canadian Journal of Philosophy* 16 (September 1986): 437–53. Both are reprinted in Geivett and Sweetman, *Contemporary Perspectives*.

39. Hume, *Dialogues,* pt. 12 (quoted from the Norman Kemp Smith edition, p. 227 [italics added]).

40. See George Mavrodes, "Religion and the Queerness of Morality," in *Rationality, Religious Belief, and Moral Commitment: New Essays in the Philosophy of Religion,* ed. Robert Audi and William J. Wainwright (Ithaca, N.Y.: Cornell University Press, 1986), pp. 213–26.

41. Ibid., p. 218.

42. Ibid., p. 220.

43. C. S. Lewis, "De Futilitate," in his *Christian Reflections,* p. 66.

44. Pliny used the phrase to describe the irony of ascribing blame to Fortune in Greek religion (Pliny *Natural History* 2.22).

45. Lewis, "De Futilitate," p. 70.

46. See Alvin Plantinga, *God, Freedom, and Evil* (Grand Rapids, Mich.: Eerdmans, 1977), p. 28.

CHAPTER 8

1. Basil Mitchell, *The Justification of Religious Belief* (New York: Oxford University Press, 1981), p. 41.

2. John Hick, *Arguments for the Existence of God* (New York: Herder & Herder, 1971), p. 51.

3. Ibid., p. 50.

4. Ibid., pp. 51–52.

5. Ibid., pp. 50–51.

6. Ibid., p. 50.

7. Antony Flew, *God and Philosophy* (London: Hutchinson, 1966), p. 102.

8. Ibid.

9. J. L. Mackie, *The Miracle of Theism: Arguments For and Against the Existence of God* (Oxford: Clarendon Press, 1982), p. 94.

10. Hick, *Arguments,* p. 47.

11. This despite claims to the contrary by Alvin Plantinga in "Discussion Article II: Existence, Necessity, and God," *New Scholasticism* 50 (Winter 1976): 71–72.

12. John Hick, *Philosophy of Religion,* 3d ed. (Englewood Cliffs, N.J.: Prentice Hall, 1983), p. 23.

13. See, for example, Richard Swinburne, *The Existence of God* (Oxford: Clarendon Press, 1979), chaps. 4, 7. Swinburne's cosmological argument is not, however, an argument for the existence of God from the beginning of the universe. Some theists who offer a cosmological argument for the existence of God clearly think that one should press explanation a bit further but do not argue at length for this. See also the discussion by William Lane Craig, who does argue for the existence of God from the beginning of the universe (*The Kalam Cosmological Argument,* [New York: Barnes & Noble, 1979], pp. 141–48). Elsewhere Craig simply says that the notion that whatever begins to exist has a cause "is so intuitively obvious that I think scarcely anyone could sincerely believe it to be false. I therefore think it somewhat unwise to argue in favor of it, for any proof of the principle is likely to be less obvious than the

principle itself" (*Apologetics: An Introduction* [Chicago: Moody Press, 1984], p. 74).

14. David Hume, *Dialogues Concerning Natural Religion*, pt. 9. (The quotation is from the Norman Kemp Smith edition [Indianapolis, Ind.: Bobbs-Merrill, 1947], pp. 190–91.)

15. Swinburne, *Existence of God*, p. 118.

16. Ibid., p. 103.

17. John Hick, *An Interpretation of Religion: Human Responses to the Transcendent* (London: Macmillan, 1989), pp. 80–81.

18. See Nicholas Rescher's pragmatist defense of the principle of sufficient reason in his essay "The Principle of Sufficient Reason, Then and Now," in his *Baffling Phenomena and Other Studies in the Philosophy of Knowledge and Valuation* (Savage, Md.: Rowman & Littlefield, 1991).

19. See Hick, *Interpretation of Religion*, pp. 122–24, 221.

20. Hick, *Arguments*, p. 30.

21. Hick, *Interpretation of Religion*, p. 123.

22. Hick, *Arguments*, pp. 30–31.

23. Hick, *Interpretation of Religion*, p. 123.

24. Alvin Plantinga, "The Prospects for Natural Theology," in *Philosophical Perspectives, 5: Philosophy of Religion, 1991*, ed. James E. Tomberlin (Atascadero, Calif.: Ridgeview, 1991), p. 312.

25. See Richard F. Vieth, *Holy Power, Human Pain* (Bloomington, Ind.: Meyer-Stone, 1988), pp. 119–20; and Richard L. Purtill, *Reason to Believe* (Grand Rapids, Mich.: Eerdmans, 1974), pp. 110–13.

26. C. S. Lewis, *The Problem of Pain* (New York: Macmillan, 1962), p. 93.

27. See Richard L. Purtill, *A Logical Introduction to Philosophy* (Englewood Cliffs, N.J.: Prentice Hall, 1989), p. 162.

CHAPTER 9

1. This is the title of pt. 4 in Hick's *EAGOL;* the first chapter, which outlines the main features of Hick's theodicy much as I have in Chapter 3, is entitled "The Starting-point."

2. John Hick, *God and the Universe of Faiths: Essays in the Philosophy of Religion* (New York: St. Martin's Press, 1973), p. 53.

3. Hick, *EAGOL*, p. 259 n. 1.

4. See ibid., pp. 210–11.

5. Hick, *Universe of Faiths*, p. 53.

6. Kurt Vonnegut, Jr., *Cat's Cradle* (New York: Dell, Random House, 1963), p. 177.

7. Hick, *EAGOL*, p. 240.

8. Ibid., p. 198; see also pp. 195–96.

9. See the chapter "Revelation and Faith" in his *Philosophy of Religion*, 3d ed. (Englewood Cliffs, N.J.: Prentice Hall, 1983), pp. 57–75.

10. John Hick, *An Interpretation of Religion: Human Responses to the Transcendent* (London: Macmillan, 1989), p. 216.

11. Hick, *Philosophy of Religion*, p. 70.

12. A well-known expression of this particular view of the revelatory status of the Incarnation is John Hick, ed., *The Myth of God Incarnate* (Philadelphia: Westminster, 1977); see also idem, *The Center of Christianity*, new and enl. ed. (San Francisco: Harper & Row, 1978).

13. M. B. Ahern, *The Problem of Evil* (New York: Schocken, 1971), p. 64.

14. Hick, *EAGOL*, p. 198.

15. Ibid., p. 317.

16. Ibid., p. 198.

17. See John Hick, *Evil and the God of Love* (London: Macmillan, 1966), p. 252, in the chapter "Recent Teleological Theodicies," not contained in the revised edition.

18. Hick, *EAGOL*, p. 257.

19. Ibid., p. 256.

20. John Hick, "The Problem of Evil in the First and Last Things," *Journal of Theological Studies* 19 (October 1968): 591.

21. Hick, *EAGOL*, p. 193.

22. See ibid., pp. 70–85.

23. Ibid., pp. 49–50.

24. See ibid., pp. 38–43.

25. Ibid., p. 37.

26. Ibid., p. 43.

27. The seven observations that follow are from *EAGOL*, pp. 193–95.

28. Ibid., p. 195.

29. Illtyd Trethowan, "Dr. Hick and the Problem of Evil," *Journal of Theological Studies* 18 (October 1967): 412. As Trethowan remarks, "There is in fact a tendency in [Hick's] book to make over-abrupt or unreal contrasts which have the general effect of exaggerating the difficulties of traditionalist thought" (409).

30. Hick, *EAGOL*, p. 77.

31. Ibid., p. 196.

32. Ibid., p. 12.

33. Hick, *Universe of Faiths*, p. 53.

34. Hick, *EAGOL*, p. 262.

35. Ibid., p. 264.

36. Ibid.

37. Ibid., p. 265.

38. See ibid., pp. 265–77.

39. Ibid., p. 265.

40. Ibid., p. 266.

41. Ibid., p. 196.

42. Ibid., p. 266.

43. See ibid., pp. 267–71.

44. Ibid., p. 272.

45. Ibid., p. 273.

46. Ibid., p. 275.

47. Ibid.

48. See ibid., pp. 275–76.

49. Ibid., p. 276.

50. Ibid., p. 281.

51. See Hick's discussion "The Virtual Inevitability of the Fall" in ibid., pp. 277–80.

52. Ibid., p. 286.

53. Ibid.

54. Ibid., pp. 238–39.

55. Ibid., pp. 289–90.

56. See Hick, "First and Last Things," 597.

57. Hick, *EAGOL*, p. 289.

58. Ibid., p. 256.

59. Ibid., pp. 256–57. In an interesting article reviewing Hick's account of natural evil, Roland Puccetti decries this analysis: "There is something suspect in the way Hick presents this contrast. I cannot speak for other antitheists, but I at least never regarded it the duty of a loving God to provide his creatures with a hedonistic paradise" ("The Loving God—Some Observations on John Hick's *Evil and the God of Love*," *Religious Studies* 2 [April 1967]: 259–60).

60. Hick, *EAGOL*, p. 266.

61. Ibid., p. 257.

62. Ibid., p. 258.

63. See ibid., pp. 260, 286, 287.

64. Hick delineates this catalogue of virtues in ibid., p. 307; see also pp. 324–26.

65. Ibid., p. 307.

66. Ibid., p. 308.

67. Ibid., p. 317.

68. Trethowan, "Dr. Hick," 411.

69. Hick, *EAGOL*, pp. 288–89.

70. Ibid., p. 289.

71. Ibid., pp. 289–90.

72. Ibid., p. 290. See also Hick, "First and Last Things," 597; idem, *Universe of Faiths*, p. 69.

73. Hick, *EAGOL*, p. 290.

74. Stuart Hackett, *The Resurrection of Theism: Prolegomena to Christian Apology* 2d ed. (Grand Rapids, Mich.: Baker, 1982), pp. 351–52. For a recent attempt to reconcile divine responsibility for moral evil with the Augustinian tradition, see Nelson Pike, "Over-Power and God's Responsibility for Sin," in *The Existence and Nature of God*, ed. Alfred J. Freddoso (Notre Dame, Ind.: University of Notre Dame Press, 1983). Unfortunately, Pike does not show how God can be responsible in his sense without being also morally blameworthy, although Pike makes this distinction.

75. See Henri Renard, *The Philosophy of Being*, rev. 2d ed. (Milwaukee, Wis.: Bruce, 1946), p. 187.

76. Hick, *EAGOL*, p. 290.

77. Trethowan, "Dr. Hick," 415.

78. See G. Stanley Kane, "The Free-Will Defense Defended," *New Scholasticism* 50 (Autumn 1976): 435.

79. Trethowan, "Dr. Hick," 414.

CHAPTER 10

1. Thomas Aquinas *Summa theologiae* 1a.84.5. This quotation is from Anton C. Pegis, ed., *Introduction to St. Thomas Aquinas* (New York: Modern Library, 1948), p. 390.

2. Jacques Maritain, *Saint Thomas and the Problem of Evil* (Milwaukee, Wis.: Marquette University Press, 1942), pp. 9–10.

3. Gottfried Wilhelm von Leibniz, *Discourse on Metaphysics, Correspondence with Arnauld, and Monadology,* trans. George R. Montgomery (La Salle, Ill.: Open Court, 1962), pp. 5–7.

4. Frederick Copleston, *A History of Philosophy, 2: Mediaeval Philosophy, Augustine to Scotus* (Westminster, Md.: Newman Press, 1950), p. 81.

5. Ibid., p. 97.

6. See Augustine *De libero arbitrio* 1.2.

7. Augustine *De libero arbitrio* 1.3. All quotations from Augustine's *De libero arbitrio voluntatis* are from idem, *On Free Choice of the Will,* trans. Anna S. Benjamin and L. H. Hackstaff (Indianapolis, Ind.: Bobbs-Merrill, 1964).

8. Augustine *De libero arbitrio* 1.2.

9. See Augustine *De libero arbitrio* 2.1, 2.2.

10. See Augustine *De libero arbitrio* 2.2.

11. Augustine *De libero arbitrio* 2.3.

12. See Augustine *De libero arbitrio* 2.17.

13. Augustine *De libero arbitrio* 2.18.

14. Augustine *De libero arbitrio* 2.18.

15. Augustine *De libero arbitrio* 2.19.

16. Copleston, *History of Philosophy,* p. 83.

17. See G. Stanley Kane, "The Free-Will Defense Defended," *New Scholasticism* 50 (Autumn 1976): 435; see also 443.

18. See Augustine *De libero arbitrio* 2.19.

19. St. Augustine, *The Confessions of St. Augustine,* trans. F. J. Sheed (New York: Sheed & Ward, 1943), p. 3.

20. Copleston, *History of Philosophy,* p. 86.

21. Ibid.

22. Augustine *De libero arbitrio* 2.18 (italics added).

23. Augustine *De libero arbitrio* 2.15.

24. Thomas Aquinas, Commentary, *I Sentences* 19.2.5 (as cited in Thomas Gilby, trans., *St. Thomas Aquinas: Philosophical Texts* [Durham, N.C.: Labyrinth, 1982], p. 163).

25. Thomas Aquinas *Summa theologiae* 1.22.2 (as cited in Gilby, *Philosophical Texts,* p. 117 [italics added]).

26. G. Stanley Kane, "Evil and Privation," *International Journal for Philosophy of Religion* 11 (1980): 53.

27. Ibid., 55.

28. See Gen. 1:31; see also 1 Tim. 4:4 and Titus 1:15.

29. Kane, "Evil and Privation," 55.

30. Kane's terminology, ibid., 56.

31. Ibid., 55.

32. Bill Anglin and Stewart Goetz, "Evil Is Privation," *International Journal for Philosophy of Religion* 13 (1982): 9.

33. Ibid., 10. See also W. S. Anglin, *Free Will and the Christian Faith* (Oxford: Clarendon Press, 1990), pp. 131–37.

34. See Norman L. Geisler and Winfried Corduan, *Philosophy of Religion*, 2d ed. (Grand Rapids, Mich.: Baker, 1988), p. 332.

35. Thomas Aquinas *Summa theologiae* 1.48.1 (as cited in Gilby, *Philosophical Texts*, pp. 164–65).

36. See, for example, James Cornman and Keith Lehrer, *Philosophical Problems and Arguments: An Introduction* (New York: Macmillan, 1969), pp. 340–49; Michael Martin, "Is Evil Evidence Against the Existence of God?" *Mind* 87 (1978): 429–32; William L. Rowe, *Philosophy of Religion: An Introduction*, 2d ed. (Belmont, Calif.: Wadsworth, 1993), pp. 79–82; and idem, "The Problem of Evil and Some Varieties of Atheism," in *Contemporary Perspectives on Religious Epistemology*, ed. R. Douglas Geivett and Brendan Sweetman (New York: Oxford University Press, 1992), pp. 33–42.

37. Rowe, *Philosophy of Religion*, p. 80.

38. See Michael Peterson, *Evil and the Christian God* (Grand Rapids, Mich.: Baker, 1982). William E. Mann refers to the problem here as "the Problem of God's Ubiquitous Meddlesomeness," in his essay "God's Responsibility for Sin," in *Divine and Human Action: Essays on the Metaphysics of Theism*, ed. Thomas V. Morris (Ithaca, N.Y.: Cornell University Press, 1988), p. 199. For another theist who assumes that there is gratuitous evil in the world, see William Hasker, "Must God Do His Best?" *International Journal for Philosophy of Religion* 16 (1984): 213–23.

39. Ronald H. Nash, *Faith and Reason: Searching for a Rational Faith* (Grand Rapids, Mich.: Zondervan, 1988), pp. 216–21. Nash says that "the presence of gratuitous evils in God's creation is consistent with God's purposes for creation" (p. 221). The reason he gives for thinking this is that the doctrine of meticulous providence is not essential to theism. However, in a letter to the author (17 December 1992), Professor Nash makes it clear that he does not repudiate the doctrine of meticulous providence.

40. Peter van Inwagen, "The Place of Chance in a World Sustained by God," in Morris, *Divine and Human Action*, p. 221.

41. Ibid., p. 220.

42. Peterson, *Evil and the Christian God*, pp. 16–17 n. 8.

43. For a similar perspective see Jane Mary Trau, "Fallacies in the Argument from Gratuitous Suffering," *New Scholasticism* 60 (1986): 485–89. Trau argues that the deductive version of the argument from gratuitous suffering

commits the fallacy *petitio principii* ("One can never be certain that there are cases of gratuitous suffering unless one is certain that there is no God" [p. 487]), and that the inductive version of this argument commits the fallacy *argumentum ad ignorantiam*.

44. See Chapter 6 for a defense of this claim.

45. Peterson, *Evil and the Christian God*, p. 89.

46. Ibid.

47. See the following sample of biblical texts used by theologians in the Christian tradition to support such a doctrine of providence: Gen. 45:4–8, 50:20; Matt. 6:25–34; Prov. 16:33; Rom. 8:28; Eph. 1:11; Col. 1:17.

48. Nash, *Faith and Reason*, pp. 220–21.

49. Peterson, *Evil and the Christian God*, p. 117.

50. Hick, *EAGOL*, p. 329.

51. Ibid., p. 333.

52. Ibid., pp. 333–34 (italics added).

53. Ibid., p. 336.

54. Alvin Plantinga, *God, Freedom, and Evil* (Grand Rapids, Mich.: Eerdmans, 1977), p. 27.

55. See Alvin Plantinga, *The Nature of Necessity* (Oxford: Clarendon Press, 1974), p. 193.

56. Plantinga, *God, Freedom, and Evil*, p. 58; and idem, *Nature of Necessity*, p. 192; see also idem, "The Free Will Defense," in *Philosophy in America: Essays*, ed. Max Black (London: Allen & Unwin, 1965), pp. 218–20.

57. Richard Swinburne, "The Problem of Evil," in *Reason and Religion*, ed. Stuart C. Brown (Ithaca, N.Y.: Cornell University Press, 1977), p. 93.

58. Bruce Reichenbach, *Evil and a Good God* (New York: Fordham University Press, 1982), p. 101.

59. Stuart Hackett, *The Resurrection of Theism: Prolegomena to Christian Apology*, 2d ed. (Grand Rapids, Mich.: Baker, 1982), p. 355.

60. Ibid., p. 355.

CHAPTER 11

1. See David Ray Griffin, *God, Power and Evil: A Process Theodicy* (Philadelphia: Westminster, 1976), pp. 174–204.

2. Hick, *EAGOL*, p. 267. See also Antony Flew, "Divine Omnipotence and Human Freedom," in *New Essays in Philosophical Theology*, eds. Antony Flew and Alasdair MacIntyre (New York: Macmillan, 1955); and J. L. Mackie, "Evil and Omnipotence," *Mind* 64 (1955): 200–12.

3. Hick, *EAGOL*, p. 267.

4. See John H. Hick, "An Irenaean Theodicy," in *Encountering Evil: Live Options in Theodicy*, ed. Stephen T. Davis (Atlanta, Ga.: John Knox Press, 1981), pp. 43–44.

5. Ibid., p. 44.

6. Ibid., p. 45.

7. Ibid., p. 39.

8. From John Hick's critique of Stephen T. Davis in Davis, *Encountering Evil*, p. 87.

9. Hick, *EAGOL*, p. 255.

10. Hick, "Irenaean Theodicy," p. 45.

11. Ibid., pp. 41–42.

12. Ibid., p. 43.

13. Ibid.

14. Ibid., p. 44.

15. Hick, *EAGOL*, p. 255.

16. Hick, "Irenaean Theodicy," p. 44.

17. See ibid., p. 45; and the section entitled "Man Created as a Fallen Being" in *EAGOL*, pp. 280–91.

18. Hick, *EAGOL*, p. 272.

19. See ibid., p. 264.

20. See ibid., pp. 249–51.

21. In his critique of Stephen Davis in Davis, *Encountering Evil*, p. 86.

22. Hick, *EAGOL*, pp. 249–50. For further development of this kind of claim, see Robert F. Brown, "The First Evil Will Must Be Incomprehensible: A Critique of Augustine," *Journal of the American Academy of Religion* 46, 3 (1978): 315–29.

23. Mackie, as cited by Hick in *EAGOL*, p. 271. The quotation is from Mackie's essay "Theism and Utopia," *Philosophy* 37 (April 1962): 157. See also Flew's earlier statement of this objection to the free-will defense in his "Divine Omnipotence."

24. Griffin, *God, Power and Evil*, p. 194; see also Hick, *EAGOL*, p. 272.

25. Griffin, *God, Power and Evil*, p. 194.

26. Hick, *EAGOL*, p. 274.

27. Alvin Plantinga, *The Nature of Necessity* (Oxford: Clarendon Press, 1974), p. 190.

28. My reticence about the use of possible-worlds semantics in this context has to do with the current controversy over the *nature* of possible worlds. The apparatus (or heuristic) of possible-worlds semantics may help in defining such notions as logical possibility and logical necessity. But when it comes to the nature of possibilia, I am in the market for an alternative account. As long as the ontological status of "possible worlds" is in dispute I do not see how an appeal to them can be very helpful in solving other metaphysical difficulties. Trying to explain the obscure by the more obscure is not very productive. (It is possible that the Flew–Mackie objection depends upon a metaphysics of possible worlds that is itself quite controversial.)

29. See Plantinga, *Nature of Necessity*, p. 171.

30. Ibid., pp. 181–83.

31. Ibid., p. 182.

32. See Gottfried Wilhelm von Leibniz, "A Vindication of God's Justice," article 59; see also articles 125, 126, 142. This Leibnizian essay is a systematic abridgment in Latin of the contents of the *Theodicee*, attached as an appendix to the same in the year 1710. See Paul Schrecker, "Notes on the Texts," in

Monadology and Other Philosophical Essays, trans. Paul Schrecker (Indianapolis, Ind.: Bobbs-Merrill, 1965), p. xxvii.

33. Illtyd Trethowan, "Dr. Hick and the Problem of Evil," *Journal of Theological Studies* 18 (October 1967): 412.

34. Germain Grisez, *Beyond the New Theism: A Philosophy of Religion* (Notre Dame, Ind.: University of Notre Dame Press, 1975), p. 294.

35. Ibid.

36. Hick, *EAGOL,* p. 236 (italics added).

37. Bill Anglin and Stewart Goetz, "Evil Is Privation," *International Journal for Philosophy of Religion* 13 (1982): 11.

38. Hick, *EAGOL,* p. 232; see also p. 279.

39. Ibid., p. 233.

40. Ibid.

41. Ibid., p. 261.

42. See ibid., p. 233.

43. Stephen T. Davis, "Free Will and Evil," in his *Encountering Evil,* pp. 72–73.

44. Hick, *EAGOL,* p. 174.

45. C. S. Lewis, *The Problem of Pain* (New York: Macmillan, 1962), p. 91.

46. Trethowan, "Dr. Hick," 413.

CHAPTER 12

1. John H. Hick, "An Irenaean Theodicy," in *Encountering Evil: Live Options in Theodicy,* ed. Stephen T. Davis (Atlanta, Ga.: John Knox Press, 1981), pp. 50–51.

2. John Hick, "Remarks" (on "The Problem of Evil"), in *Reason and Religion,* ed. Stuart C. Brown (Ithaca, N.Y.: Cornell University Press, 1977), p. 128.

3. Hick, *EAGOL,* p. 255.

4. Hick, "Remarks," p. 127.

5. Hick, *EAGOL,* p. 339.

6. Ibid.

7. Hick, "Remarks," p. 127.

8. Ibid.

9. Hick, "Irenaean Theodicy," pp. 50–51.

10. Hick, *EAGOL,* p. 341.

11. Hick, "Irenaean Theodicy," p. 52.

12. Hick, "Remarks," p. 128.

13. Ibid.

14. Hick, "Irenaean Theodicy," p. 52.

15. Ibid., p. 66.

16. Ibid., p. 67.

17. John Hick, "The Problem of Evil in the First and Last Things," *Journal of Theological Studies* 19 (October 1968): 598, 601.

18. Ibid., 598.

19. Ibid.

20. Hick, "Irenaean Theodicy," p. 52.

21. John Hick, *Death and Eternal Life* (San Francisco: Harper & Row, 1976), p. 243.

22. Hick, "First and Last Things," 600.

23. Ibid.

24. Hick, "Irenaean Theodicy," p. 51.

25. Hick, "First and Last Things," 600.

26. Hick, *Death and Eternal Life*, p. 221 (italics added).

27. Hick, "First and Last Things," 600.

28. Hick, *EAGOL*, p. 347.

29. Ibid.

30. Ibid., p. 348.

31. Ibid.

32. See Hick, *Death and Eternal Life*, pp. 399–424; see also pp. 455–58.

33. Hick, "Irenaean Theodicy," p. 65.

34. Hick, "Remarks," p. 128.

35. Hick, *EAGOL*, p. 347 (italics in the original).

36. Hick, *Death and Eternal Life*, p. 365.

37. Ibid., p. 388.

38. See ibid., pp. 366–73.

39. Ibid., p. 457.

40. Ibid., p. 460.

41. Ibid., p. 462.

42. Ibid., p. 461.

43. Ibid., p. 463.

44. See Hick, *EAGOL*, pp. 192–93.

45. Richard Swinburne, "A Theodicy of Heaven and Hell," in *The Existence and Nature of God,* ed. Alfred J. Freddoso (Notre Dame, Ind.: University of Notre Dame Press, 1983), p. 43.

46. See George P. Klubertanz and Maurice R. Holloway, *Being and God: An Introduction to the Philosophy of Being and to Natural Theology* (New York: Appleton-Century-Crofts, Meredith, 1963), p. 371.

47. Ibid., p. 372.

48. For the terminology and a very fine critique of Hick's universalism, see Paul Helm's "Universalism and the Threat of Hell," *Trinity Journal* 4 (Spring 1983): 35–43.

49. Hick, *EAGOL*, p. 343.

50. See Hick, "First and Last Things," 598.

51. Swinburne, "Theodicy of Heaven and Hell," p. 41.

52. Ibid., p. 43.

53. Ibid.

54. C. S. Lewis, *The Great Divorce* (New York: Macmillan, 1946).

55. See Norman L. Geisler, *The Roots of Evil* (Grand Rapids, Mich.: Zondervan, 1978), pp. 60–61.

56. See Hick, *EAGOL*, pp. 341–45.

57. See the discussion "Christ as a Controversialist" by the Scottish divine James Stalker in his book *Imago Christi: The Example of Jesus Christ* (London: Hodder & Stoughton, 1890), pp. 281–98.

58. See Hick, *EAGOL*, p. 339; and idem, "Remarks," p. 128.

59. Hick, *Death and Eternal Life*, pp. 460, 463.

60. Hick, *EAGOL*, p. 347.

61. Hick, "Irenaean Theodicy," p. 51.

62. John Hick, "Response" (to critique of "Irenaean Theodicy"), in Davis, *Encountering Evil*, pp. 65–66.

63. But see Hick's famous article on "eschatological verification" titled "Theology and Verification," *Theology Today* 17 (April 1960), reprinted in idem, ed., *The Existence of God* (New York: Macmillan, 1964), pp. 253–74. See also the discussion in idem, *An Interpretation of Religion: Human Responses to the Transcendent* (London: Macmillan, 1989), pp. 178–80.

64. See Lewis, *Great Divorce*, pp. 120–21.

65. Stephen T. Davis, "Critiques" (of Hick's "An Irenaean Theodicy"), in his *Encountering Evil*, p. 60.

66. Paul Edwards writes that he has "some misgivings about the moral rightness of the orgy of 'mutual forgiveness' which, according to Hick, will take place in our heavenly lives" ("Difficulties in the Idea of God," in *The Idea of God: Philosophical Perspectives*, eds. Edward H. Madden, Rollo Handy, and Marvin Farber [Springfield, Ill.: Charles C. Thomas, 1968], p. 61). Compare Roland Puccetti's remarks, as this relates to the problem of natural evil, in his article "The Loving God—Some Observations on John Hick's *Evil and the God of Love,*" *Religious Studies* 2 (April 1967): 255–68.

67. See Harry Blamires, *Knowing the Truth About Heaven and Hell: Our Choices and Where They Lead Us* (Ann Arbor, Mich.: Servant, 1988), p. 7.

68. Frederick Buechner, *Wishful Thinking: A Theological ABC* (New York: Harper & Row, 1973), p. 96.

69. Swinburne, "Theodicy of Heaven and Hell," p. 49.

70. John K. Roth, "Critiques" (of Hick's "An Irenaean Theodicy"), in Davis, *Encountering Evil*, pp. 62–63.

71. Davis, "Critiques," p. 59.

72. Swinburne, "Theodicy of Heaven and Hell," p. 49.

73. Hick, "Irenaean Theodicy," p. 52. Reference is to Augustine *Confessions* 1.1.

74. M. B. Ahern, *The Problem of Evil* (New York: Schocken, 1971), p. 64.

75. Hick, *EAGOL*, p. 347.

76. Davis, "Critiques," p. 59.

77. Hick, *EAGOL*, p. 215.

78. See Hick, "Irenaean Theodicy," p. 39.

79. In addition to John Hick's *Death and Eternal Life*, see Rudolf Frieling, *Christianity and Reincarnation*, trans. Rudolf Koehler and Margaret Koehler (Edinburgh: Floris, 1977); John J. Hearney, *The Sacred and the Psychic: Parapsychology and Christian Theology* (New York: Paulist Press, 1984); Quincy Howe, Jr., *Reincarnation for the Christian* (Philadelphia: Westminster, 1974); Geddes MacGregor, *Reincarnation in Christianity* (Wheaton, Ill.: Quest,

1978); idem, *Reincarnation as a Christian Hope* (Totowa, N.J.: Barnes & Noble, 1982); Michael Perry, *Psychic Studies: A Christian's View* (Wellingborough, Northamptonshire: Aquarian, 1984); Frederick A. M. Spencer, *The Future Life: A New Interpretation of the Christian Doctrine* (New York: Harper & Row, 1935); and Leslie D. Weatherhead, *The Christian Agnostic* (Nashville, Tenn.: Abingdon, 1965).

80. George MacDonald, quoted by C. S. Lewis in his spiritual autobiography *Surprised by Joy: The Shape of My Early Life* (San Diego: Harcourt, Brace, Jovanovich, 1955), p. 212.

81. C. S. Lewis, *The Problem of Pain* (New York: Macmillan, 1962), p. 127.

INDEX